TRANSPORTATION ISSUES, POLICIES AND R&D

TRANSPORTATION

CONGRESSIONAL ISSUES, FINANCING AND IMPROVEMENTS

TRANSPORTATION ISSUES, POLICIES AND R&D

Additional books and e-books in this series can be found on Nova's website under the Series tab.

TRANSPORTATION ISSUES, POLICIES AND R&D

TRANSPORTATION

CONGRESSIONAL ISSUES, FINANCING AND IMPROVEMENTS

FREDERICK DANIELS
EDITOR

snova
New York

Library of Congress Cataloging-in-Publication Data

ISBN: 978-1-53615-651-5

Published by Nova Science Publishers, Inc. † New York

CONTENTS

PREFACE

The nation's air, land, and marine transportation systems are designed for accessibility and efficiency, two characteristics that make them vulnerable to attack. The focus of chapter 1 is how best to implement and finance a system of deterrence, protection, and response that effectively reduces the possibility and consequences of terrorist attacks without unduly interfering with travel, commerce, and civil liberties.

Almost every conversation about surface transportation finance begins with a two-part question: What are the "needs" of the national transportation system, and how does the nation pay for them? Chapter 2 is aimed almost entirely at discussing the "how to pay for them" question.

On December 4, 2015, President Barack Obama signed the Fixing America's Surface Transportation Act (FAST Act; P.L. 114-94). As reported in chapter 3, the act authorized spending on federal highway and public transportation programs, surface transportation safety and research activities, and rail programs for five years, through September 30, 2020.

Despite significant investments in public transportation at the federal, state, and local levels, transit ridership has fallen in many of the top 50 transit markets. If strong gains in the New York area are excluded, ridership nationally declined by 7% over the past decade. Chapter 4 examines the implications for federal transit policy of the current weakness and possible future changes in transit ridership.

Congress created the Railroad Rehabilitation and Improvement Financing (RRIF) program to offer long-term, low-cost loans to railroad operators, with particular attention to small freight railroads, to help them finance improvements to infrastructure and investments in equipment. This program is discussed in chapter 5.

The Department of Transportation's (DOT) Federal Railroad Administration (FRA) and Federal Transit Administration (FTA) carry out different approaches to rail safety oversight. FRA has a more centralized safety oversight program for railroads, while FTA's program for oversight of rail transit safety largely relies on state safety agencies to monitor and enforce rail transit safety, as established in federal statute. Chapter 6 examines (1) key characteristics of FRA's and FTA's rail safety oversight programs and (2) strengths and limitations of FRA's and FTA's rail safety oversight programs.

Research sponsored by the Federal Railroad Administration (FRA) has identified driver behavior as the main cause of highway-rail grade crossing crashes and that factors such as train and traffic volume can contribute to the risk of a crash. Chapter 7 examines: (1) the focus of FRA's grade-crossing-safety research, (2) how states select and implement grade-crossing projects and what data are available from FRA to inform their decisions, and (3) the challenges states reported in implementing and assessing projects and the extent to which FHWA assesses the program's effectiveness.

Chapter 1 - The nation's air, land, and marine transportation systems are designed for accessibility and efficiency, two characteristics that make them vulnerable to terrorist attack. While hardening the transportation sector is difficult, measures can be taken to deter terrorists. The enduring challenge facing Congress is how best to implement and finance a system of deterrence, protection, and response that effectively reduces the possibility and consequences of terrorist attacks without unduly interfering with travel, commerce, and civil liberties. Transportation security has been a major policy focus since the terrorist attacks of September 11, 2001. In the aftermath of those attacks, the 107th Congress moved quickly to pass the Aviation and Transportation Security Act (ATSA; P.L. 107-71), creating the Transportation Security Administration (TSA) and mandating that security screeners employed by the federal government inspect airline passengers, their baggage, and air cargo. Despite the extensive focus on aviation and transportation security over the past decade, a number of challenges remain, including

- developing and deploying effective biometric capabilities to verify the identities of transportation workers and travelers;
- developing effective risk-based approaches to vetting and screening transportation workers accessing secured areas of airports and other sensitive areas of transportation networks;
- developing cost-effective solutions to screen air cargo and freight without impeding the flow of commerce; and
- coordination among state, local, and federal homeland security and law enforcement personnel to effectively deter and respond to criminal and terrorist acts targeting public areas of transportation facilities.

The FAA Extension, Safety, and Security Act of 2016 (P.L . 114-190) and the TSA Modernization Act (P.L. 115-254, Division K) included provisions intended to improve screening technologies, streamline the passenger screening process, mandate more rigorous background checks of airport workers, strengthen airport access controls, increase passenger checkpoint efficiency and operational performance, and enhance security in public areas of airports and at foreign airports where flights depart for the United States. Oversight of TSA actions to implement these mandates may be an area of particular interest in the 116th Congress. Particular topics may include the evolution of screening technologies and assessments of emerging screening technology solutions; the expansion of canine teams for transportation security; the expansion of the PreCheck program to expedite screening of known travelers; the use of biometrics and associated data security and privacy concerns; implementing effective approaches, regulations, and international agreements to conduct risk-based screening of air cargo shipments worldwide; protecting public areas of airports; and developing effective countermeasures to protect critical infrastructure, including airports and aircraft, from attacks using drones. Bombings of passenger trains in Europe and Asia in the past few years illustrate the vulnerability of passenger rail systems to terrorist attacks. Passenger rail systems—primarily subway systems in the United States carry about five times as many passengers each day as do airlines, over many thousands of miles of track, serving stations that are designed primarily for easy access. Transit security issues of recent interest to Congress include the quality of TSA's surface transportation inspector program. The bulk of U.U.S. overseas trade is carried by ships, and thus the economic consequences of a maritime terrorist attack could be significant. Customs and Border Protection (CBP) and the Coast Guard have implemented security screening procedures that effectively "push the borders out"—that is, they begin screening vessels and cargo before they reach a U.S. port. Two aspects of maritime security that have drawn attention recently are cybersecurity and the use of drones for coastal surveillance.

Chapter 2 - For many years, federal surface transportation programs were funded almost entirely from taxes on motor fuels deposited in the Highway Trust Fund. The tax rates, which are fixed in terms of cents per gallon, have not been increased at the federal level since 1993. Meanwhile, motor fuel consumption is projected to decline due to improved fuel efficiency, increased use of electric vehicles, and slow growth in vehicle miles traveled. In consequence, revenue flowing into the Highway Trust Fund has been insufficient to support the surface transportation program authorized by Congress since 2008. Congress has yet to address the surface transportation program's fundamental revenue issues, and has given limited consideration to raising fuel taxes in recent years. Instead, since 2008 Congress has supported the federal surface transportation program by supplementing fuel tax revenues with transfers from the U.S. Treasury general fund. The most recent reauthorization act, the Fixing America's Surface Transportation Act (FAST Act; P.L. 114-94), authorized spending on federal highway and public transportation programs through September 30, 2020. The act provided $70 billion in general fund transfers to the Highway Trust Fund from FY2016 through FY2020. This use of general fund transfers to supplement the Highway Trust Fund will have been the de facto funding policy for 12 years when the FAST Act expires. Congressional Budget Office (CBO) projections indicate that the Highway Trust Fund insufficiency relative to spending will reemerge following expiration of the FAST Act. The projections indicate a shortfall of $85 billion over the first five years following the FAST Act, and $109 billion over the first six years. As the September 2020 expiration of the FAST Act approaches, Congress may again examine adjustments to the funding and financing of the federal role in surface transportation.

- Raising motor fuel taxes could provide the Highway Trust Fund with sufficient revenue to fully fund the program in the near term, but may not be a viable long-term solution due to expected declines in fuel consumption. It would also not address the equity issue arising from the increasing number of personal and commercial vehicles that are powered electrically and therefore do not pay motor fuel taxes.
- Replacing motor fuel taxes with a mileage-based road user charge would need to overcome a variety of financial, administrative, and privacy barriers, but could be a solution in the longer term.
- Treasury general fund transfers could continue to be used to make up for the Highway Trust Fund's projected shortfalls but could require budget offsets of an equal amount.

The political difficulty of adequately funding the Highway Trust Fund could lead Congress to consider altering the trust fund system or eliminating it altogether. This might involve a reallocation of responsibilities and obligations among federal, state, and local governments. Some surface transportation needs can be met by private investment, including public-private partnerships, and federal loans from the Transportation Infrastructure Finance and Innovation Act (TIFIA) program. If it desires to promote private investment in transportation infrastructure, Congress could consider asset recycling incentive grants to state and local governments for the sale or lease of government-owned infrastructure if the proceeds are committed to new infrastructure. Tolling may be an effective way to finance specific roads, bridges, or tunnels that are likely to have heavy use and are located such that the tolls are difficult to evade. All revenue from tolls flows to the state or local agencies or private entities that operate tolled facilities; the federal government does not collect any revenue from tolls. However, a major expansion of tolling might reduce the need for federal expenditures on roads. Tolls and private investment are unlikely to provide broad financial support for surface transportation needs, and many projects are not well suited to alternative financing.

Chapter 3 - On December 4, 2015, President Barack Obama signed the Fixing America's Surface Transportation Act (FAST Act; P.L. 114-94). The act authorized spending on federal highway and public transportation programs, surface transportation safety and research activities, and rail programs for five years, through September 30, 2020. The act's authorization totaled roughly $305 billion for FY2016 through FY2020. This included $233 billion for highways and highway safety, $61 billion for public transportation, and more than $10 billion for Amtrak. Most of the funding for surface transportation bills has been drawn from the Highway Trust Fund (HTF) since its creation in 1956, but the principal revenue source for the HTF, federal motor fuel taxes, has not generated sufficient revenue to cover HTF outlays since 2008. To fill this shortfall, Congress has relied on Treasury general fund transfers to make up the difference. Although Congress was unable to agree on a long-term solution to the HTF revenue issue, the FAST Act identified roughly $70 billion in budgetary offsets to support general fund transfers sufficient to pay for the five-year bill. The FAST Act builds upon the many programmatic changes made in the previous multiyear reauthorization bill, the Moving Ahead for Progress in the 21st Century Act (MAP-21; P.L. 112- 141). The act also continues initiatives intended to increase program efficiency through performance-based planning and the streamlining of project development. Among FAST Act's major attributes are

- $225 billion authorized from the HTF over five years, an average of $45 billion annually, for Federal Highway Administration (FHWA) programs;
- $61 billion authorized from the HTF and the general fund, an average of $12.2 billion per year, for Federal Transit Administration (FTA) programs;
- a major redirection of funding toward highway freight projects via a new formula program and a competitive grant program;
- direct funding for the Transportation Infrastructure Finance and Innovation Act (TIFIA) program of $275 million, down from $1 billion in FY2015;
- competitive grant component added to the Bus and Bus Facilities Program;
- provisions on intercity passenger rail transportation included in a surface transportation act for the first time; and
- no project earmarks.

The FAST Act does not increase motor fuels taxes or provide another sustainable source of revenues to be paid into the HTF. Unless new revenue sources are found, Congress will face projections of a large gap between HTF tax receipts and spending plans when it begins debating the reauthorization of the FAST Act in 2020.

Chapter 4 - Despite significant investments in public transportation at the federal, state, and local levels, transit ridership has fallen in many of the top 50 transit markets. If strong gains in the New York area are excluded, ridership nationally declined by 7% over the past decade. This chapter examines the implications for federal transit policy of the current weakness and possible future changes in transit ridership. Although there has been a lot of research into the factors that explain transit ridership, there seems to be no comprehensive explanation for the recent decline. One complication is that national trends in public transportation ridership are not necessarily reflected at the local level; thus, different areas may have different reasons for growth or decline. But at the national level, the two factors that most affect public transportation ridership are competitive factors and the supply of transit service. Several competitive factors, notably the drop in the price of gasoline over the past few years and the growing popularity of bikeshare and ridesourcing services, appear to have adversely affected transit ridership. The amount of transit service supplied has generally grown over time, but average fares have risen faster than inflation, possibly deterring riders. The future of public transportation ridership in the short to medium term is likely to depend on population growth; the public funding commitment to supplying transit; and factors that make driving more or less attractive, such as the price of parking, the extent of highway congestion, and the implementation of fuel taxes, tolls, and mileage-based user fees. Over the long term, ridership is also likely to depend on the introduction of autonomous vehicle technology, although its timing is uncertain. Fleets of driverless taxis that can be hailed with a smartphone, a plausible scenario, promise to be much cheaper than taxis and ridesourcing today. Widespread deployment of driverless taxis could reduce transit ridership, unless restrictions or fees make them an expensive alternative in some areas. Two major federal transit policies related to these issues are the general funding of public transportation, distributed mainly by formula, and the discretionary funding of new large capital projects such as rail and bus rapid transit systems through the Capital Investment Grant (CIG) Program, also known as New Starts. One option to boost ridership without raising funding would be to tie federal formula funds to ridership or fare revenue. If the most consequential uncertainty for transit ridership is the introduction of autonomous vehicles, federal funding might focus on buses, which last about 10 years, and not new rail systems that last 30 years or more. Another option would be to redirect CIG funding from building new rail systems and lines to refurbishing rail transit in the large and dense cities where rail transit currently carries large numbers of riders. If fully autonomous ridesourcing vehicles become available, policymakers may face pressure to subsidize ridesourcing trips for disabled and elderly passengers alongside or in place of traditional transit and paratransit services.

Chapter 5 - Congress created the Railroad Rehabilitation and Improvement Financing (RRIF) program to offer long-term, low-cost loans to railroad operators, with particular attention to small freight railroads, to help them finance improvements to infrastructure and investments in equipment. The program is intended to operate at no cost to the government, and it does not receive an annual appropriation. Since 2000, the RRIF program has made 37 loans totaling $5.4 billion (valued at $5.9 billion in 2018 dollars). The program, which is administered by the Build America Bureau within the Office of the Secretary of Transportation, has approved only four loans since 2012. Congress has authorized $35 billion in loan authority for the RRIF program and repeatedly has urged the Department of Transportation (DOT) to increase the number of loans the program makes. Reports suggest the uncertain length and outcome of the RRIF loan application process and the up-front costs to prospective borrowers are among the elements of the program that have reduced its appeal compared with other financing options available to railroads. By statute, the Build America Bureau has 90 days from the time a completed application is submitted to render a decision on the application. This timeline becomes uncertain due to the Bureau's discretion in determining when a loan application is "complete." A 2014 audit indicated that some loan applications had been in process for more than a year. Unlike DOT's other prominent loan assistance program, the Transportation Infrastructure Finance and Innovation Act (TIFIA) program, RRIF requires loan recipients to pay a credit risk premium, which is intended to offset the risk of a default on their loan. The credit risk premium helps the program comply with a congressional requirement that federal loan assistance programs operate at no cost to the federal government. However, it may make RRIF loans less attractive to borrowers than other types of federal, state, or private financing. Several RRIF loans have been made to government-run intercity passenger rail projects. A number of private companies seeking to build intercity passenger rail lines also have expressed interest in RRIF loans. Changes made by Congress in the Fixing America's Surface Transportation Act (P.L. 114-94), enacted in December 2015, may lead to even greater use of the RRIF program by sponsors of passenger rail and transit-related projects, as opposed to small freight railroads. Such loans likely would be quite large relative to those RRIF typically extends to small freight railroads, raising questions about the risk to the federal government if the projects are not completed or if they fail to generate sufficient revenue to service the loans.

Chapter 6 - In 2012 and 2015, DOT was provided with additional authority to oversee the safety of rail transit. Within DOT, FTA is now implementing this authority. The DOT's Office of Inspector General has reported, though, that FTA faces challenges in carrying out its enhanced safety oversight. FRA, also in DOT, has long carried out safety oversight of freight, intercity passenger, and commuter railroads. GAO was asked to review various rail safety and oversight issues, including the differences between FRA's and FTA's rail safety oversight programs. This chapter examines (1) key characteristics of FRA's and FTA's rail safety oversight programs and (2) strengths and limitations of FRA's and FTA's rail safety oversight programs. GAO assessed FRA's and FTA's information about rail safety oversight activities against guidance from the Office of Management and Budget, leading practices developed by the transit industry, and federal standards for internal control. GAO also interviewed stakeholders, including rail operators chosen based on mode, size, and location.

Chapter 7 - Crashes at highway-rail grade crossings are one of the leading causes of railroad-related deaths. According to FRA data, in 2017, there were more than 2,100 crashes resulting in 273 fatalities. Since 2009 crashes have occurred at a fairly constant rate. The federal government provides states funding to improve grade-crossing safety through FHWA's Section 130 Program. The persistence of crashes and deaths raises questions about the effectiveness of the federal grade-crossing-safety program. GAO was asked to review federal efforts to improve grade-crossing safety. This chapter examines: (1) the focus of FRA's grade-crossing-safety research, (2) how states select and implement grade-crossing projects and what data are available from FRA to inform their decisions, and (3) the challenges states reported in implementing and assessing projects and the extent to which FHWA assesses the program's effectiveness. GAO analyzed FRA data; reviewed FRA's, FHWA's, and states' documents; reviewed a study of states' selection of projects; and interviewed FRA and FHWA headquarters and field staff, and officials from a non-generalizable sample of eight states, selected to include a mix in the number of grade crossings and crashes, and geographic diversity.

In: Transportation
Editor: Frederick Daniels
ISBN: 978-1-53615-651-5

Chapter 1

TRANSPORTATION SECURITY: ISSUES FOR THE 116TH CONGRESS*

Bart Elias, John Frittelli and David Randall Peterman

The nation's air, land, and marine transportation systems are designed for accessibility and efficiency, two characteristics that make them vulnerable to terrorist attack. While hardening the transportation sector is difficult, measures can be taken to deter terrorists. The enduring challenge facing Congress is how best to implement and finance a system of deterrence, protection, and response that effectively reduces the possibility and consequences of terrorist attacks without unduly interfering with travel, commerce, and civil liberties.

Transportation security has been a major policy focus since the terrorist attacks of September 11, 2001. In the aftermath of those attacks,

* This is an edited, reformatted and augmented version of Congressional Research Service, Publication No. R45500, dated February 11, 2019.

the 107th Congress moved quickly to pass the Aviation and Transportation Security Act (ATSA; P.L. 107-71), creating the Transportation Security Administration (TSA) and mandating that security screeners employed by the federal government inspect airline passengers, their baggage, and air cargo. Despite the extensive focus on aviation and transportation security over the past decade, a number of challenges remain, including

- developing and deploying effective biometric capabilities to verify the identities of transportation workers and travelers;
- developing effective risk-based approaches to vetting and screening transportation workers accessing secured areas of airports and other sensitive areas of transportation networks;
- developing cost-effective solutions to screen air cargo and freight without impeding the flow of commerce; and
- coordination among state, local, and federal homeland security and law enforcement personnel to effectively deter and respond to criminal and terrorist acts targeting public areas of transportation facilities.

The FAA Extension, Safety, and Security Act of 2016 (P.L . 114-190) and the TSA Modernization Act (P.L. 115-254, Division K) included provisions intended to improve screening technologies, streamline the passenger screening process, mandate more rigorous background checks of airport workers, strengthen airport access controls, increase passenger checkpoint efficiency and operational performance, and enhance security in public areas of airports and at foreign airports where flights depart for the United States. Oversight of TSA actions to implement these mandates may be an area of particular interest in the 116th Congress. Particular topics may include the evolution of screening technologies and assessments of emerging screening technology solutions; the expansion of canine teams for transportation security; the expansion of the PreCheck program to expedite screening of known travelers; the use of biometrics and associated data security and privacy concerns; implementing effective approaches, regulations, and international agreements to conduct risk-based screening of air cargo shipments worldwide; protecting public areas of airports; and developing effective countermeasures to protect critical infrastructure, including airports and aircraft, from attacks using drones.

Bombings of passenger trains in Europe and Asia in the past few years illustrate the vulnerability of passenger rail systems to terrorist attacks. Passenger rail systems—primarily subway systems in the United States carry about five times as many passengers each day as do airlines, over many thousands of miles of track, serving stations that are designed primarily for easy access. Transit security issues of recent interest to Congress include the quality of TSA's surface transportation inspector program. The bulk of U.U.S. overseas trade is carried by ships, and thus the economic consequences of a maritime terrorist attack could be significant. Customs and Border Protection (CBP) and the Coast Guard have implemented security screening procedures that effectively "push the borders out"—that is, they begin screening vessels and cargo before they reach a U.S. port. Two aspects of maritime security that have drawn attention recently are cybersecurity and the use of drones for coastal surveillance.

INTRODUCTION

The nation's air, land, and marine transportation systems are designed for accessibility and efficiency, two characteristics that make them vulnerable to attack. The difficulty and cost of protecting the transportation sector from attack raises a core question for policymakers: how much effort and resources to put toward protecting potential targets versus pursuing and fighting terrorists. While hardening the transportation sector against terrorist attack is difficult, measures can be taken to deter terrorists. The focus of debate is how best to implement and finance a system of deterrence, protection, and response that effectively reduces the possibility and consequences of terrorist attacks without unduly interfering with travel, commerce, and civil liberties.

For all modes of transportation, one can identify four principal policy objectives that would support a system of deterrence and protection: (1) ensuring the trustworthiness of the passengers and the cargo flowing through the system; (2) ensuring the trustworthiness of the transportation workers who operate and service the vehicles, assist the passengers, or handle the cargo; (3) ensuring the trustworthiness of the private companies that operate in the system, such as the carriers, shippers, agents, and brokers; and (4) establishing a perimeter of security around transportation facilities and vehicles in operation. The first three policy objectives are concerned with preventing an attack from within a transportation system, such as occurred on September 11, 2001. The concern is that attackers could once again disguise themselves as legitimate passengers (or shippers or workers) to get in position to launch an attack.

The fourth policy objective is concerned with preventing an attack from outside a transportation system. For instance, terrorists could ram a bomb-laden speedboat into an oil tanker, as was done in October 2002 to the French oil tanker *Limberg,* or they could shoot a shoulder-fired missile at an airplane taking off or landing, as was attempted in November 2002 against an Israeli charter jet in Mombasa, Kenya. Achieving all four of these objectives is difficult at best, and in some modes, is practically impossible. Where limited options exist for preventing an attack, policymakers are left with evaluating options for minimizing the consequences of an attack, without imposing unduly burdensome requirements.

AVIATION SECURITY[1]

Following the 9/11 terrorist attacks, Congress took swift action to create the Transportation Security Administration (TSA) within the U.S. Department of Transportation and gave it control over all airline passenger and baggage screening functions and deployment of armed air marshals on

[1] This section was prepared by Bart Elias, Specialist in Aviation Policy.

commercial passenger flights. In 2003, TSA was transferred to the newly formed Department of Homeland Security (DHS).[2]

To this day, the federal role in airport screening remains controversial. While airports are allowed to opt out of federal screening, alternative private screening under TSA contracts has been limited to 22 airports out of approximately 450 commercial passenger airports where passenger screening is required.[3] Congress has sought to ensure that optional private screening remains available for those airports that want to pursue this option. The TSA Modernization Act, incorporated into the FAA Reauthorization Act of 2018 (P.L. 115-254), includes language directing TSA to streamline the contracting process for private screening at airports, and directs TSA to look into the feasibility of modifying the program to allow individual airport terminals, instead of entire airports, to switch over to screening by private contractors. Proposals seeking more extensive reforms of passenger screening have not been extensively debated. Rather, aviation security legislation has largely focused on specific mandates to comprehensively screen for explosives and carry out background checks and threat assessments.

Despite the extensive focus on aviation security for more than a decade, a number of challenges remain, including

- effectively screening passengers, baggage, and cargo for explosives threats;
- developing effective risk-based methods for screening passengers and others with access to aircraft and sensitive areas;
- incorporating biometrics into the passenger screening process to verify identities;
- exploiting available intelligence information and watchlists to identify individuals who pose potential threats to civil aviation;

---

[2] See P.L. 107-296.

[3] Transportation Security Administration, *Screening Partnership Program*, https://www.tsa.gov/for-industry/screeningpartnerships.

- implementing effective systems, regulations, and international agreements to assess risk and conduct risk-based screening of air cargo shipments worldwide;
- effectively deterring and responding to security threats in public areas of airports and at screening checkpoints;
- developing effective strategies for addressing aircraft vulnerabilities to shoulder-fired missiles and other standoff weapons; and
- addressing the potential security implications of unmanned aircraft operations in domestic airspace and developing effective countermeasures to protect critical infrastructure, including airports and aircraft, from attacks using drones.

Explosives Screening Strategy for the Aviation Domain

Prior to the 9/11 attacks, explosives screening in the aviation domain was limited in scope and focused on selective screening of checked baggage placed on international passenger flights. Immediately following the 9/11 attacks, the Aviation and Transportation Security Act (ATSA; P.L. 107-71) mandated 100% screening of all checked baggage placed on domestic passenger flights and on international passenger flights to and from the United States.

In addition, the Implementing the 9/11 Commission Recommendations Act of 2007 (P.L. 110-53) mandated the physical screening of all cargo placed on passenger flights. Unlike passenger and checked baggage screening, TSA does not routinely perform physical inspections of air cargo. Rather, TSA satisfies this mandate through the Certified Cargo Screening Program. Under the program, manufacturers, warehouses, distributors, freight forwarders, and shippers carry out screening inspections using TSA-approved technologies and procedures both at airports and at off-airport facilities in concert with certified supply-chain security measures and chain-of-custody standards. Internationally, TSA works with other governments, international trade organizations, and industry to assure that all U.S.-bound air cargo shipments carried aboard passenger aircraft meet the requirements of the mandate.

Additionally, TSA works closely with Customs and Border Protection (CBP) to carry out risk-based targeting of cargo shipments, including use of the CBP Advance Targeting System-Cargo (ATS-C), which assigns risk-based scores to inbound air cargo shipments to identify shipments of elevated risk. Originally designed to combat drug smuggling, ATS-C has evolved over the years, particularly in response to an October 2010 cargo aircraft bomb plot that originated in Yemen, to assess shipments for explosives threats or other terrorism-related activities. CBP and TSA continue to pilot test the Air Cargo Advance Screening (ACAS) system, initiated in 2010, under which freight forwarders and airlines voluntarily submit key data elements of cargo manifests for predeparture vetting.

P.L. 115-254 requires TSA to establish an air cargo security division and review and improve the Known Shipper Program and Certified Cargo Screening Program to enhance their effectiveness and address any identified vulnerabilities. The act also requires U.S. Customs and Border Protection to work with TSA to establish a formal ACAS program for inbound international cargo modelled on the long-running ACAS pilot program. It directs TSA to examine the feasibility of expanding the use of computed tomography to air cargo and examine other emerging screening technologies that may enhance air cargo screening.

Given the focus on the threats to aviation posed by explosives, a significant focus of TSA acquisition efforts has been on explosives screening technologies. The Transportation Security Acquisition Reform Act (P.L. 113-245) required TSA to develop a five-year technology investment plan and mandated formal justifications and certifications that technology investments are cost-beneficial. The act also required tighter inventory controls and processes to ensure efficient utilization of procured technologies. P.L. 115-254 requires TSA to update this plan annually to accompany its budget request. The act also requires TSA to establish an innovation task force to work with industry to identify, cultivate, and accelerate the development and implementation of innovative transportation security technologies.

A major thrust of TSA's acquisition and technology deployment strategy is improving the capability to detect concealed explosives and bomb-making components carried by airline passengers. The October 31, 2015, downing of a Russian passenger airliner departing Sharm el-Sheikh, Egypt, reportedly following the explosion of a bomb aboard the aircraft,[4] renewed concerns over capabilities to detect explosives in baggage and cargo and monitoring of airport workers with access to aircraft, particularly overseas.

In response to a 2009 incident aboard a Northwest Airlines flight, the Obama Administration accelerated deployment of Advanced Imaging Technology (AIT) whole body imaging devices and other technologies at passenger screening checkpoints. This deployment responded to the 9/11 Commission recommendation to improve the detection of explosives on passengers.[5] In addition to AIT, next generation screening technologies for airport screening checkpoints include advanced technology X-ray systems for screening carry-on baggage, bottled liquids scanners, cast and prosthesis imagers, shoe scanning devices, and portable explosives trace detection equipment.

The use of AIT has raised a number of policy questions. Privacy advocates have objected to the intrusiveness of AIT, particularly when used for primary screening.[6] To allay privacy concerns, TSA eliminated the use of human analysis of AIT images and does not store imagery. In place of human image analysts, TSA has deployed automated threat detection capabilities using automated targeting recognition (ATR) software. Another concern raised about AIT centered on the potential medical risks posed by backscatter X-ray systems, but those systems are no longer in use for airport screening, and current millimeter wave systems emit nonionizing millimeter waves generally not considered harmful. More recently, the effectiveness of AIT and ATR has been brought into question.

---

[4] Andrew Roth, "Russia: Terrorist Attack Brought Down Jetliner over Sinai," *Washington Post,* November 18, 2015, p. A8.

[5] National Commission on Terrorist Attacks upon the United States, *The 9/11 Commission Report*, New York, NY: W. W. Norton & Co., 2004.

[6] See, e.g., American Civil Liberties Union. ACLU Backgrounder on Body Scanners and "Virtual Strip Searches," New York, NY, January 8, 2010.

In 2015, the DHS Office of Inspector General completed covert testing of passenger screening checkpoint technologies and processes and consistently found failures in technology and procedures coupled with human error that allowed prohibited items to pass into secure areas.[7]

Even prior to the revelations of weaknesses in passenger checkpoint screening technologies and procedures, the use of AIT was controversial. Past legislative proposals specifically sought to prohibit the use of whole body imaging for primary screening (see, for example, H.R. 2200, 111th Congress). Primary screening using AIT is now commonplace at larger airports, but checkpoints at many smaller airports have not been furnished with AIT equipment and other advanced checkpoint detection technologies. This raises questions about TSA's long-range plans to expand AIT to ensure more uniform approaches to explosives screening across all categories of airports.

Through FY2018, TSA deployed about 960 AIT units. It has not planned for procurements beyond this level, although many smaller airports are not equipped with this capability. TSA plans to manage this risk to a large extent through risk-based passenger screening measures, primarily through increased use of voluntary passenger background checks under the PreCheck trusted traveler program. However, this program, likewise, is not available at many smaller airports: Currently, the program's incentive of expedited screening is offered at fewer than half of all commercial passenger airports.

The FAA Extension, Safety, and Security Act of 2016 (P.L. 114-190) directed TSA to initiate a demonstration program at three to six large airports to examine passenger checkpoint reconfigurations that increase efficiencies and reduce vulnerabilities, and a separate demonstration program at three airports to develop and test next-generation screening system prototypes designed to expedite passenger handling. P.L. 115-254 instructs TSA to continue operation of its systems integration facility at Washington Reagan National Airport for testing and evaluating advanced

---

[7] Statement of John Roth, Inspector General, Department of Homeland Security, Before the Committee on Oversight and Government Reform, U.S. House of Representatives, Concerning TSA: Security Gaps, November 3, 2015.

transportation security screening technologies, and to ensure timely assessments of new screening technologies. It also directs TSA to promote a diverse security technology industry to better enable small business innovators to develop and commercialize new transportation security technologies. The act requires TSA to formally establish its innovation task force to accelerate the development of innovative transportation security technologies and capabilities. The act also directs DHS to conduct a review to determine whether the Transportation Security Laboratory in Atlantic City, NJ, whose core mission is to perform research, development, and validation of explosives detection and mitigation technologies, should be managed by TSA or by another DHS entity. The laboratory was originally transferred to TSA from the Federal Aviation Administration (FAA), but has been in the hands of the DHS Science and Technology Directorate for more than a decade.

Risk-Based Passenger Screening

TSA has initiated a number of risk-based screening initiatives to focus its resources and apply directed measures based on intelligence-driven assessments of security risk. These include PreCheck; modified screening procedures for children 12 and under; and a program for expedited screening of known flight crew and cabin crew members. Programs have also been developed for modified screening of elderly passengers similar to those procedures put in place for children.

PreCheck is modeled on CBP programs such as Global Entry, SENTRI, and NEXUS. Under the program, participants vetted through a background check process are processed through expedited screening lanes where they can keep shoes on and keep liquids and laptops inside carry-on bags. As of December 2018, PreCheck expedited screening lanes were available at more than 200 airports. The cost of background checks under the PreCheck program is recovered through application fees of $85 per passenger for a five-year membership. TSA's goal is to process 50% of passengers through PreCheck expedited screening lanes, thus reducing the need for standard security screening lanes, but it has struggled to increase program membership.

One concern raised over the PreCheck program is the lack of biometric authentication to verify participants at screening checkpoints. A predecessor test program, the Registered Traveler program, which used private vendors to issue and scan participants' biometric credentials, was scrapped by TSA in 2009 because it failed to show a demonstrable security benefit. In 2016, biometric identity authentication was reintroduced at 13 airports under a private trusted traveler program known as Clear. Participants in Clear, which is separate from PreCheck and not operated or funded by TSA, use an express lane to verify identity using a fingerprint or iris scan rather than interacting with a TSA document checker.[8]

Previously, the extensive use of a program called "managed inclusion" to route selected travelers not enrolled in PreCheck through designated PreCheck expedited screening lanes also raised objections. The Government Accountability Office (GAO) found that TSA had not fully tested its managed inclusion practices, and recommended that TSA take steps to ensure and document that testing of the program adheres to established evaluation design practices.[9]

TSA phased out the managed inclusion program in the fall of 2015. Since September 2015, TSA behavior detection officers and explosives trace detection personnel no longer direct passengers not enrolled in PreCheck to expedited screening lanes, but pre-assessments using canine teams have continued at some major airports. Questions remain regarding whether PreCheck is fully effective in directing security resources to unknown or elevated-risk travelers. Nonetheless, it has improved screening efficiency. TSA has estimated annual savings in direct screener workforce costs totaling $110 million as a result of PreCheck and other risk-based

---

[8] Scott McCartney, "The Airport Security Shortcut That Isn't PreCheck," *Wall Street Journal*, June 22, 2016, http://www.wsj.com/articles/the-airport-security-short-cut-that-isnt-precheck-1466616335.

[9] U.S. Government Accountability Office, *Aviation Security: Rapid Growth in Expedited Passenger Screening Highlights Need to Plan Effective Security Assessments*, GAO-15-150, December 2014.

initiatives.[10] A study suggested that considerably greater efficiency gains might be realized if TSA could double the annual number of PreCheck screenings, which would require increasing the number of PreCheck-eligible travelers to about 15 to 20 million.[11] PreCheck expansion was addressed in recent legislation,[12] and oversight of TSA efforts to expand PreCheck may be a specific topic of interest during the 116th Congress.

Language in P.L. 115-254 directs TSA to work with at least two private-sector entities to expand PreCheck enrollment options and forge at least two agreements for marketing the program, setting enrollment targets of 7 million by the end of FY2019, 10 million by the end of FY2020, and 15 million by the end of FY2021. The act also directs TSA to explore cost-effective options for conducting recurrent background checks of program participants, although this could raise concerns over impacts on enrollments if procedures for recurrent checks impose additional burdens on participants.

The act requires TSA to ensure that PreCheck expedited screening lanes are open and available to program participants during peak and high-volume travel times and take steps to provide expedited screening at standard screening lanes when PreCheck lanes are not available. It also instructs TSA to ensure that only trusted traveler program members and members of the Armed Forces are permitted to use PreCheck screening lanes.

P.L. 115-254 also directs TSA and CBP to work together on the deployment of biometric technologies for the entry-exit program for international travelers and other uses. According to the TSA Biometrics Roadmap,[13] TSA also plans to integrate biometrics technology for identity verification of PreCheck travelers, and seeks to eventually expand the voluntary use of biometrics to all domestic air travelers. Plans for increased

---

[10] Department of Homeland Security, Transportation Security Administration, Fiscal Year 2016 Congressional Justification, Aviation Security.

[11] Sheldon H. Jacobson, Arash Khatibi, and Ge Yu, "When Should TSA PreCheck Be Offered at No Cost to Travelers?" *Journal of Transportation Security,* 10, June 2017, pp. 23-39.

[12] See P.L. 114-190 and P.L. 115-254.

[13] Transportation Security Administration, *TSA Biometrics Roadmap*, September 2018, https://www.tsa.gov/sites/default/files/tsabiometricsroadmap.pdf.

use of biometrics raise privacy and data-protection concerns that may be of particular interest to congressional oversight committees.

In addition to passenger screening, TSA, in coordination with participating airlines and labor organizations representing airline pilots, has developed a known crewmember program to expedite security screening of airline flight crews.[14] In July 2012, TSA expanded the program to include flight attendants.[15]

TSA has also developed a passenger behavior detection program to identify potential threats based on observed behavioral characteristics. TSA initiated early tests of its Screening Passengers by Observational Techniques (SPOT) program in 2003. By FY2012, the program deployed almost 3,000 behavior detection officers at 176 airports, at an annual cost of about $200 million. Questions remain regarding the effectiveness of the behavioral detection program, and privacy advocates have cautioned that it could devolve into racial or ethnic profiling. While some Members of Congress have sought to shutter the program, Congress has not moved to do so. For example, H.Amdt. 127 (113th Congress), an amendment to the FY2014 DHS appropriations measure that sought to eliminate funding for the program, failed to pass a floor vote. Congress also has not taken specific action to revamp the program, despite the concerns raised by GAO and the DHS Office of Inspector General.[16]

P.L. 115-254 directed TSA to utilize risk-based strategies in deploying federal air marshal teams on international and domestic flights. However, a more controversial TSA initiative using air marshals to shadow passengers whose behavioral profiles based on past itineraries indicated they might

---

[14] See http://www.knowncrewmember.org/.

[15] Transportation Security Administration, *Press Release: U.S. Airline Flight Attendants to Get Expedited Airport Screening in Second Stage of Known Crewmember Program*, Friday, July 27, 2012, http://www.tsa.gov/press/releases/ 2012/07/27/us-airline-flight-attendants-get-expedited-airport-screening-second-stage.

[16] U.S. Government Accountability Office, *Aviation Security: TSA Should Limit Future Funding for Behavior Detection Activities*, GAO-14-159, November 2013; Department of Homeland Security, Office of Inspector General, *Transportation Security Administration's Screening of Passengers by Observation Techniques (Redacted)*, OIG-13-91, Washington, DC, May 29, 2013; Department of Homeland Security, Statement of Charles K. Edwards, Deputy Inspector General, Before the United States House of Representatives, Committee on Homeland Security, Subcommittee on Transportation Security, November 13, 2013.

pose an elevated security risk was reportedly shuttered in December 2018 after media reports and some Members of Congress raised concerns over the privacy implications of the program.[17]

The Use of Terrorist Watchlists in the Aviation Domain

Airlines were formerly responsible for checking passenger names against terrorist watchlists maintained by the government. Following at least two instances in 2009 and 2010 in which such checks failed to identify individuals who may pose a threat to aviation, TSA took responsibility for checking passenger names under the Secure Flight program. In November 2010, DHS announced that 100% of passengers flying to or from U.S. airports are being vetted using the Secure Flight system.[18]

Secure Flight vets passenger name records against a subset of the Terrorist Screening Database (TSDB). On international flights, Secure Flight operates in coordination with the use of watchlists by CBP's National Targeting Center-Passenger, which relies on the Advance Passenger Information System (APIS) and other tools to vet both inbound and outbound passenger manifests. In addition to flights of U.S. and foreign airlines, all inbound and outbound international flights using chartered and private aircraft must transmit passenger and crew manifests to CBP at least one hour prior to departure.

In addition to these systems, TSA conducts risk-based analysis of passenger data carried out by the airlines through use of the Computer-Assisted Passenger Prescreening System (CAPPS). In January 2015, TSA gave notification that it would start incorporating the results of CAPPS assessments, but not the underlying data used to make such assessments, into Secure Flight, along with each passenger's full name, date of birth,

---

[17] Jana Winter and Jenn Abelson, "TSA Says It No Longer Tracks Regular Travelers as if They May Be Terrorists," *Boston Globe*, December 15, 2018.

[18] Department of Homeland Security, "DHS Now Vetting 100 Percent of Passengers on Flights Within or Bound For U.S. Against Watchlists," Press Release, November 30, 2010.

and PreCheck traveler number (if applicable). These data are used within the Secure Flight system to perform risk-based analyses to determine whether passengers receive expedited, standard, or enhanced screening at airport checkpoints.[19] P.L. 115-254 removed statutory references to CAPPS, replacing them with references to the Secure Flight Program to clarify that these various passenger vetting elements are fully encompassed under Secure Flight. The act also directed TSA to conduct and publicly disseminate a review of its privacy impact assessment of the Secure Flight Program.

Central issues surrounding the use of terrorist watchlists in the aviation domain that may be considered during the 116th Congress include the speed with which watchlists are updated as new intelligence information becomes available; the extent to which all information available to the federal government is exploited to assess possible threats among passengers and airline and airport workers; the ability to detect identity fraud or other attempts to circumvent terrorist watchlist checks; the adequacy of established protocols for providing redress to individuals improperly identified as potential threats; and the adequacy of coordination with international partners.[20] In addition, there has been a growing interest in finding better ways to utilize watchlists to prevent terrorist travel, particularly travel of radicalized individuals seeking to join forces with foreign terrorist organizations such as the Islamic State (IS).

Language in P.L. 114-190 directed TSA to assess whether recurrent fingerprint-based criminal background checks could be carried out in a cost-effective manner to augment terrorist watchlist checks for PreCheck program participants. Additionally, the act directed TSA to expand criminal background checks for certain airport workers.

---

[19] Department of Homeland Security, Transportation Security Administration, "Privacy Act of 1974; Department of Homeland Security Transportation Security Administration-DHS/TSA-019 Secure Flight Records System of Records," 80 *Federal Register* 233-239, January 5, 2015.

[20] For additional information see CRS Report RL33645, *Terrorist Watchlist Checks and Air Passenger Prescreening*, by William J. Krouse and Bart Elias, available to congressional clients upon request.

Perimeter Security, Access Controls, and Worker Vetting

Airport perimeter security, access controls, and credentialing of airport workers are generally responsibilities of airport operators. There is no common access credential for airport workers. Rather, each airport separately issues security credentials to airport workers. These credentials are often referred to as Security Identification Display Area (SIDA) badges, and they convey the level of access that an airport worker is granted.

TSA requires access control points to be secured by measures such as posted security guards or electronically controlled locks. Additionally, airports must implement programs to train airport workers to challenge anyone not displaying proper identification.

Airports may also deploy surveillance technologies, access control measures, and security patrols to protect airport property from intrusion, including buildings and terminal areas. Such measures are paid for by the airport, but must be approved by TSA as part of an airport's overall security program. State and local law enforcement agencies with jurisdiction at the airport are generally responsible for patrols of airport property, including passenger terminals. They also may patrol adjacent properties to deter and detect other threats to aviation, such as shoulder-fired missiles (see "Mitigating the Threat of Shoulder-Fired Missiles to Civilian Aircraft").

TSA requires security background checks of airport workers with unescorted access privileges to secure areas at all commercial passenger airports and air cargo facilities. Background checks consist of a fingerprint-based criminal history records check and security threat assessment, which include checking employee names against terrorist database information. Certain criminal offenses committed within the past 10 years, including aviation-specific crimes, transportation-related crimes, and other felony offences, are disqualifying. Airports must collect applicant biographical information and fingerprints to submit to TSA to process background checks. Many airports use a service known as the

Transportation Security Clearinghouse to coordinate the processing of background check applications.[21]

P.L. 114-190 directed TSA to update the eligibility criteria and disqualifying criminal offenses for SIDA access credentials based on other transportation vetting requirements and knowledge of insider threats to security. The law proposes that TSA expand the criminal history look-back period from the current 10 years to 15 years, and that individuals be disqualified if they have been released from prison within 5 years of their application. The statute directs TSA to establish a formal waiver process for individuals denied credentials. It also calls for full implementation of recurrent vetting of airport workers with SIDA access credentials using the Federal Bureau of Investigation's (FBI's) Rap Back service to identify disqualifying criminal offences. Language in P.L. 115-254 requires TSA to provide congressional oversight committees with data on the number of airport workers being continuously vetted though the Rap Back service. It also directs TSA to identify means of using homeland security and intelligence resources to educate TSA personnel on means to better mitigate insider threats. The law also requires TSA to establish a centralized database of individuals who have had security access or aircraft-operator credentials revoked for failing to comply with aviation security requirements.

P.L. 114-190 directed TSA to conduct random physical inspections of airport workers at SIDA access points and in SIDA areas. P.L. 115-254 clarifies that TSA-led random inspections of aviation workers be targeted, strategic, and focused on providing the greatest level of security effectiveness, rather than being "random" in the true sense of the word. The law also directs TSA to continue its covert testing of employee access controls and provide measures of the effectiveness of such operations to airport operators, and as appropriate, to airlines. The act also establishes more stringent standards for individuals applying for SIDA access, requiring that such individuals provide their social security number in order to strengthen vetting effectiveness.

---

[21] See https://www.tsc-csc.com.

Explosives Screening Technology and Canines

Explosives screening technologies at passenger screening checkpoints primarily consist of the AIT whole body imaging systems; advanced technology X-ray imagers for carry-on items; and explosives trace detection systems used to test swab samples collected from individuals or carryon items for explosives residue. TSA began introducing Computed Tomography (CT) scanning technology at passenger screening checkpoints in FY2018 on a trial basis, and plans to expand the use of CT technology for scanning carry-on items throughout FY2019, with an aim of deploying more than 150 units at 14 major airports. TSA asserts that CT technology offers automated capabilities to help improve detection of explosives and other threats.[22] TSA concedes, however, that the introduction of CT technology, at least initially, will require more resources to clear increased numbers of false alarms compared to X-ray technology, and seeks to increase screener numbers at those airports where CT will be deployed to minimize these impacts on passenger screening. P.L. 115-254 directs TSA to proceed with these CT pilot programs and also to examine the feasibility of using CT technology to screen cargo carried on passenger aircraft. The act also directs TSA to assess other emerging screening technologies that may be used to enhance air cargo screening.

For checked baggage screening, TSA utilizes a combination of CT-based explosives detection systems and chemical trace detection technology. TSA deploys either high-speed (greater than 900 bags per hour), medium-speed (400 to 900 bags per hour), or reduced-size (100 to 400 bags per hour) CT-based systems, depending on airport needs and configurations. TSA is also funding the development of new algorithms to more reliably detect homemade explosives threats in checked baggage and reduce false positives. TSA pays for or reimburses airports for modifying baggage-handling facilities and installing new inspection systems to accommodate explosives detection technologies.

---

[22] Department of Homeland Security, Transportation Security Administration, *Budget Overview, Fiscal Year 2019 Congressional Justification*, https://www.dhs.gov/sites/default/files/publications/Transportation%20Security%20Administration.pdf.

The TSA's National Explosives Detection Canine Team Program trains and deploys canines and handlers at transportation facilities to detect explosives. The program includes approximately 370 TSA teams and 675 state and local law enforcement teams trained by TSA under partnership agreements. More than 350 of the TSA teams are dedicated to passenger screening at 46 airports. Following airport bombings in Brussels, Belgium, and Istanbul, Turkey, in 2016, there has been interest in increasing deployments of canine teams in nonsterile areas of airport terminals. P.L. 114-190 authorized TSA to provide training to foreign governments in airport security measures including the use of canine teams. The act also directed TSA to utilize canine teams to minimize passenger wait times and maximize security effectiveness of checkpoint operations.

P.L. 115-254 directs TSA to establish a working group to assess ways to support a decentralized, nonfederal domestic breeding program for explosives detection canines and to modernize canine breeding, medical, technical, and training standards. It further instructs TSA to develop guidance for the procurement and deployment of third-party domestic canines to enhance public area security at transportation hubs, including airports. Large hub airports that do not have their full allocation of explosives detection canine teams would be able to directly acquire canines from TSA-approved third-party sources, but canines procured in this manner would be trained by TSA personnel. Additionally, the act directs TSA to issue standards for the primary screening of air cargo by private entities using dogs and handlers not owned or employed by TSA.

Protecting Public Areas of Airports

Incident response at airports is primarily the responsibility of airport operators and state or local law enforcement agencies, with TSA acting as a regulator in approving an airport's comprehensive security program. Federal law enforcement may also be involved in developing and reviewing response plans, but will typically not have a lead role in event response. However, federal law enforcement may assume a lead investigative role following a security incident, particularly if the event is determined to be an act of terrorism.

P.L. 115-254 directs TSA to establish a working group to collaborate with public and private stakeholders to develop nonbinding recommendations for enhancing security in public areas of transportation facilities. The act also directs TSA to increase funding under the law enforcement reimbursable program for airports to increase the presence of law enforcement officers in public areas to provide visible deterrents to terrorists, including in baggage claim and ticketing areas and on airport access roads, as well as at screening checkpoints.

On November 1, 2013, a lone gunman targeting TSA employees fired several shots at a screening checkpoint at Los Angeles International Airport (LAX), killing one TSA screener and injuring two other screeners and one airline passenger. In a detailed postincident action report, TSA identified several proposed actions to improve checkpoint security, but did not support proposals to arm certain TSA employees or provide screeners with bulletproof vests, and did not recommend mandatory law enforcement presence at checkpoints.

The Gerardo Hernandez Airport Security Act of 2015 (P.L. 114-50), named in honor of the TSA screener killed in the LAX incident and enacted in September 2015, requires airports to adopt plans for responding to security incidents and to create a mechanism for sharing information among airports regarding best practices for airport security incident planning, management, and training. It also requires TSA to identify ways to expand the availability of funding for checkpoint screening law enforcement support through cost savings from improved efficiencies mainly achieved through implementing PreCheck expedited screening protocols. TSA partially reimburses local law enforcement agencies for support at screening checkpoints, and P.L. 115-254 directs TSA to increase funding for the reimbursable program to expand protection of public areas of airports as well as screening checkpoints.

Foreign Last Point of Departure Airports

TSA regulates foreign air carriers that operate flights to the United States to enforce requirements regarding the acceptance and screening of passengers, baggage, and cargo carried on those aircraft.[23] As part of this regulation, TSA inspects foreign airports from which commercial flights proceed directly to the United States. Officials known as Transportation Security Administration Representatives (TSARs) assess country compliance with international standards for aviation security and plan and coordinate U.S. airport risk analysis and assessments of foreign airports.

TSARs also administer and coordinate TSA response to terrorist incidents and threats to U.S. citizens and transportation assets and interests overseas.

Fifteen foreign last point of departure airports (eight in Canada, two in the Bahamas, one in Bermuda, one in Aruba, two in Ireland, and one in Abu Dhabi) have Customs and Border Protection (CBP) preclearance facilities where passengers are admitted to the United States prior to departure. Passengers arriving on international flights from these preclearance airports deplane directly into the airport sterile area upon arrival at the U.S. airport of entry, where they can board connecting flights or leave the airport directly, rather than being routed to customs and immigration processing facilities. CBP has announced its intention to expand customs preclearance to additional countries and airports. While agreements to offer preclearance at airports in Stockholm, Sweden, and Punta Cana, Dominican Republic, were finalized in 2016, preclearance operations at these airports have not yet been established. Plans to offer preclearance at other airports are still being negotiated.[24] Assessing screening measures at preclearance airports is a particular priority for TSA. TSA is also working to increase checked baggage preclearance processing so checked baggage does not have to be rescreened by TSA at the U.S. airport of entry, which has been the practice.

---

[23] See 49 C.F.R. Part 1546.

[24] J.S. Customs and Border Protection, *Preclearance Locations,* https://www.cbp.gov/border-security/ports-entry/ operations/preclearance.

Language in P.L. 114-190 requires TSA to conduct security risk assessments at all last point of departure airports, and authorizes the donation of security screening equipment to such airports to mitigate security vulnerabilities that put U.S. citizens at risk. P.L. 115-254 mandates that any such donated screening equipment be restored to original commercial settings and must not contain TSA-specific security standards or algorithms. Recipients of donated screening equipment must satisfactorily demonstrate that they are capable of properly maintaining it and must ensure that, once the equipment is retired from service, it does not get into the hands of terrorists or otherwise compromise security. The act also directs DHS, in coordination with the Department of State, to review and improve international aviation security standards and dissemination and implementation processes for security directives and emergency amendments to security requirements issued to domestic and foreign air carriers. It instructs TSA to work with the International Civil Aviation Organization to raise minimum standards for aviation security. P.L. 115-254 also directs TSA to work with FAA to track public charter flights between the United States and Cuba, and to brief congressional oversight committees on aviation security measures at Cuban airports that have air service to the United States.

Mitigating the Threat of Shoulder-Fired Missiles to Civilian Aircraft

The terrorist threat posed by small man-portable shoulder-fired missiles was brought into the spotlight soon after the 9/11 terrorist attacks by the November 2002 attempted downing of a chartered Israeli airliner in Mombasa, Kenya. Since then, Department of State and military initiatives have sought bilateral cooperation and voluntary reductions of shoulder-fired missiles, formally referred to as man-portable air defense systems (MANPADS), worldwide.

The most visible DHS initiative to address the threat was the multiyear Counter-MANPADS program carried out by the DHS Science &

Technology Directorate. The program concluded in 2009 with extensive testing and FAA certification of two systems capable of protecting airliners against heat-seeking missiles. The systems have not been deployed on commercial airliners in the United States, however, due largely to high acquisition and life-cycle costs. U.S. airlines have not voluntarily invested in these systems for operational use, and argue that the costs for such systems should be borne, at least in part, by the federal government.

MANPADS are mainly seen as a security threat to civil aviation overseas, but a MANPADS attack in the United States could have a considerable impact on the airline industry. While major U.S. airports have conducted vulnerability studies, efforts to reduce vulnerabilities to potential MANPADS attacks face significant logistic challenges. While Congress has not formally debated the issue since the conclusion of the DHS program in 2009, any future terrorist attempts to use standoff weapons, including shoulder-fired missiles, to attack civilian aircraft could quickly escalate this to a major national security priority.

Security Issues Regarding the Operation of Unmanned Aircraft

The proliferation of civilian drones, also known as unmanned aircraft systems (UAS), raises potential security risks, including the possibility that terrorists could use a drone to carry out an attack against a ground target. It is also possible that drones themselves could be targeted by terrorists or cybercriminals seeking to tap into sensor data transmissions or to cause mayhem by hacking or jamming command and control signals. Two principal concerns are that drones could be used to attack critical infrastructure or high-profile targets and that unauthorized drone operations in close proximity to airports could disrupt air transportation. The 116th Congress may have a particular interest in policies and technologies to mitigate safety and security threats posed by unmanned aircraft.

Terrorists could potentially use drones to carry out small-scale attacks using explosives, or as platforms for chemical, biological, or radiological attacks. In September 2011, the FBI disrupted a homegrown terrorist plot to attack the Pentagon and the Capitol with large model aircraft packed with high explosives.

Widely publicized drone incidents include an unauthorized flight at a political rally in Dresden, Germany, in September 2013 that came in close proximity to German Chancellor Angela Merkel; a January 2015 crash of a small hobby drone on the White House lawn in Washington, DC; a series of unidentified drone flights over landmarks and sensitive locations in Paris, France, in 2015; and drone sightings around London Gatwick and Heathrow airports in December 2018 that grounded numerous airline flights. These incidents have raised additional concerns about safety and security threats posed by small unmanned aircraft.

Domestically, there have been numerous reports of drones flying in close proximity to airports and manned aircraft, in restricted airspace, and over stadiums and outdoor events. In September 2017, a hobby drone collided with a National Guard Black Hawk helicopter assigned to patrol the skies over New York harbor during a meeting of the United Nations General Assembly, causing damage to one of the helicopter's rotor blades.

Numerous other safety incidents involving drones have been reported in the United States and abroad, but few have been tied to terrorism. However, ISIS is known to have used drones in conflict zones to conduct reconnaissance and drop explosives. While the payload capacities of small unmanned aircraft would likely limit the damage a terrorist attack using conventional explosives could inflict, drone attacks using chemical, biological, or radiological weapons could be more serious.

Regulations for small unmanned aircraft used for commercial purposes require TSA to carry out security threat assessments of certificated operators as it does for civilian pilots.[25] However, this requirement does not apply to recreational users, who are already permitted to operate small drones at low altitudes.

---

[25] See 14 CFR §61.18.

Moreover, while FAA has issued general guidance to law enforcement regarding unlawful UAS operations,[26] it is not clear that law enforcement agencies have sufficient training or technical capacity to respond to this potential threat.[27]

Technology may help manage security threats posed by unmanned aircraft. Integrating tracking mechanisms as well as incorporating "geo-fencing" capabilities, designed to prevent flights over sensitive locations or in excess of certain altitude limits, into unmanned aircraft systems may help curtail unauthorized flights.[28]

Language in P.L. 114-190 directed FAA to establish a pilot program to detect and mitigate unmanned aircraft operations in the vicinity of airports and other critical infrastructure. Additionally, the act directed FAA to develop an air traffic management system for small UASs that could include measures to detect and deter security threats posed by UASs.

The National Defense Authorization Act for FY2017 (P.L. 114-328) authorized the Armed Forces and the Department of Energy to take necessary actions to mitigate threats posed by a UAS to certain security-related facilities in the United States. The act authorizes the military to detect, monitor, and track UASs; issue warnings to operators; disrupt control of a UAS, including interrupting or jamming control signals; seize or take control of the UAS; confiscate the unmanned aircraft; or use reasonable force to disable or destroy the UAS. P.L. 115-254 more broadly authorizes the Department of Justice and DHS to take similar defensive actions to protect people, facilities, or assets from credible threats posed by UASs. The act also expands the mission of the Coast Guard to include carrying out protective measures to safeguard its facilities and assets,

---

[26] Federal Aviation Administration, *Law Enforcement Guidance for Suspected Unauthorized UAS Operations*, https://www.faa.gov/uas/resources/policy_library/media/FAA_UAS-PO_LEA_Guidance.pdf.

[27] Statement of Chief Richard Beary, President of the International Association of Chiefs of Police, Subcommittee on Oversight and Management Efficiency, Committee on Homeland Security, U.S. House of Representatives, March 18, 2015.

[28] See, e.g., Todd Humphreys, "Statement on the Security Threat Posed by Unmanned Aerial Systems and Possible Countermeasures," Submitted to the Subcommittee on Oversight and Management Efficiency, House Committee on Homeland Security, March 16, 2015.

including Coast Guard vessels and aircraft, from threats posed by unmanned aircraft.

P.L. 115-254 also directs FAA to coordinate with the various agencies authorized to engage in counter-unmanned aircraft (C-UAS) activities to review standards, policies, and practices with respect to maintaining safety for airspace users, protecting individuals and property on the ground, and not interfering with avionics, navigation, and air traffic control systems. Additionally, the review is to assess the adequacy of those agencies' coordination with FAA regarding C-UAS operations, the adequacy of training for personnel operating C-UAS systems, information sharing regarding airspace authorizations, and best practices for consistent C-UAS operations. The act directs FAA to work with the Department of Defense (DOD), DHS, and other relevant agencies to ensure that technologies developed to mitigate risks posed by an errant or hostile UAS do not adversely impact safe airport operations and air traffic and air navigation services. The act also directs FAA to work with DOD to streamline deployment of C-UAS and requires FAA to develop a comprehensive strategy for identifying and responding to public safety threats posed by UASs. It also requires FAA to implement a pilot program using remote detection capabilities to identify UASs in order to carry out enforcement actions against UAS operators not in compliance with applicable aviation laws and regulations.

P.L. 115-254 establishes a formal prohibition against civilians arming unmanned aircraft with dangerous weapons. Additionally, the act establishes criminal penalties for flying a drone over the White House grounds, the Vice President's residence, sites where the President or other individuals protected by the Secret Service are visiting, or other buildings or grounds hosting a special event of national significance. It also establishes criminal penalties for using a drone in a manner that interferes with wildfire suppression efforts or related law enforcement or emergency response activities.

Aviation Cybersecurity

There is growing concern over cybersecurity threats to aircraft, air traffic control systems, and airports. Executive Order 13636 provides broad guidance for DHS to work with FAA to identify cybersecurity risks, establish voluntary cybersecurity measures, and share information on cybersecurity threats within the broader cybersecurity framework. Additionally, 49 U.S.C. §44912 specifically directs TSA to periodically review threats to civil aviation with a particular focus on specified threats, including the potential disruption of civil aviation service resulting from a cyberattack.

TSA has indicated that its approach to cybersecurity thus far has not been through regulation, but rather through voluntary collaboration with industry. Under this framework, TSA formed the Transportation Systems Sector Cybersecurity Working Group, which created a cybersecurity strategy for the transportation sector in 2012.[29] Also, in coordination with the FBI and industry partners, TSA launched the Air Domain Intelligence Integration Center and an accompanying analysis center in 2014 to share information and conduct analysis of cyberthreats to civil aviation.[30]

In recognition of those threats, FAA has developed a software assurance policy for all FAA-owned and FAA-controlled information systems.[31] However, according to an April 2015 GAO report, while FAA has taken steps to protect air traffic control systems from cyberthreats, it faces continuing challenges in mitigating cyberthreats, particularly as it transforms air traffic control systems under its NextGen modernization

---

[29] Department of Homeland Security, "Executive Order 13636—Improving Critical Infrastructure Cybersecurity, Section 10(b) Report: TSA's Approach to Voluntary Industry Adoption of the NIST Cybersecurity Framework," http://www.dhs.gov/sites/default/files/publications/ExecutiveOrder_13636Sec10%28b%29Reportv5.pdf.

[30] Rachael King, "Aviation Industry and Government to Share Cyber Threats in New Intelligence Center," *Wall Street Journal CIO Journal*, April 15, 2014, http://blogs.wsj.com/cio/2014/04/15/aviation-industry-and-government-to-sharecyberthreats-in-new-intelligence-center/.

[31] Federal Aviation Administration, "Order 1370.109: National Policy, Software Assurance Policy," effective October 23, 2009.

initiative.[32] While FAA has adopted an evolving framework to address the cybersecurity of its systems, a January 2018 GAO report warned that new aircraft tracking technologies that will transform air traffic control in the coming years under NextGen have unmitigated cybersecurity vulnerabilities, including vulnerabilities to jamming, hacking, and spoofing of signals, that could compromise air traffic operations as well as pose a threat to national security and military aircraft operations.[33]

For systems onboard aircraft, FAA requires cybersecurity to be addressed in the existing airworthiness certification process. Large commercial aircraft and aviation systems manufacturers now typically collaborate with software security companies to attain high levels of assurance for software embedded in avionics equipment. Despite efforts to design aircraft systems to be resilient to cyberthreats, in April 2015 TSA and the FBI issued warnings that the increasing interconnectedness of these systems makes them vulnerable to unauthorized access and advised airlines to look out for individuals trying to tap into aircraft electronics and for evidence of tampering or network intrusions.[34]

FAA separately addresses cybersecurity of government-owned air traffic control systems and certified aircraft systems. However, GAO has cautioned that FAA's current approach to cybersecurity does not adequately address the interdependencies between aircraft and air traffic systems, and consequently may hinder efforts to develop a comprehensive and coordinated strategy.[35] While it identified no easy fix, GAO recommended that FAA develop a comprehensive cybersecurity threat model, better clarify cybersecurity roles and responsibilities, improve management security controls and contractor oversight, and fully

[32] Government Accountability Office, *Air Traffic Control: FAA Needs a More Comprehensive Approach to Address Cybersecurity as Agency Transitions to NextGen*, GAO-15-370, April 2015.

[33] Government Accountability Office, Homeland Defense: Urgent Need for DOD and FAA to Address Risks and Improve Planning for Technology That Tracks Military Aircraft, GAO-18-177, January 2018.

[34] Kim Zetter, "Feds Warn Airlines to Look Out for Passengers Hacking Jets," *Wired*, April 21, 2015, http://www.wired.com/2015/04/fbi-tsa-warn-airlines-tampering-onboard-wifi/.

[35] Government Accountability Office, Air Traffic Control: FAA Needs a More Comprehensive Approach to Address Cybersecurity As Agency Transitions to NextGen, GAO-15-370, April 2015.

incorporate National Institute of Standards and Technology information security guidance throughout the system life cycle.

Language in P.L. 114-190 mandated development of a comprehensive strategic framework for reducing cybersecurity risks to the national airspace system, civilian aviation, and FAA information systems. P.L. 115-254 directs FAA to review and update the framework to address known cybersecurity risks to the aviation system and short-term and long-term objectives for addressing these risks. The act also directs FAA to address cybersecurity in the certification of aircraft avionics systems and component software, and the cybersecurity of systems and technologies relating to the air traffic control system. The act also directs FAA to develop an integrated cybersecurity testbed for air traffic control modernization technologies. It orders a National Academy of Sciences study to develop recommendations on how to increase the size, quality, and diversity of FAA's cybersecurity workforce.

P.L. 115-254 directs TSA to implement the framework for improving critical infrastructure cybersecurity developed by the National Institute of Standards and Technology to manage cybersecurity risks and conduct cybersecurity vulnerability assessments, including cybersecurity evaluations of the PreCheck program as well as transportation worker credentialing programs that contain data on individuals. The act also directs TSA to coordinate with international counterparts to harmonize validation processes, allowing reciprocal recognition of security and screening technology approvals that comply with agreed-upon standards relating to performance as well as information security and cybersecurity. The act also directs DHS to review global aviation security standards and practices, including assessments of the cybersecurity risks of security screening equipment.

In November 2018, TSA released a new cybersecurity roadmap providing a broad framework for how it will work with transportation industry and government stakeholders to address cybersecurity risks, including risks to aviation.[36] The specific roles of TSA and FAA in

---

[36] Transportation Security Administration, *TSA Cybersecurity Roadmap 2018,* https://www.tsa.gov/sites/default/files/documents/tsa_cybersecurity_roadmap_adm_approved.pdf.

regulating cybersecurity, particularly in areas such as aircraft and avionics certification and air traffic control, which have historically been FAA responsibilities, may be a specific topic for congressional oversight during the 116th Congress.

TRANSIT AND PASSENGER RAIL SECURITY[37]

Bombings of and shootings on passenger trains in Europe and Asia have illustrated the vulnerability of passenger rail systems to terrorist attacks. Passenger rail systems—primarily subway systems—in the United States carry about five times as many passengers each day as do airlines, over many thousands of miles of track, serving stations that are designed primarily for easy access. The increased security efforts around air travel have led to concerns that terrorists may turn their attention to "softer" targets, such as transit or passenger rail. A key challenge Congress faces is balancing the desire for increased rail passenger security with the efficient functioning of transit systems, the potential costs and damages of an attack, and other federal priorities.

The volume of ridership and number of access points make it impractical to subject all rail passengers to the type of screening all airline passengers undergo. Consequently, transit security measures tend to emphasize managing the consequences of an attack. Nevertheless, steps have been taken to try to reduce the risks of an attack as well. These include vulnerability assessments; emergency planning; emergency response training and drilling of transit personnel (ideally in coordination with police, fire, and emergency medical personnel); increasing the number of transit security personnel; installing video surveillance equipment in vehicles and stations; and conducting random inspections of bags, platforms, and trains.

The challenges of securing rail passengers are dwarfed by the challenge of securing bus passengers. There are some 76,000 buses

[37] This section was prepared by David Randall Peterman, Analyst in Transportation Policy.

carrying 19 million passengers each weekday in the United States. Some transit systems have installed video cameras on their buses, but the number and operating characteristics of transit buses make them all but impossible to secure.

In contrast with the aviation sector, where TSA provides security directly, security in surface transportation is provided primarily by the transit and rail operators and local law enforcement agencies. TSA's main roles are oversight, coordination, intelligence sharing, training, and assistance. However, it provides some operational support through its Visible Intermodal Prevention and Response (VIPR) teams, which conduct operations with local law enforcement officials, including periodic patrols of transit and passenger rail systems to create "unpredictable visual deterrents." Several presidential Administrations have sought to reduce the size of the VIPR program, the value of which has yet to be demonstrated,[38] but Congress has sought to increase the size of the program.

Congressional efforts to promote the security of passenger rail and transit include providing grants to service providers, requiring those providers considered to be high-risk targets (by DHS) to have security plans approved by DHS, and requiring DHS to conduct security background checks and immigration status checks on all transit and railroad frontline employees. According to TSA, its three primary objectives for reducing risk in transit are to

- increase system resilience by protecting high-risk/high-consequence assets (i.e., critical tunnels, stations, and bridges);
- expand visible deterrence activities (i.e., canine teams, passenger screening teams, and antiterrorism teams); and
- engage the public and transit operators in the counterterrorism mission.[39]

---

[38] Department of Homeland Security, Office of the Inspector General, Federal Air Marshal Service Needs to Demonstrate How Ground-Based Assignments Contribute to TSA's Mission, OIG-18-70, July 24, 2018.

[39] Department of Homeland Security, Transportation Security Administration, Surface Transportation Security FY2016 Congressional [Budget] Justification, p. 11.

TSA surface transportation security inspectors conduct assessments of transit systems (and other surface modes) through the agency's Baseline Assessment for Security Enhancement (BASE) program. The agency has also developed a security training and security exercise program for transit. TSA's program for securing surface transportation is known as Risk Mitigation Activities for Surface Transportation (RMAST).

The intent of the RMAST program is to focus TSA's limited surface security resources on high-risk entities and locations. However, GAO reported in 2017 that TSA had not identified or prioritized high-risk entities for the RMAST program to focus on.[40]

The surface transportation inspector program has been a focus of congressional interest. Issues of concern to Congress have included whether the inspectors promoted from screening passengers at airports have sufficient expertise in surface transportation security; the administrative challenge of having the surface inspectors managed by airport-based federal security directors who themselves typically have no surface transportation experience; and the security value of the tasks performed by surface inspectors.[41] The number of surface inspectors declined from 404 in FY2011 to 222 (full-time equivalent positions) in FY2018. TSA attributed the decrease to efficiencies achieved through focusing efforts on the basis of risk.[42] However, in 2017 GAO reported that surface transportation inspectors were spending more time on the surface transportation mode that TSA had identified as the lowest risk than on the

---

40 Government Accountability Office, Transportation Security Administration: Surface Transportation Inspector Activities Should Align More Closely With Identified Risks, GAO-18-180, December 2017, p. 30.

41 U.S. House of Representatives, Committee on Homeland Security, Subcommittee on Transportation Security, Hearing on TSA's Surface Inspection Program: Strengthening Security or Squandering Resources?, May 31, 2012, http://homeland.house.gov/hearing/subcommittee-hearing-tsa%E2%80%99s-surface-inspection-programstrengthening-security-or-squandering.

42 Peter Neffenger, Administrator, Transportation Security Administration, U.S. Department of Homeland Security, Statement to the United States Senate Committee on Commerce, Science, and Transportation, Hearing on Transportation Security, April 6, 2016; Department of Homeland Security, Transportation Security Administration, Surface Transportation Security FY2014 Congressional [Budget] Justification, p. 14.

one identified as the highest risk.[43] Surface inspection field offices are located near airports, and surface inspectors may spend a significant portion of their time on tasks related to aviation safety, but TSA does not have complete information on the extent to which surface inspectors are tasked to work on aviation security.[44]

GAO reported in 2014 that lack of guidance to TSA's surface inspectors resulted in inconsistent reporting of rail security incidents and that TSA had not consistently enforced the requirement that rail agencies report security incidents, resulting in poor data on the number and types of incidents.[45] GAO also found that TSA did not have a systematic process for collecting and addressing feedback from surface transportation stakeholders regarding the effectiveness of its information-sharing effort.[46] In a 2015 hearing, GAO testified that TSA had put processes in place to address these issues.[47]

DHS provides grants for security improvements for public transit, passenger rail, and occasionally other surface transportation modes under the Transit Security Grant Program. The vast majority of the funding goes to public transit providers. CRS estimates that, on an inflation-adjusted basis, funding for this program has declined 84% since 2009, when Congress allocated $150 million in the American Recovery and Reinvestment Act of 2009, in addition to routine appropriations (see Table 1).

---

[43] Government Accountability Office, Transportation Security Administration: Surface Transportation Inspector Activities Should Align More Closely With Identified Risks, GAO-18-180, December 2017, pp. 24-26.

[44] Ibid., p. 20: Several surface inspectors estimated spending 20%-50% of their work time on aviation tasks.

[45] Government Accountability Office, Passenger Rail Security: Consistent Incident Reporting and Analysis Needed to Achieve Program Objectives, GAO-13-20, December 19, 2012.

[46] Government Accountability Office, Transportation Security Information Sharing: Stakeholder Satisfaction Varies; TSA Could Take Additional Actions to Strengthen Efforts, GAO-14-506, June 24, 2014.

[47] Government Accountability Office, Surface Transportation Security: TSA Has Taken Steps Designed to Develop Process for Sharing and Analyzing Information and to Improve Rail Security Incident Reporting, GAO-15-205T, given before the U.S. House of Representatives, Committee on Homeland Security, Subcommittees on Transportation Security and Counterterrorism & Intelligence, September 17, 2015.

Table 1. Congressional Funding for Transit Security Grants, FY2002-FY2018

Fiscal Year	Appropriation (millions of nominal dollars)	Appropriation (millions of 2018 dollars)
2002	$63[a]	$86
2003	65	87
2004	50	65
2005	108	137
2006	131	161
2007	251	301
2008	356	413
2009	498[b]	575
2010	253	288
2011	200	223
2012	88[c]	96
2013	84	90
2014	90	95
2015	87	92
2016	87	91
2017	88	90
2018	88	88

Source: FY2002: Department of Defense FY2002 Appropriations Act, P.L. 107-117; FY2003: FY2003 Emergency Wartime Supplemental Appropriations Act, P.L. 108-11; FY2004: Department of Homeland Security FY2004 Appropriations Act, P.L. 108-90; FY2005-FY2011: U.S. Government Accountability Office, *Homeland Security: DHS Needs Better Project Information and Coordination among Four Overlapping Grant Programs*, GAO-12-303, February 2012, Table 1; FY2012-2018: DHS, Transit Security Grant Program annual funding opportunity announcements.

Notes: The Transit Security Grant Program was formally established in FY2005; in FY2003-FY2004, grants were made through the Urban Areas Security Initiative. Does not include funding provided for security grants for intercity passenger rail (Amtrak), intercity bus service, and commercial trucking. Nominal dollar amounts adjusted to constant 2018 dollars using the Total Non-defense column from Table 10: Gross Domestic Product and Deflators Used in the Historical Tables: 1940-2023, published in the Historical Tables volume of the Budget of the United States Government, Fiscal Year 2019 (https://www.whitehouse.gov/omb/historical-tables/).

[a]Appropriated to Washington Metropolitan Area Transit Authority and the Federal Transit Administration.

[b]Includes $150 million provided in the American Recovery and Reinvestment Act.

[c]Congress did not specify an amount for transit security grants, but provided a lump sum for state and local grant programs, leaving funding allocations to the discretion of DHS.

In a 2012 report, GAO found potential for duplication among four DHS state and local security grant programs with similar goals, one of which was the public transportation security grant program.[48] Despite this finding, Congress has not supported consolidation of the programs, though appropriators have expressed concern that grant programs have not focused on areas of highest risk and that significant amounts of previously appropriated funds have not yet been awarded to recipients.

In P.L. 114-50, Congress directed TSA to ensure that all passenger transportation providers it considers as having high-risk facilities have in place plans to respond to active shooters, acts of terrorism, or other security-related incidents that target passengers.

PORT AND MARITIME SECURITY[49]

The bulk of U.S. overseas trade is carried by ships, and thus the economic consequences of a maritime terrorist attack could be significant. In the aftermath of the 9/11 attacks, the U.S. Customs Service (now Customs and Border Protection, CBP) and the Coast Guard realized that they needed to "push the borders out"—that is, they needed to begin screening vessels and cargo before they reached a U.S. port. While the previous screening methods that occurred at U.S. ports were sufficient to intercept other illicit cargo (e.g., drug smuggling) they could be too late in the case of intercepting a terrorist bomb. Thus, Customs instituted the "24-hour rule," requiring importers to submit shipment information to Customs a day before the shipment arrived at the *overseas* port of loading rather than submitting this information within days of its arrival at a U.S. port. Customs analyzes this information and other intelligence to flag shipments it believes are higher risk or have an unknown risk. Under the Container Security Initiative, those riskier shipments are examined by imaging machines or possibly unloaded before being loaded on a vessel. (It is

---

[48] United States Governmental Accountability Office, Homeland Security: DHS Needs Better Project Information and Coordination among Four Overlapping Grant Programs, GAO-12-303, February 2012.

[49] This section was prepared by John Frittelli, Specialist in Transportation Policy.

practically impossible to examine shipping containers once they are aboard a vessel or while the ship is at sea).

Similarly, the Coast Guard recognized the need to extend terrorist screening beyond U.S. ports. It required ships to announce and report their intended arrival four days before entering a U.S. harbor. The Coast Guard examines the vessel's particulars, its crew, and past history to evaluate the security risk. The Coast Guard pushed for establishing international standards for port security at the International Maritime Organization so that overseas ports sending cargo to the United States would abide by the same security regulations as U.S. ports. The Coast Guard also visits foreign ports to assess their security measures.

In addition to pushing the borders out, these agencies have instituted multiple layers of security that cover the four main elements of maritime transportation: ports, vessels, cargo, and workers. CBP's Customs Trade Partnership Against Terrorism (C-TPAT) program identifies a series of practices that importers are to follow that are designed to cover a shipper's entire supply chain— from the overseas point of origin to final delivery in the United States. For instance, C-TPAT includes procedures and independent checks when loading a shipping container and applying the seal on its doors to prevent tampering while in route. In addition to container inspection equipment installed at overseas ports, CBP has installed radiation portal monitors at each truck exit gate in U.S. ports.

The Coast Guard requires vessel owners, port authorities and their terminal operators to submit security plans that describe their access control measures, drills and exercises to respond to a security incident, and other measures to secure their facilities. The Coast Guard recognizes that U.S. ports vary greatly in terms of their geographies and types of cargo they handle. The port security plans allow the industry to develop plans specific to their vulnerabilities. An important goal of the Coast Guard is "maritime domain awareness"—knowledge of the varied legitimate vessel activity taking place in a harbor (cargo, fishing, recreational) so as to spot any abnormal or suspicious activity. One aspect of this is requiring many vessels to be equipped with Automatic Identification Systems (transponders). The Coast Guard, along with TSA, has also instituted a port worker background check for longshoremen, truck drivers, vessel crews, and others that need access to port terminals. A Transportation Worker Identification Credential (TWIC) card must be obtained from the TSA and renewed every five years.

Congress authorized much of the Coast Guard's role in maritime security in the Maritime Transportation Security Act of 2002 (MTSA; P.L. 107-295) and CBP's role in the Security and Accountability for Every Port Act of 2006 (SAFE Port Act; P.L. 109-347). Congress modified these maritime security programs in Division J of the FAA Reauthorization Act of 2018 (P.L. 115 254).

Two aspects of maritime security that have drawn attention recently are cybersecurity and the use of drones for coastal surveillance. The development of electronic navigation ("e-navigation"), involving the replacement of paper charts with electronic charts (already commonplace) or the replacement of channel marker buoys with virtual aids to navigation (in progress), could create vulnerabilities to cyberattack. In June 2017, a cyberattack on Maersk Line, the largest container carrier, prevented the carrier from taking bookings and required it to close its U.S. terminals for two to three days. A less severe attack affected COSCO Shipping in July 2018. P.L. 115-254 incorporated cybersecurity as a required element in MTSA security plans for terminal and vessel operators. The Coast Guard has provided guidance for vessels and ports to address cyber vulnerabilities, and has incorporated cybersecurity into existing enforcement and compliance programs.[50] The Coast Guard has added cybersecurity training to the requirements for mariner licensing and for port security officer qualifications.

Greater use of unmanned aircraft systems potentially offers significant efficiencies in performing various Coast Guard missions, including coastal surveillance. Congress has provided funding for the use of drones aboard national security cutters.[51] The Coast Guard has tested both hand-held drones and larger drone aircraft to extend the surveillance range of its

---

[50] Coast Guard, Navigation and Vessel Inspection Circular (NVIC) 05-17; Guidelines for Addressing Cyber Risks at Maritime Transportation Security Act (MTSA) Regulated Facilities, July 12, 2017.

[51] H.Rept. 114-215, DHS Appropriations Bill, 2016; p. 59.

patrol vessels. Since 2015, the Coast Guard has been testing UASs in the Arctic for missions such as surveying ice conditions, marine environmental monitoring, marine safety, and search and rescue.[52] The unmanned aircraft being tested each summer can be launched from land or a Coast Guard cutter.[53] The Coast Guard Authorization Act of 2018 (P.L. 115-282, §812) requests a study by the National Academy of Sciences as to how drones could be used to enhance the Coast Guard's maritime domain awareness. The act also allows the Coast Guard to lease but not design its own large UASs if funding is provided for design and construction of Offshore Patrol Cutters (§304).[54]

---

[52] 80 *Federal Register* 18431, April 6, 2015.

[53] Coast Guard Compass, "Research, Development, Test and Evaluation Spotlight: Arctic Technology Evaluation 2018," September 11, 2018; http://coastguard.dodlive.mil/2018/09/research-development-test-and-evaluation-spotlightarctic-technology-evaluation-2018/.

[54] Similar language was enacted in the National Defense Authorization Act for FY2017 (P.L. 114-328, §899).

In: Transportation
Editor: Frederick Daniels
ISBN: 978-1-53615-651-5

Chapter 2

FUNDING AND FINANCING HIGHWAYS AND PUBLIC TRANSPORTATION (UPDATE)*

Robert S. Kirk and William J. Mallett

SUMMARY

For many years, federal surface transportation programs were funded almost entirely from taxes on motor fuels deposited in the Highway Trust Fund. The tax rates, which are fixed in terms of cents per gallon, have not been increased at the federal level since 1993. Meanwhile, motor fuel consumption is projected to decline due to improved fuel efficiency, increased use of electric vehicles, and slow growth in vehicle miles traveled. In consequence, revenue flowing into the Highway Trust Fund has been insufficient to support the surface transportation program authorized by Congress since 2008.

Congress has yet to address the surface transportation program's fundamental revenue issues, and has given limited consideration to raising fuel taxes in recent years. Instead, since 2008 Congress has supported the federal surface transportation program by supplementing fuel tax revenues with transfers from the U.S. Treasury general fund. The

* This is an edited, reformatted and augmented version of Congressional Research Service, Publication No. R45350, dated October 24, 2018.

most recent reauthorization act, the Fixing America's Surface Transportation Act (FAST Act; P.L. 114-94), authorized spending on federal highway and public transportation programs through September 30, 2020. The act provided $70 billion in general fund transfers to the Highway Trust Fund from FY2016 through FY2020. This use of general fund transfers to supplement the Highway Trust Fund will have been the de facto funding policy for 12 years when the FAST Act expires. Congressional Budget Office (CBO) projections indicate that the Highway Trust Fund insufficiency relative to spending will reemerge following expiration of the FAST Act. The projections indicate a shortfall of $85 billion over the first five years following the FAST Act, and $109 billion over the first six years.

As the September 2020 expiration of the FAST Act approaches, Congress may again examine adjustments to the funding and financing of the federal role in surface transportation.

- Raising motor fuel taxes could provide the Highway Trust Fund with sufficient revenue to fully fund the program in the near term, but may not be a viable long-term solution due to expected declines in fuel consumption. It would also not address the equity issue arising from the increasing number of personal and commercial vehicles that are powered electrically and therefore do not pay motor fuel taxes.
- Replacing motor fuel taxes with a mileage-based road user charge would need to overcome a variety of financial, administrative, and privacy barriers, but could be a solution in the longer term.
- Treasury general fund transfers could continue to be used to make up for the Highway Trust Fund's projected shortfalls but could require budget offsets of an equal amount.

The political difficulty of adequately funding the Highway Trust Fund could lead Congress to consider altering the trust fund system or eliminating it altogether. This might involve a reallocation of responsibilities and obligations among federal, state, and local governments.

Some surface transportation needs can be met by private investment, including public-private partnerships, and federal loans from the Transportation Infrastructure Finance and Innovation Act (TIFIA) program. If it desires to promote private investment in transportation infrastructure, Congress could consider asset recycling incentive grants to state and local governments for the sale or lease of government-owned infrastructure if the proceeds are committed to new infrastructure.

Tolling may be an effective way to finance specific roads, bridges, or tunnels that are likely to have heavy use and are located such that the tolls are difficult to evade. All revenue from tolls flows to the state or local agencies or private entities that operate tolled facilities; the federal government does not collect any revenue from tolls. However, a major expansion of tolling might reduce the need for federal expenditures on roads. Tolls and private investment are unlikely to provide broad financial support for surface transportation needs, and many projects are not well suited to alternative financing.

INTRODUCTION

Almost every conversation about surface transportation finance begins with a two-part question: What are the "needs" of the national transportation system, and how does the nation pay for them? This chapter is aimed almost entirely at discussing the "how to pay for them" question. Since 1956, federal surface transportation programs have been funded largely by taxes on motor fuels that flow into the Highway Trust Fund (HTF). A steady increase in the revenues flowing into the HTF due to increased motor vehicle use and occasional increases in fuel tax rates accommodated growth in surface transportation spending over several decades. In 2001, though, trust fund revenues stopped growing faster than spending. In 2008 Congress began providing Treasury general fund transfers to keep the HTF solvent.[1]

Every year since 2008, there has been a gap between the dedicated tax revenues flowing into the HTF and the cost of the surface transportation spending Congress has authorized. Congress has filled these shortfalls by transfers, largely from the general fund, that have shifted a total of $143.6 billion to the HTF (roughly 22% of outlays).[2] The last $70 billion of these transfers were authorized in the Fixing America's Surface Transportation Act (FAST Act; P.L. 114-94), which was signed by President Barack Obama on December 4, 2015.[3] The FAST Act funds federal surface transportation programs from FY2016 through FY2020. When the act

---

[1] Based on Federal Highway Administration (FHWA) data. Balances in the HTF accrued in previous years were large enough to keep the fund sufficient until FY2008.

[2] Based on actual and projected outlays FY2009 through late FY2021, when the HTF is projected to approach a zero balance.

[3] CRS Report R44388, *Surface Transportation Funding and Programs Under the Fixing America's Surface Transportation Act (FAST Act; P.L. 114-94)*, coordinated by Robert S. Kirk.

expires the de facto policy of relying on general fund transfers to sustain the HTF will be 12 years old.

Congressional Budget Office (CBO) projections indicate that the imbalance between motor fuel tax receipts and HTF expenditures will persist beyond FY2020. In consequence, funding and financing surface transportation is expected to continue to be a major issue for Congress.

The Highway Trust Fund Revenue Dilemma

The HTF has two separate accounts—highways and mass transit. The primary revenue sources for these accounts are an 18.3-cent-per-gallon federal tax on gasoline and a 24.3-cent-per-gallon federal tax on diesel fuel. Although the HTF has other sources of revenue, such as truck registration fees and a truck tire tax, and is also credited with interest paid on the fund balances held by the Treasury, fuel taxes in most years provide 85% to 90% of the amounts paid into the fund by highway users. The transit account receives 2.86 cents per gallon of fuel taxes, with the remainder of the tax revenue flowing into the highway account. An additional 0.1-cent-per-gallon fuel tax is reserved for the Leaking Underground Storage Tank (LUST) Fund, which is not part of the transportation program.

Since the trust fund was created in 1956, Congress has increased federal motor fuel taxes four times: in 1959, 1982, 1990, and 1993. Since the 1993 increase, additional changes to the taxation structure have modestly boosted trust fund revenues. However, since 2001, revenue flowing into the HTF has not met expectations in most years.[4] The American Jobs Creation Act of 2004 (P.L. 108-357), for example, provided the trust fund with increased future income by changing elements of federal "gasohol" taxation. In 2005, the Safe, Accountable, Flexible, Efficient Transportation Equity Act: A Legacy for Users (P.L. 109-59;

[4] See Congressional Budget Office, *How Would Proposed Fuel Economy Standards Affect the Highway Trust Fund?* May 2012, p. 3. A drop in outlays in FY2006 helped bring the HTF briefly into balance in FY2006 and FY2007.

SAFETEA) sought to bolster the trust fund by addressing tax fraud. SAFETEA also provided for the transfer of some general fund revenue associated with transportation-related activities to the trust fund. It was believed at the time of SAFETEA's passage that the tax changes, a $12.5 billion unexpended balance in the trust fund, and higher fuel tax revenue due to expected economic growth would be sufficient to finance the surface transportation program through FY2009.[5] This prediction proved to be incorrect. Trust fund revenue has generally lagged inflation since FY2007. The shortfalls resulting from the overly optimistic forecasts associated with SAFETEA were rectified by Treasury general fund contributions. In September 2008, Congress enacted a bill that transferred $8 billion from the general fund to shore up the HTF. Other transfers followed (see Table 1).

When the HTF was conceived, annual vehicle miles traveled (VMT), and therefore motor fuel tax revenue, were rising rapidly. That is no longer the case. The Federal Highway Administration (FHWA) projects that VMT will grow at an average of roughly 1.2% per year over the next 20 years.[6] Meanwhile, other policy changes are weakening the link between driving activity and motor fuel tax revenues. Under rules issued in 2012, new passenger cars and light trucks are expected to attain an average fuel economy of 41.0 miles per gallon in model year 2021 and 49.7 miles per gallon in model year 2025.[7] Improved fuel economy is slowly reducing the average amount of fuel used per mile of travel. The expanding fleets of hybrid and electric vehicles, respectively, pay less or nothing by way of fuel taxes, raising equity issues that are likely to become more prominent as the electric/hybrid vehicle fleet expands.[8] On April 2, 2018, the Trump

---

[5] Jeff Davis, "Ten Years of Highway Trust Fund Bankruptcy: Why Did It Happen, and What Have We Learned?," *Eno Transportation Weekly*, August 27, 2018, pp. 8-12.

[6] Federal Highway Administration, *FHWA Forecasts of Vehicle Miles Traveled (VMT): Spring 2018*, Washington, DC, May 2018, https://www.fhwa.dot.gov/policyinformation/tables/vmt/vmt_forecast_sum.pdf.

[7] CRS Report R45204, *Vehicle Fuel Economy and Greenhouse Gas Standards: Frequently Asked Questions*, by Richard K. Lattanzio, Linda Tsang, and Bill Canis.

[8] Congressional Budget Office, *How Would Proposed Fuel Economy Standards Affect the Highway Trust Fund?*, May 2012, http://cbo.gov/sites/default/files/cbofiles/attachments/05-02-CAFE_brief.pdf. Because of the gradual turnover in the car and truck fleet and because the new standards will not take effect until model year 2017, CBO estimates that

Administration announced its intent to revise the Corporate Average Fuel Economy (CAFE) standards for the model years 2022-2025.[9] This change could slow the increase in the average fuel economy of the motor vehicle fleet.

Table 1. Transfers to the Highway Trust Fund (in billions of dollars; reflects sequestration for FY2013 and FY2014)

Public Law	Effective Date	Highway Account	Mass Transit Account	Highway Trust Fund Total
P.L. 110-318	Sept. 15, 2008	8.017	0	8.017
P.L. 111-46	Aug. 7, 2009	7.000	0	7.000
P.L. 111-147	Mar. 18, 2010	14.700	4.800	19.500
P.L. 112-141	July 6, 2012			
From LUST	For FY2012	2.400	0	2.400
From general fund	For FY2013	5.884	0	5.884
From general fund	For FY2014	9.651	2.042	11.693
P.L. 113-159	Aug. 8, 2014	7.765	2.000	9.765
From LUST	Aug. 8, 2014	1.000	0	1.000
P.L. 114-41	July 31, 2015	6.068	2.000	8.068
P.L. 114-94				
From general fund	Dec. 4, 2015	51.900	18.100	70.000
From LUST	Dec. 4, 2015	0.100	0	0.100
From LUST	Oct. 1, 2016	0.100	0	0.100
From LUST	Oct. 1, 2017	0.100	0	0.100
General fund total		110.985	28.942	139.927
LUST fund total		3.700	0	3.700
Total transfers		114.685	28.942	143.627

Sources: Public laws as indicated. Sequestration amounts from FHWA.

Notes: Transfers are from the Treasury's general fund unless indicated. LUST refers to the Leaking Underground Storage Tank Trust Fund administered by the Environmental Protection Agency.

An increase in the existing fuel tax rates would provide immediate relief to the trust fund. As a rule of thumb, adding a penny to federal motor fuel taxes provides the trust fund with roughly $1.5 billion to $1.7 billion

the standards will reduce "gasoline tax revenues between 2012 and 2022 by less than 1 percent."

[9] CRS In Focus IF10871, *Vehicle Fuel Economy and Greenhouse Gas Standards*, by Richard K. Lattanzio, Linda Tsang, and Bill Canis.

per year.[10] The prospect of reduced motor fuel consumption, however, casts doubt on the ability of the motor fuel taxes to support increased surface transportation spending beyond the next decade, even with significant increases in tax rates.

What Congress Faces

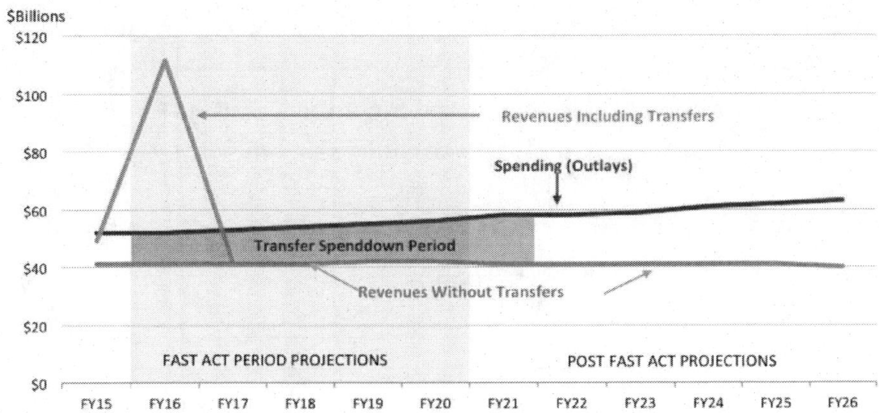

Source: CRS, based on CBO, Highway Trust Fund Projections: April 2018 HTF Baseline 2017-2028.

Notes: Includes highway account and mass transit accounts combined. Revenues include interest on HTF balances. The shading between spending and revenues indicates the period that the HTF balance is maintained by the FAST Act transfers from the general fund and the LUST fund.

Figure 1. Highway Trust Fund Funding Gap.

CBO projects that from FY2021 to FY2026 the gap between dedicated surface transportation revenues and spending will average $19 billion annually (Table 2).[11] In 2020, as Congress considers surface transportation

[10] Joseph Kile, *Testimony: The Status of the Highway Trust Fund and Options for Paying for Highway Spending*, Congressional Budget Office, June 18, 2015, p. 9, https://www.cbo.gov/sites/default/files/114th-congress-2015-2016/reports/50297-TransportationTestimony-Senate.pdf.

[11] Congressional Budget Office, *Projections of Highway Trust Fund Accounts Under CBO's April 2019 Baseline*, April 2018, https://www.cbo.gov/system/files?file=2018-06/51300-2018-04-highwaytrustfund.pdf. The $19 billion figure represents the average annual gap

reauthorization, it could again face a choice between finding new sources of income for the surface transportation program and settling for a smaller program, which might look very different from the one currently in place. Figure 1 shows the impact of the general fund transfers within the context of the underlying imbalance between HTF revenues and projected spending for FY2018-FY2026.

The Underlying Problem: HTF Spending Exceeds Revenues

Table 2. Projected HTF Revenue and Spending (Outlays) Imbalance (in billions of dollars)

Fiscal Year	HTF Revenue	HTF Outlays	Difference
2021	41	58	-17
2022	41	59	-17
2023	41	59	-18
2024	41	61	-20
2025	41	62	-21
2026	40	63	-23
5-YR: FY2021-2025 total	205	299	-94
5-YR: FY2021-2025 average	41	60	-19
6-YR: FY2021-2026 total	245	362	-117
6-YR: FY2021-2026 average	41	60	-19

Source: CRS calculations based on CBO, Highway Trust Fund Projections: April 2018 HTF Baseline 2017-2028.

Notes: Includes combined figures from both the highway account and the mass transit account. The "HTF Revenue" column includes interest on the HTF balances. Numbers may not add due to rounding.

Table 2 provides projections of the gap between HTF receipts and outlays following the expiration of the FAST Act at the end of FY2020. In recent decades, Congress has typically sought to reauthorize surface transportation programs for periods of five or six years. As the table

---

between projected receipts from the motor fuel and other excise taxes that flow into the Highway Trust Fund and the anticipated cost of maintaining the surface transportation program at its current "baseline" level. Because of beginning of year (BOY) HTF balances for FY2021, a five-year surface transportation bill (FY2021-FY2025) could be funded with roughly $85 billion in transfers or increased revenues.

indicates, a five-year reauthorization beginning in FY2021 faces a projected gap between revenues and outlays of roughly $94 billion. A six-year reauthorization would face a gap of almost $117 billion.[12] These projections assume that spending on federal highway and public transportation programs would remain as it is today, adjusted for anticipated inflation.

The Resulting Funding Shortfalls

When the FAST Act expires at the end of FY2020, the balance in the HTF is expected to be $14 billion—an amount equal to almost three months of outlays. CBO projects that this balance, plus incoming revenue, will allow the Federal Highway Administration (FHWA) and the Federal Transit Administration (FTA) to pay their obligations to states and transit agencies until sometime in FY2021. However, without a reduction in the size of the surface transportation programs, an increase in revenues, or further general fund transfers, the balance in the HTF is projected to be close to zero near the end of FY2021 (see Table 3). At that point, both FHWA and FTA would likely have to delay payments for completed work.[13]

Based strictly on projected income and expenses, the HTF would move from a positive balance of $14 billion at the start of FY2021 to a negative balance of $85 billion at the end of FY2025. However, current law does not allow the HTF to incur negative balances. Unless this is changed, $85 billion represents the minimum amount the House Ways and Means Committee and the Senate Committee on Finance would need to find over the FY2021-FY2025 period in some combination of additional revenue and budget offsets for general fund transfers, should Congress choose to continue funding surface transportation at the current, or "baseline," level,

[12] Since the early 1990s Congress has begun the reauthorization debates with a goal of a six-year bill. The most recent bill, the FAST Act, however, provided five years of funding.

[13] Federal Highway Administration, *Action: Procedures for Reimbursements During a Cash Shortfall*, July 1, 2014, https://www.transportation.gov/sites/dot.gov/files/docs/Guidance-Memo-Cash-Allocation-Final-3.pdf.

adjusted for inflation.[14] Because the HTF currently provides all but about $2 billion of annual spending authorized for the highway and transit programs (the main exception being the FTA Capital Investment Grants Program), these numbers have implications for the size of the program Congress may approve to follow the FAST Act.

Table 3. Projected Negative Cash Flow and HTF Cumulative Shortfalls (in billions of dollars)

	2021	2022	2023	2024	2025	2026
Start-of-year HTF balancea	14	-3	-22	-41	-63	-85
Revenues minus outlays	-17	-17	-18	-20	-21	-23
End-of-year HTF shortfall	-3	-22	-41	-63	-85	-109

Source: CBO, Highway Trust Fund Projections: April 2018 HTF Baseline 2017-2028.

Notes: Includes combined figures from both the highway account and the mass transit account. Numbers do not add due to rounding. CBO provides data for each account rounded to the nearest billion dollars for its HTF baseline projections.

[a] Under current law, the HTF cannot incur negative balances.

Highway and transit spending based solely on the revenue projected to flow into the HTF under current law would be limited to roughly $41 billion in FY2021, significantly less than the "baseline" FY2021 outlays of roughly $58 billion. The projected stagnation and eventual FY2026 decline in HTF revenue implies that once expected inflation is factored in, FHWA and FTA would have less contract authority in each year to spend on projects through FY2026.[15]

Reducing expenditures would not provide immediate relief from the demands on the HTF. Because transportation projects can take years to complete, both the highway and public transportation programs must make payments in future years pursuant to commitments that have already been incurred. As of FY2019, obligated but unspent contract authority for highway projects in progress is projected to be roughly $62 billion. This

[14] FHWA estimates that it must also maintain a working balance of $5 billion. Maintaining this working balance increases the funding shortfall five-year total to $90 billion.

[15] Contract authority is a type of budget authority that is available for obligation even without an appropriation. However, appropriators must eventually provide liquidating appropriation authority, which is not recorded as budget authority, to permit the eventual outlays. Contract authority is the type of budget authority used by the HTF.

does not count another $22 billion in available but unobligated contract authority. For public transportation programs the equivalent figures for FY2019 are projected to be almost $18 billion in unpaid obligations and another $11 billion in unobligated contract authority.[16] The obligated amounts represent legal obligations of the U.S. government and must be paid out of future years' HTF receipts.

On February 9, 2018, President Trump signed the Bipartisan Budget Act of 2018 (P.L. 115-123), which raised the ceilings on non-defense discretionary spending for FY2018 and FY2019 by $63.3 billion and $67.5 billion, respectively. House and Senate leaders agreed to work with the appropriators to ensure that at least $10 billion per year of these additional outlays would be provided for infrastructure, including surface transportation.[17] The Consolidated Appropriations Act, 2018 (P.L. 115-141), provided additional infrastructure funding from the general fund in accordance with the Bipartisan Budget Act, including $2.834 billion for programs normally funded from the HTF. These funds were not credited to the HTF, however, and have no impact on HTF solvency.

EXISTING HIGHWAY FUEL TAXES[18]

The first federal tax on gasoline (1 cent per gallon) was imposed in 1932, during the Hoover Administration, as a deficit-reduction measure following the depression-induced fall in general revenues. The rate was raised to help pay for World War II (to 1.5 cents per gallon) and raised again during the Korean War (to 2 cents per gallon). The Highway Revenue Act of 1956 (P.L. 84 627) established the HTF and raised the rate

[16] Office of Management and Budget, *Budget of the U.S. Government FY2019: Appendix* (Washington, DC: 2018), pp. 875, 899-900. Estimates are for start-of-year FY2019.

[17] "Bipartisan Budget Agreement: a Memorandum from the House and Senate Leaders," February 8, 2018.

[18] This discussion tracks the changes in the rate of the gasoline tax. Over time other fuels such as diesel have been taxed at different rates. For instance, the current tax on diesel fuel is 6 cents per gallon higher than the gasoline tax. For a tabular history of the rates of the various federal fuel taxes, see Federal Highway Administration, *Highway Statistics: Table FE101-A*, https://www.fhwa.dot.gov/policyinformation/statistics/2015/fe101a.cfm.

to 3 cents per gallon to pay for the construction of the Interstate Highway System. The Federal-Aid Highway Act of 1959 (P.L. 86-342) raised the rate to 4 cents per gallon. The gasoline tax remained at 4 cents from October 1, 1959, until March 31, 1983. During this period, revenues grew automatically from year to year as fuel consumption grew along with increases in vehicle miles traveled.

Since 1983 lawmakers have passed legislation raising the tax rates on highway fuel use three times. Although infrequent, these rate increases were quite large in a proportional sense. The gasoline tax was raised on April 1, 1983, from 4 to 9 cents per gallon, a 125% increase; on September 1, 1990, from 9 to 14 cents (not counting the additional 0.1 cent for LUST), or 55%; and on October 1, 1993, from 14 to 18.3 cents, or 31%.[19]

How the Rates Have Been Raised Since 1983

Increasing the rate of the fuel taxes has never been popular. The last three increases were accomplished with difficulty and were influenced by the broader budgetary environment and the politics of the time.[20]

The "Great Compromise" and the Highway "User Fee"

The increase in the fuel tax rate under the Surface Transportation Assistance Act of 1982 (STAA; P.L. 97-424, Title V) occurred in the lame-duck session of the 97th Congress. In the "Great Compromise," supporters of increased highway spending had come to an agreement with transit supporters (mostly from the Northeast) that a penny of a proposed 5-cents-per-gallon increase would be dedicated to a new mass transit account within the HTF. This meant that support for the bill during the lame-duck session was widespread and bipartisan. President Reagan's opposition to an increase in the "gas tax" softened during the lame-duck

[19] CRS Report RL30304, *The Federal Excise Tax on Motor Fuels and the Highway Trust Fund: Current Law and Legislative History*, by Sean Lowry.

[20] Federal Highway Administration, *Financing Federal-aid Highways; Appendix M, Federal Excise Taxes on Highway Motor Fuel*, last modified February 20, 2015, http://www.fhwa.dot.gov/reports/fifahiwy/ffahappm.htm.

session. On November 23, 1982, he announced that he would support passage of STAA because "Our country's outstanding highway system was built on the user fee principle—that those who benefit from a use should share in its cost."[21] Nonetheless, the bill faced a series of filibusters in the Senate, which were eventually overcome by four cloture votes. The conference report was again filibustered, and President Reagan helped secure the votes needed for cloture. President Reagan signed STAA into law on January 6, 1983, more than doubling the highway fuel tax to 9 cents per gallon.[22]

50/50 Share: Deficit Reduction/Highway Trust Fund

The Omnibus Budget Reconciliation Act of 1990 (OBRA90; P.L. 101-508), enacted November 5, 1990, was passed under the pressure of impending final FY1991 sequestration orders issued by President George H. W. Bush under Title II of P.L. 99-177, the Balanced Budget and Emergency Deficit Control Act of 1985, also known as the Gramm-Rudman-Hollings Act (GRH). OBRA90 included budget cuts, tax changes, and the Budget Enforcement Act (P.L. 101-508), which rescinded the FY1991 sequestration orders. OBRA90 also raised the tax on gasoline by 5 cents per gallon, to 14 cents. Half the increase went to the HTF (2 cents to the highway account and 0.5 cents to the mass transit account), with the other 2.5 cents per gallon to be deposited in the general fund for deficit reduction. This was the first time since 1957 the motor fuel tax had been used as a source of general revenue. Section 9001 expressed the sense of Congress that all motor fuel taxes should be directed to the HTF as soon as possible.

More for Deficit Reduction

The Omnibus Budget Reconciliation Act of 1993 (OBRA93; P.L. 103-66) Section 13241(a) made further changes in regard to fuel taxes:

---

[21] U.S. President (Reagan), "Remarks to Reporters Announcing the Administration's Proposal for a Highway and Bridge Repair Program: Nov. 23, *1982*," *The American Presidency Project; Public Papers.*

[22] See Jeff Davis, *Reagan Devolution: The Real Story of the 1982 Gas Tax Increase*, Eno Center for Transportation, Washington, DC, 2015, pp. 1-40.

- The 2.5-cents-per-gallon fuel tax dedicated to deficit reduction in OBRA90 was redirected to the HTF beginning October 1, 1995, and its authorization was extended to September 30, 1999.
- The highway account received 2 cents per gallon and the mass transit account 0.5 cents per gallon of the rededicated amount.
- An additional permanent 4.3-cents-per-gallon fuel tax took effect in October 1993 and was dedicated to deficit reduction.

This brought the gasoline tax to 18.3 cents per gallon, although for two years (October 1, 1993, to October 1, 1995) 6.8 cents per gallon of this was deposited in the general fund. On October 1, 1995, the amount going to the general fund dropped to 4.3 cents per gallon, and the amount dedicated to the HTF increased to 14 cents per gallon. Subsequently, under the Taxpayer Relief Act of 1997 (P.L. 105-34), all motor fuel tax revenue was redirected to the HTF. (The LUST fund continues to receive the revenue from an additional 0.1 cents-per-gallon tax.)

ALTERNATIVES FOR HTF REVENUE

The political difficulty of increasing motor fuel taxes has led to interest in alternative approaches for supporting the HTF. Among options that have been proposed are the following:

"Fixing" the Gas Tax

A differently designed gas tax might be indexed to both inflation (either inflation generally or highway construction cost inflation) and fuel-efficiency improvements.[23] This new design could be imposed after raising

[23] There are many inflation indexes that could be used. Which one is most appropriate might become an issue of controversy. The most commonly used index is the U.S. Bureau of Labor Statistics' consumer price index (CPI), which, for example, is used to adjust certain aviation user fees. Other examples are the Bureau of Economic Analysis price indexes for

the current gas tax rate to compensate for the loss in purchasing power since the last rate increase in 1993.[24]

If the motor fuel taxes for gasoline and diesel had been adjusted in 2017 to keep pace with the change in the Bureau of Labor Statistics' consumer price index since 1993, the 18.3-cents-pergallon gasoline tax would now be 31.7 cents per gallon, and the 24.3-cents-per-gallon diesel tax would be 42.1 cents per gallon. Consequently, the first step in implementing this method of "fixing" the gas tax would be to raise the base tax rate for gasoline by roughly 13.4 cents per gallon and to raise the rate for diesel by roughly 17.8 cents per gallon. Future adjustments would depend on the inflation rate in future years.

Tax-rate adjustments to make up for revenue lost due to greater fuel efficiency could be determined by dividing miles driven by vehicle category by the total amount of fuel consumed by that category and comparing the quotient to the previous year. Although fuel-economy standards for new vehicles are to rise over the next few years, the average efficiency of the entire vehicle fleet will rise slowly because of the large number of older vehicles on the road.

Switching to Sales Taxes

Under the sales tax concept, the federal motor fuel taxes would be assessed as a percentage of the retail price of fuel rather than as a fixed amount per gallon. Some states already levy taxes on motor fuels in this way, either alongside or in place of fixed cents-per-gallon taxes on motor fuel purchases.

If fuel prices rise in the future, sales tax revenues could rise from year to year even if consumption does not increase. Conversely, however, a decline in motor fuel prices could lead to a drop in sales tax revenue. Many

---

gross government fixed investment and the Federal Highway Administration's National Highway Construction Cost Index (NHCCI).

[24] Institute on Taxation and Economic Policy, *A Federal Gas Tax for the Future*, Washington, DC, September 2013, pp. 1-13, http://www.itep.org/pdf/fedgastax0913.pdf.

states that tied fuel taxes to prices after the price shocks of the 1970s encountered revenue shortfalls in the 1980s, when fuel prices fell dramatically. Over a 20 year period, most of these variable state fuel taxes disappeared.[25] In 2013, Virginia eliminated its cents-per-gallon fuel taxes in favor of a sales tax on fuel and a general sales tax increase that was dedicated to transportation purposes. The Virginia law mandates that the tax be imposed on the average wholesale price (calculated twice each year) but sets price floors; if prices of motor fuels fall beneath those floors, the amount of fuel tax charged per gallon is not reduced further.[26]

A federal sales tax on motor fuel would likely be at best an interim solution to the long-term problem of financing transportation infrastructure because, as with the current motor fuel tax, it relies on fuel consumption to fund transportation programs. To the extent that improved vehicle efficiency or adoption of hybrid or electric vehicles leads to long-term declines in fuel usage, a sales tax on fuel may not lead to increases in trust fund revenues.[27]

Vehicle Miles Traveled Charges (VMT)

Economists have long favored mileage-based user charges as an alternative source of highway funding. Under the user charge concept, motorists would pay fees based on distance driven and, perhaps, on other costs of road use, such as wear and tear on roads, traffic congestion, and air

---

[25] Jeffrey Ang-Olson, Martin Wachs, and Brian D. Taylor, *Variable-Rate State Gasoline Taxes*, Institute of Transportation Studies, University of California, Berkeley, Working Paper, UCB-ITS-WP-99-3, July 1999. See also, M. Madowitz and K. Novan, "Gasoline taxes and revenue volatility: An Application to California," *Energy Policy*, vol. 59, 2013, pp 663-673, http://www.sciencedirect.com/science/article/pii/S0301421513002577.

[26] Virginia House Bill 2313, 2013 session. The price floor is the wholesale price as of February 20, 2013. The taxes are paid when the fuel is removed from a refinery or tank farm terminal. This is often referred to as collecting at the "rack."

[27] A fuel price floor could be established, but its impact would depend on how high the floor is set and whether the floor is indexed to inflation. The outcome could still fail to meet revenue expectations.

pollution. The funds collected would be spent for surface transportation purposes.[28]

The concept is not new: federal motor fuel taxes are a form of indirect road user charge insofar as road use is loosely related to fuel consumption. Some states have charged trucks by the mile for many years, and toll roads charge drivers based on miles traveled and the number of axles on a vehicle, which is used as a proxy for weight. Recent technological developments, as well as the evident shortcomings of motor fuel taxes, have led to renewed interest in the user charge concept, including funding for pilot programs included in the FAST Act.

VMT charges, also referred to as mileage-based road user charges, could range from a flat centper-mile charge based on a simple odometer reading to a variable charge based on vehicle movements tracked by Global Positioning System (GPS). Other proposals envision VMT charges that would mimic the way Americans now pay their fuel taxes by collecting the charge at the pump, but a different method would be required to obtain payment from electric vehicle users.

Implementation of a VMT charge would have to overcome a number of potential disadvantages relative to the motor fuel tax, including public concern about personal privacy; higher collection and enforcement costs (estimates range from 5% to 13% of collections); the administrative challenge of collecting the charge from roughly 265 million vehicles; and the setting and adjusting of VMT rates, which would likely be as controversial as increasing motor fuel taxes. Another issue is how to collect the charge from drivers who have no bank accounts or credit/debit cards. A nationwide VMT charge would be analogous to a national toll. This raises the prospect that vehicles using toll roads might be charged

---

[28] See CRS Report R44540, *Mileage-Based Road User Charges*, by Robert S. Kirk and Marc Levinson. For additional discussion of mileage-based charges, see Transportation Research Board, National Cooperative Highway Research Program, *Implementable Strategies for Shifting to Direct Usage-Based Charges for Transportation Funding*, NCHRP Project 20-24(69), Web-Only Document 143, October 2009, http://onlinepubs.trb.org/onlinepubs/nchrp/ nchrp_w143.pdf. See also Paul Sorensen, Liisa Ecola, and Martin Wachs, *Mileage-Based User Fees for Transportation Funding: A Primer for State and Local Decisionmakers*, Rand Corporation, 2012, pp. 1-34, http://www.rand.org/content/dam/rand/pubs/tools/TL100/TL104/RAND_TL104.pdf.

twice, although this effectively happens now in that toll-road users also pay tax on the motor fuel they consume while using the toll road. Technically, it would be possible for a VMT charge to replace an existing toll, but this could cause complications with respect to the servicing of bonds funded by toll-road revenue.

VMT Charges and Non-Highway Programs

Since 1982, the HTF has financed most federal public transportation programs as well as highway programs. If a VMT charge were to be used strictly for highway purposes, it might reasonably be characterized as a user fee even if the amount paid by each individual driver does not correspond precisely to the social cost (such as pollution and traffic congestion costs) of that user's driving. A VMT charge that funded both highways and public transportation might arguably be seen more as a tax than a user fee. This distinction raises a number of legal issues.[29] Any legislation establishing a VMT charge would, at a minimum, have to clearly identify what the charge would be spent on. If the existing HTF were to be retained, legislation would have to specify what share of the revenue would be credited to the separate highway and mass transit accounts within the fund.

Carbon Taxes

A carbon tax would be assessed on emissions of carbon dioxide and other greenhouse gases. Its scope might include manufacturing facilities, power plants, and transportation.[30] A share of revenues from a carbon tax

---

[29] There may be legal considerations depending on whether the VMT charge is structured as a fee or tax. See, for example, U.S. Const. Art. 1, §8, cl. 1 ("all Duties, Imposts and Excises shall be uniform throughout the United States"). Legally, the two are distinguished by the relationship between the amount charged by the government and the services rendered to the payor. For example, the Supreme Court has explained that a tax may be administered "arbitrarily and [without regard to] benefits bestowed by the Government on a taxpayer and go solely on ability to pay, based on property or income," while a user fee is a specific charge imposed for a benefit that accrues only to the payors. *Nat'l Cable Television Ass'n v. United States*, 119 U.S. 336, 340-41 (1974).

[30] CRS Report R42731, *Carbon Tax: Deficit Reduction and Other Considerations*, by Jonathan L. Ramseur, Jane A. Leggett, and Molly F. Sherlock.

could be dedicated to federal transportation programs, either directly or via existing transportation trust funds such as the HTF or the Airport and Airway Trust Fund. The revenues could either replace or supplement current transportation taxes such as the motor fuel taxes. In December 2016, CBO estimated that a carbon tax of $25 per metric ton would increase federal revenues by $977 billion between 2017 and 2026 after adjusting for tax revenue losses related to increased business costs. The projection assumed the tax would increase at an annual rate of 2%, indexed for inflation. CBO estimated that the tax would reduce cumulative emissions from the taxed sources by roughly 9%.[31] The effect of a carbon tax on the HTF would depend on the design of the tax and the use of the revenue it generates.

Electric Vehicle Fees/Taxes

Since electric vehicles do not burn taxed motor fuels, their wider use could further weaken the sustainability of the HTF. In the near term, however, the impact of electric vehicles on HTF revenue is expected to be modest. In 2017 plug-in vehicles accounted for 1.1% of U.S. light vehicle sales,[32] and the roughly 982,000 plug-in vehicles sold in the United States since their 2010 introduction comprise roughly 0.9% of registered automobiles.[33] If each electric vehicle is assumed to replace a light duty vehicle that consumes 475 gallons of petroleum-based fuel per year, roughly $85 million in annual revenue is lost to the HTF.[34] Even if electric

---

[31] Congressional Budget Office, *Options for Reducing the Deficit: 2017 to 2026*, Publication 52142, Washington, DC, December 2016, pp. 211-212, https://www.cbo.gov/sites/default/files/114th-congress-2015-2016/reports/52142-budgetoptions2.pdf.

[32] Electric Drive Transportation Association, *Electric Drive Sales Dashboard*, June 2018, https://electricdrive.org/ index.php?ht=d/sp/i/20952/pid/20952. Year 2017 plug-in vehicle sales were 194,479 of 17,464,777 vehicle sales. Sales since introduction are 981,744 through September 2018.

[33] Federal Highway Administration, *State Motor-Vehicle Registrations—2016*, Table MV-1, Washington, DC, November 2017, https://www.fhwa.dot.gov/policyinformation/statistics/2016/mv1.cfm.

[34] Federal Highway Administration, *Annual Vehicle Distance Traveled in Miles and Related Data—2016*, Table VM-1, Washington, DC, December 2017, https://www.fhwa.dot.gov/policyinformation/statistics/2016/vm1.cfm.

vehicle sales grow rapidly, a significant impact on HTF revenues is likely to be roughly five to seven years away.

As of 2017, 18 states had some form of tax or fee on electric vehicles.[35] In most cases, the revenue from such fees is dedicated to transportation. Although sales and mileage fees have been considered, the most common form of tax is a flat fee paid annually at registration. Congress could consider imposing a similar federal fee. However, if Congress structures a federal registration fee in a way that mandates the states to implement the federal program, unrelated to the provision of federal funds, the fee might be challenged in court on constitutional grounds.[36]

Other Options to Preserve the Highway Trust Fund

A wide range of additional proposals has been suggested to generate revenue for the HTF. These proposals largely originated from the work of two commissions established pursuant to SAFETEA and of groups such as the American Association of State Highway and Transportation Officials (AASHTO) and the Transportation Research Board (TRB).[37] For example, AASHTO's "Matrix of Illustrative Surface Transportation Revenue Options" lists 33 potential HTF revenue options with yield estimates in tabular form.[38] Many of these options involve taxes on freight movements or energy. It should be emphasized that the revenue estimates from these

---

[35] American Road & Transportation Builders Association, *State Electric Vehicle Fees*, Washington, DC, 2017, http://transportationinvestment.org/wp-content/uploads/2017/12/state-electric-vehicle-fees-handout.pdf.

[36] CRS Report R45323, *Federalism-Based Limitations on Congressional Power: An Overview*, coordinated by Andrew Nolan and Kevin M. Lewis.

[37] The Transportation Research Board, through its research programs, has prepared several reports on future surface transportation finance that discuss VMT and other options, including National Cooperative Highway Research Program (NCHRP), *Future Financing Options to Meet Highway and Transit Needs*, NCHRP Project 20-24, Web-Only Document 102, December 2006, http://onlinepubs.trb.org/onlinepubs/nchrp/nchrp_w102.pdf; and Transportation Research Board, *The Fuel Tax and Alternatives for Transportation Funding*, Special Report 285, January 2006, http://onlinepubs.trb.org/onlinepubs/sr/sr285.pdf.

[38] American Association of State Highway and Transportation Officials, "Matrix of Illustrative Surface Transportation Revenue Options," 2015, p. 2, http://downloads.transportation.org/TranspoRevenueMatrix2014.pdf.

exercises are merely suggestive; the revenue obtained from any given measure would depend on changes in the price of motor fuels, growth in the number of annual auto registrations, and other factors.

THE FUTURE OF THE TRUST FUND

The HTF was set up as a temporary device that was supposed to disappear when the Interstate System was finished. It has endured, and its breadth of financing has expanded well beyond the Interstates, most significantly with the 1982 creation of the mass transit account within the HTF to support public transportation spending. But the HTF is not essential to a federal role in transportation funding. Congress routinely funds large infrastructure projects, such as those constructed by the Army Corps of Engineers, from general fund appropriations. Before 1956, it funded highway projects using annual appropriations. As recently as the 1990s, significant highway programs such as the Appalachian Development Highway System were funded from the general fund.

If Congress chooses not to impose new taxes and fees dedicated to the HTF, it could still maintain or expand the surface transportation program with general fund monies. Any of the revenues from the HTF financing options discussed above could also be deposited into the general fund rather than the HTF if Congress considers alternatives to the trust fund financing model. Possible alternatives include the following:

Eliminate the Trust Fund

This would do away with the complicated budget framework of contract authority, obligations, and apportionments.[39] Surface transportation would be forced to compete with other federal programs for

[39] Joshua Schank, "Life and Death of the Highway Trust Fund: How We Pay for Transportation," Eno Center for Transportation, December 2014, https://www.enotrans.org/store/research-papers/the-life-and-death-of-the-highwaytrust-fund-2.

funding each year, possibly affecting the level of funding provided for transportation.

There could be advantages to moving away from trust fund financing of surface transportation. Until recently, one of the most intractable arguments in reauthorization debates concerned which states were "donors" to transportation programs and which were "donees." Donor states were states whose highway users were estimated to pay more to the highway account of the HTF than they received. Donee states received more than they paid. The donor-donee dispute was unique to the federal highway program, and occurred largely because of the ability to track federal fuel tax revenues by state. This issue has faded as HTF shortfalls have been resolved with injections of general fund transfers to the fund. These general fund monies transferred into the HTF have nothing to do with highway tax revenues, but have made nearly all states donees. The donor-donee issue would likely disappear entirely if transportation-related taxes were deposited into the general fund instead of the trust fund. This would provide Congress with greater flexibility to allocate funding among various transportation modes and between transportation and nontransportation uses. However, treating fuel taxes as just another source of federal revenue would weaken the long-standing link between road user charges and program spending.

Most trust-fund outlays take the form of formula grants over which states have a great deal of spending discretion. While there are numerous federal requirements attached to trust fund expenditures, there have been until recently relatively few performance-oriented goals that the states are required to meet in selecting projects to be undertaken with federal monies. Performance measures might be easier to implement without formula programs that automatically apportion funding to the states. However, this may not be the case; performance measures in recent years have been imposed on the Federal-Aid highway programs as they are currently structured, although implementation has been slow.[40]

---

[40] Jeff Davis, "Regulatory Freeze Continues as Agencies Extend Deadlines and Regroup," *Eno Transportation Weekly*, February 8, 2017, pp. 1-3.

Eliminating the trust fund might also allow for creativity in thinking about the provision of transportation infrastructure across the modal boundaries that now define much of federal transportation spending. Historically, important parts of U.S. transportation infrastructure, such as the transcontinental railroads and the Panama Canal, were authorized by specific congressional enactments rather than grant programs. Reconsidering the trust fund structure might reopen discussion of this approach.

Devote HTF Revenues Exclusively to Highways

This option would leave transit and other surface transportation programs to be funded entirely by annual appropriations of general funds or devolved to the states. Such a change would have political implications. Since the early 1990s, public transportation and cycling advocates, environmentalists, and a wide range of other groups have become full-fledged supporters of the surface transportation program. They might be less enthusiastic about supporting a program that does not address their interests.

"Devolve" Surface Transportation Programs to the States

The federal government could devolve most federal responsibility for highways and public transportation to the states. Under devolution proposals, the federal taxes that now support surface transportation programs, mostly fuel taxes, would be reduced accordingly, leaving individual states to raise their own taxes to pay for highway and transit projects as they see fit. A small program, funded by much-reduced motor fuel taxes, would remain in place at the federal level to maintain roads on federal lands, fund highway safety efforts, and support other programs Congress decides not to devolve.[41]

By enacting the FAST Act, Congress chose to support the current funding model by transferring funds into the HTF, mostly from the Treasury general fund. Whether such general fund support should continue is likely to become a major point of contention when Congress debates reauthorizing surface transportation programs beyond FY2020.

MAKING A GENERAL FUND SHARE PERMANENT

By FY2020, the last year of the FAST Act, federal highway programs will have been funded for 12 years under a de facto policy of providing a Treasury general fund share. Congress could address the inadequacy of motor fuel taxes to meet surface transportation needs by making the general fund share permanent.

The public transportation titles of surface transportation bills already fund the Capital Investment Grants program through appropriations from the general fund. The Federal Aviation Administration (FAA) budget is also supported by a combination of trust funds and general funds; the general fund amount is supposed to approximate the value of the airways system to military and other government users and to "societal" nonusers (people who do not fly but, for example, benefit from the delivery of freight via aircraft).[42] A similar argument could be made regarding the public good benefits of a well-functioning highway system to justify an annual general fund appropriation to support spending on roads.[43]

Should Congress agree on a future policy of providing an annual general fund share for federal highway funding, the financing structure of

---

[41] CRS Report R44811, *Surface Transportation Devolution*, by Robert S. Kirk.

[42] The provision of a general fund share for the FAA is not required by statute but is the historical norm. When the Airport and Airway Trust Fund was running sufficient balances to do so, it was not uncommon for presidential budgets to propose funding the entire FAA budget with trust fund revenues. Since the 1971 creation of the Airport and Airway Trust Fund, however, this only occurred in FY2000.

[43] Joseph E. Stiglitz, *Economics of the Public Sector* (New York, NY: W.W. Norton Co., 1986), p. 599.

the federal-aid highways program could change. Congress would have the choice of appropriating the general fund share to the HTF and maintaining the programmatic status quo, or it could fund some programs from the trust fund and fund others via appropriations. Congress could also consider a two-pronged approach to authorization. It could authorize the trust funded programs separately from the appropriated programs. This would give Congress the option of approving a very long authorization for trust-funded projects that typically take many years to plan and complete. The long-term authorization could be paired with a series of short-term bills funded with appropriated general funds for programs whose projects are more likely to be completed quickly.[44]

TOLL FINANCING OF FEDERAL-AID SYSTEM HIGHWAYS

Toll roads have a long history in the United States, going back to the early days of the republic. During the 18th century, most were local roads or bridges that could not be built or improved with local government tax revenue alone. However, beginning with the Federal Aid Road Act of 1916 (39 Stat. 355), federal law has included a prohibition on the tolling of roads that benefited from federal funds.[45] During the late 1940s and early 1950s, the prospect of toll revenues allowed states to build thousands of miles of limited-access highways without federal aid and much sooner than would have been the case with traditional funding. Despite this, the tolling prohibition was reiterated in the Federal-Aid Highway Act and Highway Revenue Act of 1956 (70 Stat. 374), which authorized funds for the Interstate System, created the HTF, and raised the fuel taxes to pay for their construction. Over the last three decades the prohibition has been moderated so that exceptions to the general ban on tolling now cover the vast majority of federal-aid roads and bridges. There remains a ban on the tolling of existing Interstate System highway surface lane capacity. While

[44] See Jeff Davis, *Why Not a Ten-Year Year Surface Transportation Bill? (Executive Summary)*, Eno Center for Transportation, February 26, 2015, p. 1.

[45] CRS Report R44910, *Tolling U.S. Highways and Bridges*, by Robert S. Kirk.

new toll facilities have opened in several states, some of those projects have struggled financially.

Generally, there are several levels of restrictions on tolling of federal-aid highways. Non-Interstate System highways and bridges may be converted to toll roads but only after reconstruction or replacement. Existing Interstate System surface lane capacity may not be converted to toll roads except under the auspices of two small pilot programs. Interstate System bridges and tunnels may be converted if they are reconstructed or replaced. New capacity on the federal-aid highway system, including Interstate Highways, generally may be tolled. There are no federal restrictions on tolling of roads that are not part of the federal-aid system.

Options for Expanded Use of Tolling

Highway toll revenue nationwide came to $14.457 billion in FY2016, according to FHWA. While the amount of toll revenue has grown significantly in recent years, toll revenue as a share of total spending on highways has been relatively steady for more than half a century, ranging from roughly 5% to 7%.[46] On average, facility owners collected $2.41 million per mile of toll road or bridge in FY2016, but revenue per mile varies greatly among toll facilities.[47] All revenue from tolls flows to the state or local agencies or private entities that operate tolled facilities; the federal government does not collect any revenue from tolls. However, a major expansion of tolling might reduce the need for federal expenditures on roads. There are three possible means of increasing revenue from tolling:

---

[46] Federal Highway Administration, *Highway Statistics: Summary to 1975*, Table HF-211, 1977, pp. 107-136. Also *Highway Statistics: Summary to 1995*, Table SF-210; *Highway Statistics*, various years, Tables SF-21, HF-10, and HF10a; *Our Nation's Highways: 2010,* Figure 6-6: Toll Facility Revenue: 1993-2008, http://www.fhwa.dot.gov/ policyinformation/ pubs/pl10023/fig6_6.cfm.

[47] Federal Highway Administration, *Funding for Highways and Disposition of Highway-User Revenues, All Units of Government, 2015*, Table HF-10, May 2017.

- Increase the Extent of Toll Roads. FHWA statistics identify 6,001 tolled miles of roads, bridges, and tunnels as of January 1, 2017,[48] a net increase of 1,280 miles, or 27%, over 1990.[49] Toll-road mileage comprises 0.6% of the 1,022,815 miles of public roads eligible for federal highway aid.[50] While there may be many existing roads on which tolling would be financially feasible, the vast majority of mileage on the federal-aid system probably has too little traffic to make toll collection economically viable.
- Increase the Average Toll per Mile. Raising tolls can be politically challenging, especially when revenue is used for purposes other than building and maintaining the toll facility. Trucking interests frequently raise opposition to rate changes that increase truck tolls relative to automobile tolls. Where roads are operated by private concessionaires, the operators' contracts with state governments typically specify the maximum rate at which tolls can rise. Additionally, large increases can encourage motorists to use competing nontolled routes, thereby reducing their revenue-raising potential.
- Increase Toll-Road Usage. To a great extent, increasing toll road usage is dependent on policies that effectively increase the number of miles tolled and establish toll rates that maximize revenues without discouraging use. However, toll road use is also determined by broad economic and social trends. The financing of many of the toll roads constructed in the 20th century was based on the assumption that the new roads would lead to increased vehicle usage. Although vehicle miles traveled declined in the wake of the recession that began in 2007, vehicle use has been rising again since 2014. If this trend continues it bodes well for toll revenues,

---

[48] Federal Highway Administration, *Toll Facilities in the United States: Toll Mileage Trends—2007 to 2017*, Washington, DC, April 4, 2018, https://www.fhwa.dot.gov/policy information/tollpage/page05.cfm.

[49] Federal Highway Administration, *Toll Facilities in the United States: Bridges-Roads-Tunnels-Ferries*, Publication No: FHWA-PL-91-009, 1991, p. v.

[50] Federal Highway Administration, *Public Road Length-2016: Miles by Functional System and Federal-Aid Highways, National Summary*, Table HM-18, Washington, DC, September 18,2018, https://www.fhwa.dot.gov/policyinformation/statistics/2016/hm18.cfm.

which would rise with increasing traffic. On the other hand, if demographic trends and social changes eventually lead to slower growth in personal motor vehicle use, then toll revenues may be constrained in the longer term.

The constraints on these means of increasing revenue from tolling suggest that imposing tolls on individual transportation facilities is likely to be of only limited use in supporting the overall level of highway capital spending. Furthermore, some states, particularly those with low population densities, may have few or no facilities suitable for tolling.[51] Toll collection itself can be costly; collection costs on many existing toll roads exceed 10% of revenues. For these reasons, while tolls may be an effective way of financing specific facilities—especially major roads, bridges, or tunnels that are likely to be used heavily and are located such that the tolls are difficult to evade— they would likely be less effective in providing broad financial support for surface transportation programs.

VALUE CAPTURE

Value capture represents an attempt to cover part or all of the cost of transportation improvements from landowners or developers who benefit from the resulting increase in the value of real property. Value capture revenue mechanisms include tax increment financing, special assessments, development impact fees, negotiated exactions, and joint development.[52] The federal role in value capture strategies may be limited, as the Government Accountability Office (GAO) has noted,[53] but it is worth

---

[51] CRS Report R45250, *Rural Highways*, by Robert S. Kirk.

[52] Adeel Lari, David Levinson, and Zhirong Zhao, et al., *Value Capture for Transportation Finance: Technical Research Report*, Center for Transportation Studies, University of Minnesota, June 2009, http://www.cts.umn.edu/ research/featured/value-capture. Tax increment financing uses the increase in property tax revenue within a defined area resulting from an infrastructure improvement to cover the cost of the improvement.

[53] Government Accountability Office, *Public Transportation: Federal Role in Value Capture Strategies for Transit Is Limited, but Additional Guidance Could Help Clarify Policies*, GAO-10-781, July 2010, http://www.gao.gov/ new.items/d10781.pdf.

describing these strategies to provide a fuller picture of the ways in which they might supplement or supplant more commonly used funding and financing mechanisms.

Value capture is not a new idea. Land developers built and operated streetcar systems in the late 19th century as a way to sell houses on the urban fringe, for example. Much of the recent experience with value capture has been associated with public transit. GAO found that the most widely used mechanism is joint development, in which a real estate project at or near a transit station is pursued cooperatively between the public and private sectors. An example might involve a transit agency leasing the unused space over a station, its "air rights," to a developer in exchange for a regular payment.

Joint development has generated relatively small amounts of money for transit agencies. For example, the Washington Metropolitan Area Transit Authority received about $10 million from joint development in FY2016, about 1% of its operating revenue.[54] However, less widely used strategies, such as special assessment districts, are estimated to generate significant amounts of funding for specific projects. In a special assessment district, properties within a defined area are assessed a special tax for a specific purpose. A special assessment district in Seattle produced $25 million of the $53 million (47%) needed to fund the South Lake Union streetcar project.[55]

There has been less use of value capture in highway projects, but this appears to be changing. Texas, for example, has authorized the use of tax increment financing through the creation of transportation reinvestment zones to help fund highway projects.[56] Special assessment districts also

---

[54] Washington Metropolitan Area Transit Authority, *FY2019 Proposed Budget*, p. 17, https://www.wmata.com/about/records/public_docs/upload/FY2019-Proposed-Budget-Book-12-12-2017-Final.pdf.

[55] Government Accountability Office, *Public Transportation: Federal Role in Value Capture Strategies for Transit Is Limited, but Additional Guidance Could Help Clarify Policies*, GAO-10-781, July 2010, pp. 16, 20, http://www.gao.gov/new.items/d10781.pdf.

[56] Sharada Vadali, Rafael Manuel-Aldrete, and Arturo Bujanda, et al., *Transportation Reinvestment Zone Handbook*, Texas Transportation Institute, College Station, TX, 2011, http://ntl.bts.gov/lib/37000/37800/37821/0-6538-P1_Handbook_resub_editjd_sv.pdf; Texas Department of Transportation, "Transportation Reinvestment Zone," http://www.txdot.gov/government/programs/trz.html.

have been set up in several states, including Florida and Virginia, to fund highway projects. In Virginia a special assessment district was used to help fund the expansion of Route 28 near Washington Dulles International Airport beginning in the late 1980s.[57]

PUBLIC-PRIVATE PARTNERSHIPS (P3S)

Growing demands on the transportation system and constraints on public resources have led to calls for more private-sector involvement in the provision of highway and transit infrastructure through public-private partnerships (P3s), which can be designed to lessen demands on public-sector funding.[58] Private involvement can take a variety of forms, including design-build and design-build-finance-operate agreements. Typically, the "public" in public-private partnerships refers to a state government, local government, or transit agency. The federal government, nevertheless, exerts influence over the prevalence and structure of P3s through its transportation programs, funding, and regulatory oversight.[59]

To be viable, P3s involving private financing typically require an anticipated project-related revenue stream from a source such as vehicle tolls, freight container fees, or, in the case of transit station development, building rents. Private-sector resources may come from an initial payment to lease an existing asset in exchange for future revenue, as with the Indiana Toll Road and Chicago Skyway, or they may arise from a newly developed asset that creates a new revenue stream. Either way, a facility user fee, such as a toll, is often the key to unlocking private-sector participation and resources.

---

[57] For more information, see Route 28 Corridor Improvements LLC, "Route 28 Public/Private Partnership: Moving Right Along," http://www.28freeway.com.

[58] See, for example, Bipartisan Policy Center, *Bridging the Gap Together: A New Model to Modernize U.S. Infrastructure*, May 2016, https://bipartisanpolicy.org/library/modernize-infrastructure/.

[59] CRS Report R45010, *Public-Private Partnerships (P3s) in Transportation*, by William J. Mallett.

In some cases, private-sector financing is backed by "availability payments," regular payments made by government to the private entity based on negotiated quality and performance standards of the facility. Aversion in the private sector to the risk that too few users will be willing to pay for use of a new facility, known as demand risk, has made availability payment P3s more common over the past few years. As a result, state and local governments are retaining demand risk more often.[60]

It is frequently asserted that hundreds of billions of dollars of private funds are available globally for infrastructure investment.[61] To date, however, the number of transportation P3s in the United States is relatively small, as is the amount of long-term private financing provided. According to one source, from 1993 through September 2017 there were 30 surface transportation P3s involving long-term financing, with total project costs totaling $39 billion. This includes the 99 year lease of the Chicago Skyway; the I-595 managed lanes project in Florida; and the Purple Line light rail transit project in Maryland.[62] P3s and private investment in infrastructure, including surface transportation, are relatively larger in many other countries, including Canada, Australia, and the United Kingdom.[63]

While private investment may grow in the future, many impediments remain. Some of the major ones include the relative attractiveness of the tax-exempt financing available to state and local government, political opposition to tolling and privatization, and difficulties associated with project development. Private-sector financing generated through P3s might best be seen as a supplement to traditional public-sector funding rather than as a substitute.

---

[60] "Demand Risk P3s Are An Unhappy Family," *Public Works Financing*, September 2014, p. 19.

[61] Bipartisan Policy Center, *Bridging the Gap Together: A New Model to Modernize U.S. Infrastructure*, May 2016, p. 67, https://bipartisanpolicy.org/library/modernize-infrastructure/.

[62] "U.S./Canada Transportation P3 Market 1993-2017," *Public Works Financing*, September 2017, pp. 9-12.

[63] EY, *Public-Private Partnerships and the Global Infrastructure Challenge*, 2015, figure 1, https://www.ey.com/Publication/vwLUAssets/Health/%24FILE/EY_PPP_Thought_Leadership.pdf.

In addition to attracting private capital, P3s may generate new resources for highway and transit infrastructure in at least two ways. First, P3s may improve efficiency through better management and innovation in construction, maintenance, and operation—in effect providing more infrastructure for the same price. Private companies may be more able to examine the full life-cycle cost of investments, whereas public agency decisions are often tied to short-term budget cycles. Such cost reductions may not materialize, however, if the public sector has to spend a substantial amount of time on procurement, oversight, dispute resolution, and litigation.

Second, P3s may reduce government agencies' costs by transferring the financial risks of building, maintaining, and operating infrastructure to private investors. These risks include construction delays, unexpectedly high maintenance costs, and the possibility that demand will be less than forecast. There is a danger, however, that this transfer of risk may prove illusory if major miscalculations force the public agency to renegotiate contracts or provide financial guarantees.[64] Moreover, as GAO points out, not all the risks can or should be shifted to the private sector. For instance, private investors are unlikely to accept the risk of higher construction costs due to delays in the environmental review process.[65]

ASSET RECYCLING

Asset recycling is the sale or lease to the private sector of government-owned infrastructure assets and the investment of the proceeds in new infrastructure. For a few years, the national government of Australia had a policy of making 15% incentive payments to state and territory governments if they agreed to sell or lease assets to the private sector and then "recycle" these payments to other infrastructure projects. Over the roughly three-year period the asset recycling initiative was in effect, the

---

[64] E. Engel, R. Fischer, and A. Galetovic, "Privatizing Highways in the United States," *Review of Industrial Organization*, vol. 29, 2006, pp. 27-53.

[65] Government Accountability Office, *Highway Public-Private Partnerships*, February 2008.

national government entered into four agreements with incentive payments totaling A$3.175 billion (approximately US$2.4 billion). One of the agreements involved the lease of 49% of the electricity network businesses owned by the State of New South Wales and the investment of the proceeds in the Sydney Metro, Parramatta Light Rail, and several road projects.[66] A similar program for the United States was proposed in a draft bill on infrastructure investment circulated by House Transportation and Infrastructure Committee Chairman Bill Shuster in 2018. The draft bill proposed to provide a federal payment of 15% of the assessed value of a leased infrastructure asset to eligible project sponsors, allotting $3 billion for this purpose from FY2019 through FY2023. No similar proposal has been introduced as legislation. Infrastructure assets that qualify for recycling in the draft bill include highways, public transit, airports, ports and port terminals, publicly owned railroads, intercity bus facilities, intermodal transportation facilities, and drinking and wastewater facilities.[67]

MUNICIPAL BONDS

Municipal bonds, debt instruments used by states and all types of local government, are a major source of financing for transportation infrastructure. The interest on municipal bonds is generally exempt from federal income tax; consequently, an investor will usually accept a lower interest rate than on a non-tax-exempt bond, and the borrower can finance a project at a lower cost. The forgone tax revenue is the federal government's contribution to a project financed with municipal bonds. CBO estimates that the cost to the federal government of tax-exempt bonds

---

[66] Honorable Paul Fletcher, Minister for Urban Infrastructure, "Building our Future: Strengthening Australia through Critical and Innovative Infrastructure Investment," media release, May 3, 2016, http://minister.infrastructure.gov.au/pf/releases/2016/May/budget-infra_02-2016.aspx.

[67] "The Shuster Infrastructure Proposal," https://transportation.house.gov/uploadedfiles/infra_001_xml.pdf.

in state and local transportation and water infrastructure investment is 26 cents per dollar financed.[68]

Private activity bonds (PABs) are a type of municipal bond in which a state or local government acts as a financial intermediary for a business or individual.[69] PABs are not eligible for federal tax exemption unless Congress grants an exception for a certain purpose and other requirements are met. Congress has approved limited use of tax-exempt private activity bonds for airports, docks and wharves, mass commuting facilities, high-speed intercity rail facilities, and qualified highway or surface freight transfer facilities (26 U.S.C. §142). In the case of qualified highway or surface freight transfer facilities, the Secretary of Transportation must approve the issuance of PABs, and the aggregate amount allocated must not exceed $15 billion (26 U.S.C. §142(m)(2)). The authorization for the sale of qualified highway or surface freight transfer facilities was a provision in SAFETEA, enacted in 2005. As of August 1, 2018, $8.38 billion of the $15 billion had been issued to finance 23 projects, and another $2.63 billion had been allocated to five other projects.[70] There have been proposals to increase the bond issuance cap so that PABs, which are seen as an important support for P3 deals, can continue to be issued in the future. While municipal bonds are a popular financing method, there are a number of potential disadvantages to their use. Because they are issued by state and local governments, the federal government has less control over the types of projects supported and the amount of the federal contribution than it does with grant and loan programs. Tax-exempt bonds, moreover, can be an inefficient way to subsidize state and local debt because borrowing costs are reduced by less than the forgone federal revenue. As CBO notes, "the remainder of that tax expenditure accrues to bond buyers

---

[68] Congressional Budget Office, *Federal Support for Financing State and Local Transportation and Water Infrastructure*, October 2018, p. 2, https://www.cbo.gov/system/files?file=2018-10/54549-InfrastructureFinancing.pdf.

[69] Joint Tax Committee, *Overview of Selected Provisions Relating to the Financing of Surface Transportation Infrastructure*, June 23, 2015, JCX-97-15, https://www.jct.gov/publications.html?func=showdown&id=4796.

[70] Department of Transportation, Build America Bureau, "Private Activity Bonds: Current Status," September 20, 2018, https://www.transportation.gov/buildamerica/programs-services/pab.

in the highest income tax brackets."[71] Also, tax-exempt bonds are unattractive to investors that do not have a federal tax liability, such as pension funds and foreign individuals and organizations, shrinking the potential funds available to state and local governments.

Tax credit bonds, an alternative type of tax-preferred municipal bond, might help to overcome some of these limitations. Tax credit bonds typically do not pay interest. Instead, the investor receives a tax credit, an amount that is the same for investors in different tax brackets. Tax credit bonds, therefore, are more efficient than tax-exempt bonds because the revenue forgone by the federal government equals the reduction in borrowing costs that state and local governments receive. Unused tax credits may be carried forward to another year or sold to another entity with tax liability. With some types of tax credit bonds known as issuer credit or direct pay bonds, the credit is paid to the issuer (a state or local government) by the Treasury, and the investor gets interest similar to taxable securities. Consequently, tax credit bonds can be attractive to investors with no federal tax liability.

Federal authority exists for state and local governments to issue some types of tax credit bonds, but under current authority none can be used to finance transportation projects. Tax credit bonds authorized by the American Recovery and Reinvestment Act of 2009 (P.L. 111-5), known as Build America Bonds, were used to finance a wide range of projects including transportation. The authorization to issue these bonds expired December 31, 2010.

TRANSPORTATION INFRASTRUCTURE FINANCE AND INNOVATION ACT (TIFIA)

An existing federal mechanism for providing credit assistance to relatively large transportation infrastructure projects is the Transportation

---

[71] Congressional Budget Office, "Answer to a Question for the Record Following a Hearing on the Long-Term Financing of the Highway Trust Fund Conducted by the House Committee on Ways and Means," July 24, 2015, https://www.cbo.gov/sites/default/files/114th-congress-2015-2016/reports/50418-QFRs_HTF_1.pdf.

Infrastructure Finance and Innovation Act (TIFIA) program, enacted in 1998.[72] TIFIA provides federal credit assistance in the form of secured loans, loan guarantees, and lines of credit.

Federal credit assistance reduces borrowers' costs and lowers project risk, thereby helping to secure other financing at rates lower than would otherwise be possible. Another purpose of TIFIA funding is to leverage nonfederal funding, including investment from the private sector. Loans must be repaid with a dedicated revenue stream, typically a project-related user fee, such as a toll, but sometimes dedicated tax revenue. As of September 2018, according to DOT, TIFIA had provided assistance of about $30 billion to more than 70 projects. The overall cost of the projects supported is estimated to be nearly $110 billion.[73]

The FAST Act (P.L. 112-141) authorized $275 million for TIFIA in both FY2016 and FY2017, $285 million in FY2018, and $300 million in both FY2019 and FY2020.[74] Because the government expects its loans to be repaid, an appropriation need cover only administrative costs and the subsidy cost of credit assistance. According to the Federal Credit Reform Act of 1990, the subsidy cost is "the estimated long-term cost to the government of a direct loan or a loan guarantee, calculated on a net present value basis, excluding administrative costs."[75] According to DOT, $1 in TIFIA funding historically has provided about $10 in credit assistance, a 10% subsidy cost, although in recent years each dollar has provided closer to $14.[76]

The FAST Act also allowed states to use funds they receive from two other highway programs to pay for the subsidy and administrative costs of credit assistance. These two programs are the Nationally Significant

---

[72] 23 U.S.C. §601 et seq.

[73] U.S. Department of Transportation, "Projects Financed by TIFIA," http://www.dot.gov/tifia/projects-financed.

[74] Highway and Transportation Funding Act of 2014 (P.L. 113-159); Highway and Transportation Funding Act (P.L. 114-21); Surface Transportation and Veterans Health Care Choice Improvement Act of 2015 (P.L. 114-41).

[75] Federal Credit Reform Act of 1990 (§502 5A), enacted as §13201 of Omnibus Budget Reconciliation Act of 1990 (P.L. 101-508).

[76] Department of Transportation, "Letters of Interest for Credit Assistance Under the Transportation Infrastructure Finance and Innovation Act (TIFIA) Program," 81 *Federal Register* 13030-13036, March 11, 2016.

Freight and Highway Projects Program (NSFHPP), authorized at $950 million in FY2019, and the National Highway Performance Program (NHPP), authorized at $23.7 billion in FY2019. If states decide to use their formula funding in this way, the potential amount of loans and other credit assistance may be much greater than would be possible using the $275 million direct authorization alone. The Better Utilizing Investments to Leverage Development (BUILD) Transportation Discretionary Grants program (formerly TIGER program), funded by general fund appropriations, also can be used by grant recipients to pay the subsidy and administrative costs of a TIFIA loan.[77]

Several changes to the TIFIA program in the FAST Act were aimed at making it easier to finance smaller projects, particularly those in rural areas. These provisions included

- providing authority for a TIFIA loan to a state infrastructure bank (SIB) to capitalize a "rural project fund";
- adding transit-oriented development (TOD) infrastructure as an eligible project (TOD infrastructure is a "project to improve or construct public infrastructure that is located within walking distance of, and accessible to, a fixed guideway transit facility,[78] passenger rail station, intercity bus station, or intermodal facility");[79]
- allowing up to $2 million of TIFIA budget authority each fiscal year to pay the application fees for projects costing $75 million or less instead of requiring payment by the project sponsor;
- modifying or setting the minimum project cost thresholds for credit assistance at $10 million for TOD projects, the capitalization

---

[77] A maximum of 20% ($300 million) of the funding appropriated in FY2018 was available to pay the subsidy and administrative costs of TIFIA credit assistance. Department of Transportation, "Notice of Funding Opportunity for the Department of Transportation's National Infrastructure Investments Under the Consolidated Appropriations Act, 2018," 83 *Federal Register* 18651-18661, April 27, 2018.

[78] Fixed guideway transit generally includes rail transit, passenger ferries, and bus rapid transit.

[79] FAST Act, §2001.

of a rural project fund, and local government infrastructure projects; and
- providing for a streamlined application process for loans of $100 million or less.

In addition, the FAST Act authorized the creation of a new National Surface Transportation and Innovative Finance Bureau within DOT to administer federal transportation financing programs, specifically the TIFIA program, the SIB program, the Railroad Rehabilitation and Improvement Financing (RRIF) Program, and the allocation of authority to issue private activity bonds for qualified highway or surface freight transfer facilities. To fulfill this mandate, DOT established the Build America Bureau in July 2016. The bureau also will be responsible for establishing and promoting best practices for innovative financing and P3s, and for providing advice and technical expertise in these areas. The bureau will administer the discretionary Nationally Significant Freight and Highway Projects grant program, known as INFRA grants, and will have responsibilities related to procurement and project environmental review and permitting.

NATIONAL INFRASTRUCTURE BANK

Congress has considered several proposals to create a national infrastructure bank to help finance infrastructure projects. One purported advantage of a national infrastructure bank over other loan programs, such as TIFIA, is that it would have more independence in its operation, such as in project selection, and have greater expertise at its disposal. Additionally, a national infrastructure bank would likely be set up to help a much wider range of infrastructure projects, including water, energy, and telecommunications infrastructure. Proponents claim that the best projects, or at least those that are the most financially viable, would be selected from across these sectors.

In many formulations, capitalization of a national infrastructure bank comes from an appropriation, but in others the bank is authorized to raise its own capital through bond issuance. By issuing securities that are not tax exempt, it could tap pools of private capital that do not invest in tax-exempt bonds, such as pension funds and foreign citizens, the traditional source of much project finance. Tax-exempt municipal securities are unattractive to some investors, either because individual issues are too small to interest them or because the investors do not benefit from the tax preference. Taxable bonds with long maturities might be attractive to some of these investors.[80] An infrastructure bank also might also choose to reduce the federal government's share of project costs, putting greater reliance on nonfederal capital and user fees.

Most infrastructure bank proposals assume the bank would improve the allocation of public resources by funding projects with the highest economic returns regardless of infrastructure system or type. Selection of the projects with the highest returns, however, might conflict with the traditional desire of Congress to ensure funding for various purposes. In the extreme case, major transportation projects might not be funded if the bank were to exhaust its lending authority on water or energy projects offering higher returns.

Limitations of a national infrastructure bank include its duplication of existing programs like TIFIA and the Wastewater and Drinking Water State Revolving Funds. An infrastructure bank may not be the lowest-cost means of increasing infrastructure spending. CBO has pointed out that a special entity that issues its own debt would not be able to match the lower interest and issuance costs of the U.S. Treasury.[81] In some formulations, a

---

[80] U.S. Congress, Senate Committee on Banking, Housing, and Urban Affairs, Testimony of Felix Rohatyn, Co-Chair of the Commission on Public Infrastructure, *Hearing on Condition of Our Nation's Infrastructure and Proposals for Needed Improvement*, 110th Cong., 2nd Sess., March 11, 2008; U.S. Congress, House Committee on Transportation and Infrastructure, Testimony of Bernard Schwartz, President and CEO, BLS Investments, *Hearing on Financing Infrastructure Investments*, 110th Cong., 2nd Sess., June 10, 2008.

[81] U.S. Congress, House Committee of the Budget and Committee on Transportation and Infrastructure, Testimony of Peter R. Orszag, Director, Congressional Budget Office, *Hearing on Financing Infrastructure Investment*, 110th Cong., 2nd Sess., May 8, 2008.

national infrastructure bank exposes the federal government to the risk of default.[82]

STATE INFRASTRUCTURE BANKS

State infrastructure banks (SIBs) already exist in many states. In 32 states and Puerto Rico, SIBs were created pursuant to a federal program originally established in surface transportation law in 1995 (P.L. 104-59).[83] Several other states, among them California, Florida, Georgia, Kansas, Ohio, and Virginia, have state investment banks that are unconnected to the federal program.[84] Local governments have also begun to embrace the idea. The City of Chicago has established a nonprofit organization, the Chicago Infrastructure Trust, as a way to attract private investment for public works projects,[85] and Dauphin County, PA, has established an infrastructure bank funded from a state tax on liquid fuels to make loans to the 40 municipalities and private project sponsors within its borders.[86]

One of the biggest stumbling blocks to federally authorized SIBs has been capitalization. States can capitalize the banks using some of their apportioned and allocated highway and transit funds, and any amount of rail program funds. Under the FAST Act, capitalization of a rural project fund may now be made by a loan from the TIFIA program. Federal funds have to be matched with state funds, generally on an 80% federal, 20% state basis.

---

[82] U.S. Congress, House Committee on Ways and Means, Subcommittee on Select Revenue Measures, Testimony of Samuel Staley, *Hearing on the National Infrastructure Banks*, 111th Cong., 2nd sess., May 13, 2010.

[83] Federal Highway Administration, "State Infrastructure Banks (SIBs)," http://www.fhwa.dot.gov/ipd/finance/tools_programs/federal_credit_assistance/sibsi.

[84] Robert Puentes and Jennifer Thompson, *Banking on Infrastructure: Enhancing State Revolving Funds for Transportation*, Brookings Institution, September 2012, https://www.brookings.edu/wp-content/uploads/2016/06/12-state-infrastructure-investment-puentes.pdf.

[85] Chicago Investment Trust, http://chicagoinfrastructure.orgi.

[86] Jeff Frantz, "Dauphin County Creates Infrastructure Bank for Road Improvements," *PennLive*, March 1, 2013, http://www.pennlive.com/midstate/index.ssf/2013/03/dauphin_county_creates_infrast.html.

In: Transportation
Editor: Frederick Daniels
ISBN: 978-1-53615-651-5

Chapter 3

SURFACE TRANSPORTATION FUNDING AND PROGRAMS UNDER THE FIXING AMERICA'S SURFACE TRANSPORTATION ACT (FAST ACT; P.L. 114-94)*

Robert S. Kirk, William J. Mallett, David Randall Peterman, John Frittelli, Bill Canis and Linda Luther

SUMMARY

On December 4, 2015, President Barack Obama signed the Fixing America's Surface Transportation Act (FAST Act; P.L. 114-94). The act authorized spending on federal highway and public transportation programs, surface transportation safety and research activities, and rail programs for five years, through September 30, 2020. The act's authorization totaled roughly $305 billion for FY2016 through FY2020.

* This is an edited, reformatted and augmented version of Congressional Research Service, Publication No. R44388, dated February 18, 2016.

This included $233 billion for highways and highway safety, $61 billion for public transportation, and more than $10 billion for Amtrak.

Most of the funding for surface transportation bills has been drawn from the Highway Trust Fund (HTF) since its creation in 1956, but the principal revenue source for the HTF, federal motor fuel taxes, has not generated sufficient revenue to cover HTF outlays since 2008. To fill this shortfall, Congress has relied on Treasury general fund transfers to make up the difference. Although Congress was unable to agree on a long-term solution to the HTF revenue issue, the FAST Act identified roughly $70 billion in budgetary offsets to support general fund transfers sufficient to pay for the five-year bill.

The FAST Act builds upon the many programmatic changes made in the previous multiyear reauthorization bill, the Moving Ahead for Progress in the 21st Century Act (MAP-21; P.L. 112- 141). The act also continues initiatives intended to increase program efficiency through performance-based planning and the streamlining of project development. Among FAST Act's major attributes are

- $225 billion authorized from the HTF over five years, an average of $45 billion annually, for Federal Highway Administration (FHWA) programs;
- $61 billion authorized from the HTF and the general fund, an average of $12.2 billion per year, for Federal Transit Administration (FTA) programs;
- a major redirection of funding toward highway freight projects via a new formula program and a competitive grant program;
- direct funding for the Transportation Infrastructure Finance and Innovation Act (TIFIA) program of $275 million, down from $1 billion in FY2015;
- competitive grant component added to the Bus and Bus Facilities Program;
- provisions on intercity passenger rail transportation included in a surface transportation act for the first time; and
- no project earmarks.

The FAST Act does not increase motor fuels taxes or provide another sustainable source of revenues to be paid into the HTF. Unless new revenue sources are found, Congress will face projections of a large gap between HTF tax receipts and spending plans when it begins debating the reauthorization of the FAST Act in 2020.

FAST Act: Overview

On December 4, 2015, President Barack Obama signed the Fixing America's Surface Transportation Act (FAST Act; P.L. 114-94). The act authorizes spending on federal highway and public transportation programs and surface transportation safety and research activities for five years, through September 30, 2020. The act also authorizes passenger rail programs for five years, through FY2020. The act's authorization totals about $305 billion for FY2016 through FY2020. This includes $233 billion for highways and highway safety, $61 billion for public transportation, and more than $10 billion for Amtrak.

The five-year duration of the act reestablishes the pattern of five- or six-year surface transportation authorization bills (often bound together by a series of short-term authorization acts) that dates back to the early 1990s. The bill also provides sufficient funds for a modest increase in spending for both highways and public transportation over expected inflation. This is a change from the pattern of declines in real spending for highways since the early 2000s.[1] On the programmatic side, the changes were small in comparison with the previous reauthorization act, the Moving Ahead for Progress in the 21st Century Act (MAP-21; P.L. 112-141), which made major changes in programmatic structure and operations but provided for only two years of funding (FY2013-FY2014). Although the FAST Act creates several new discretionary programs, well over 92% of spending from the Highway Trust Fund (HTF) will be distributed by formula under the law.

The FAST Act makes two important changes in transportation programs. It is the first surface transportation act to emphasize the national importance of moving freight, and funds two new freight programs. It is also the first law to treat intercity passenger rail as an integral part of the

[1] U.S. Congressional Budget Office, *Approaches to Making Federal Highway Spending More Productive*, February 11, 2016, pp. Figure 1-4, https://www.cbo.gov/publication/50150. Escalation in the prices of construction materials prior to the recession of 2007 explains some of the decline in real spending.

federal surface transportation program; previously, Amtrak was authorized under separate legislation.

SURFACE TRANSPORTATION FINANCE AND THE HIGHWAY TRUST FUND (HTF)

Almost all of federal highway funding and about 80% of federal public transportation funding comes from the HTF. The HTF is financed from a number of sources, including taxes on fuels, tires, truck and trailer sales, and a weight-based heavy-vehicle use tax.[2] However, approximately 90% of trust fund revenue comes from excise taxes on motor fuels, 18.3 cents per gallon on gasoline and 24.3 cents per gallon on diesel. The HTF consists of two separate accounts— highway and mass transit. The highway account receives an allocation equivalent to 15.44 cents of the gasoline tax, and the mass transit account receives the revenue generated by 2.86 cents of the tax.[3] Because the fuel taxes are set in terms of cents per gallon rather than as a percentage of the sale price, their revenues do not increase with inflation. The fuel tax rates were last raised in 1993.

Sluggish economic growth and improved vehicle efficiency have depressed the growth of fuel consumption and therefore the growth of fuel tax revenue. Since FY2008, the revenues flowing into the highway account of the HTF have been insufficient to fund the expenditures authorized under the Federal-Aid Highway Program. Prior to the enactment of the FAST Act, resolving this discrepancy required seven general fund and other transfers totaling $73.3 billion (of which $62.5 billion went into the

---

[2] Federal Highway Administration, *Highway Statistics 2014: Federal Highway-User Fees; Table FE-21B*, Washington, DC, 2015, http://www.fhwa.dot.gov/policyinformation/statistics/2014/fe21b.cfm.

[3] Nonfuels taxes accrue only to the highway account. A separate 0.1-cent-per-gallon tax on all fuels goes into the leaking underground storage tank (LUST) trust fund, which is administered by the U.S. Environmental Protection Agency and the states.

highway account) over a seven-year period. Without these transfers, FHWA might have faced delays in reimbursing states for completed work.[4]

Under the FAST Act, $70 billion will be transferred from the general fund to the HTF to fund the projected difference between HTF revenues and authorized spending for FY2016 through FY2020.[5] An additional $300 million was provided by transfers from the Leaking Underground Storage Tank (LUST) trust fund.[6] This mixing of revenue sources lessens the relevance of the arguments that HTF funds should be used only on highways. It also reduces the salience of states' complaints that they are not receiving a fair share of highway spending relative to their highway tax payments to the HTF (the so-called donor-donee state issue). Under the FAST Act, the general fund transfers allow for spending levels for all states that will likely exceed their highway tax payments.

A gap between dedicated HTF revenues and outlays is expected to persist after the FAST Act expires at the end of FY2020. The Congressional Budget Office (CBO) projects that beginning in FY2021, revenues credited to the highway and transit accounts of the HTF will be insufficient to meet the fund's obligations.[7] CBO projects that over the five years following the expiration of the FAST Act, from FY2021 through FY2025, HTF receipts will fall $96 billion short of the amount needed to fund highway and public transportation programs at the current level, adjusted only for projected inflation. Congress will face the need to

---

[4] Of these totals $3.4 billion was transferred from the Leaking Underground Storage Tank (LUST) Trust Fund to the highway account of the HTF during FY2012 and FY2014 combined.

[5] Joint Committee on Taxation, Estimated Revenue Effects of the Revenue Provisions Contained in the Conference Agreement for H.R. 22, The "Fixing America's Surface Transportation ("Fast") Act," committee print, 114th Cong., 1st sess., December 3, 2015, JCX-140-15, pp. 1-2, https://www.jct.gov/publications.html?func=startdown&id=4854.

[6] Since September 15, 2008, a total of $143.627 billion has been transferred to the HTF from Treasury general funds and the LUST trust fund, including $114.685 billion to the highway account.

[7] Congressional Budget Office, "Cost estimate for the conference agreement on H.R. 22, the FAST Act," as posted on the website of the House Committee on Rules on December 1, 2015, December 2, 2015, Table 5, https://www.cbo.gov/ sites/default/files/114th-congress-2015-2016/costestimate/hr22_1.pdf. Because requests for reimbursement from the HTF may occur at any time, and because Treasury transfers tax receipts to the HTF occur only twice each month, FHWA deems it prudent to maintain a $4 billion minimum in the highway account to prevent having to delay payments to states due to insufficient funds.

approve some combination of new taxes,[8] an increase in existing dedicated taxes, further general fund transfers, an increase in federally supported debt financing, or reductions in the scope of the federal surface transportation program, if the FAST Act is to be replaced or extended in 2021.[9]

HIGHWAYS

The Federal-Aid Highway Program (FAHP) is an umbrella term for the separate highway programs administered by the Federal Highway Administration (FHWA).[10] These programs are almost entirely focused on highway construction, and generally do not support operations (such as administrative salaries or fuel costs) or routine maintenance (such as mowing roadway fringes or filling potholes). Each state is required to have a State Transportation Improvement Plan, which sets priorities for the state's use of FAHP funds. State departments of transportation (state DOTs) largely determine which projects are funded, award the contracts, and oversee project development and construction. More recently, metropolitan planning organizations (MPOs) have played a growing role in project decision-making in urban areas, but federal project funding continues to flow through state DOTs.

The FAHP, unlike most other federal programs, does not rely on appropriated budget authority. Instead, FHWA exercises contract authority over monies in the HTF, and may obligate (promise to pay) funds for projects funded with contract authority prior to an appropriation. Once funds have been obligated, the federal government has a legal commitment to provide the funds. This approach shelters highway construction projects from annual decisions about appropriations.

---

[8] Section 6020 of the FAST Act provides $95 million of Highway Research and Development Program (23 U.S.C. 503 (b)) funds for a pilot program to provide grants to the states to "demonstrate user-based alternative revenue mechanisms that utilize a user fee structure." This could include grants to test the design and implementation of a vehicle miles traveled charge (VMT).

[9] CRS Report R42877, *Funding and Financing Highways and Public Transportation*, by Robert S. Kirk and William J. Mallett.

[10] CRS Report R44332, *Federal-Aid Highway Program (FAHP): In Brief*, by Robert S. Kirk.

Highway Program Terminology

Distribution of funds is FHWA notification of the availability of federal funds, usually for four years. The states do not actually receive federal money up front for highway project spending.

Apportionment is the distribution of funds among the states as prescribed by a statutory formula.

Allocation is an administrative distribution of funds (often for specific projects) under programs that do not have statutory distribution formulas.

Reimbursement occurs once a project is approved, the work is started, costs are incurred, and the state submits a voucher to FHWA. The reimbursable structure is designed to curb waste, fraud, and abuse.

Contract authority is a type of budget authority that is available for obligation without an appropriation (although appropriators must eventually provide **liquidating authority** to pay the obligations).

Obligation of contract authority for a project by FHWA legally commits the federal government to reimburse the state for the federal share of a project. This can be done prior to an appropriation.[11]

Limitation on obligations, known as ObLim or Oblimit, is used to control annual FHWA spending in place of an appropriation. The ObLim sets a limit on the total amount of contract authority that can be obligated in a single fiscal year. For practical purposes, the ObLim is analogous to an appropriation.[12]

Under the FAST Act, 92% of FAHP funding is distributed through five core programs.[13] These are the National Highway Performance Program (NHPP), the Surface Transportation Block Grant Program (STBG), the Highway Safety Improvement Program (HSIP), the Congestion Mitigation and Air Quality Improvement Program (CMAQ), and the National Highway Freight Program. The STBG was formerly known as the Surface Transportation Program, but was renamed in the FAST Act.

All five core programs are formula programs, meaning that each state's share of each program's total annual authorization is based on a mathematical calculation set out in the law. The remaining programs,

[11] For a more detailed discussion, see Federal Highway Administration, *Financing Federal-Aid Highways*, FHWA-PL07-017, Washington, March 2007, pp. 9-10, http://www.fhwa.dot.gov/reports/financingfederalaid/approp.htm#b.

[12] Ibid., pp. 19-22. To be contract authority, the authorization must refer to Title 23, Chapter 1 of the *U.S. Code*, and it must be funded out of the HTF.

[13] Federal Highway Administration, *Fixing America's Surface Transportation Act or "FAST Act,"* Washington, DC, December 2015, http://www.fhwa.dot.gov/fastact/. Most FHWA funds are available for obligation for four years.

generally referred to as discretionary programs, are administered more directly by FHWA, but the funding distribution of some of these programs (such as the Construction of Ferry Boats and Ferry Terminal Facilities Program) is formulaic as well. The FAHP does not provide money in advance. Rather, a state receives bills from private contractors for work completed and pays those bills according to its own procedures. The state submits vouchers for reimbursement to FHWA. FHWA certifies the claims for payment and notifies the Department of the Treasury, which disburses money electronically to the state's bank, often on the same day the voucher is submitted by the state.[14]

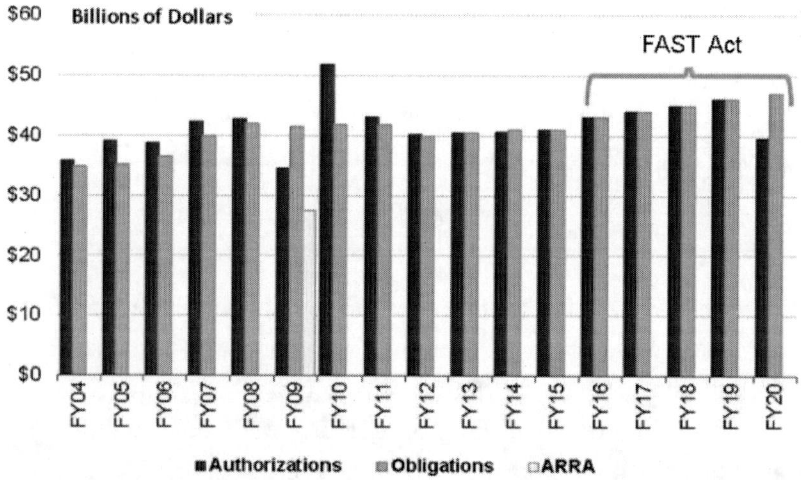

Source: Federal Highway Administration.

Notes: Totals are unadjusted for inflation. The FY2009 authorization figure reflects rescission of $8.708 billion, and the FY2010 figure reflects the restoration of the rescission. Authorizations are contract authority. Obligations are annual FAHP obligation limitations plus exempt obligations. ARRA refers to funding under the American Recovery and Reinvestment Act of 2009 (P.L. 111-5). FY2020 authorization column reflects the $7.569 billion rescission scheduled for July 1, 2020, under Section 1438 of the FAST Act.

Figure 1. Federal-Aid Highway Funding: FY2004-FY2020.

---

[14] Federal Highway Administration, *Financing Federal-Aid Highways*, FHWA-PL-07-017, Washington, DC, March 2007, pp. 17-18, http://www.fhwa.dot.gov/reports/financingfederalaid/financing_highways.pdf.

Table 1. Highway Authorizations: FAST Act (contract authority from the highway account of the HTF, except as noted, in millions of dollars)

Program	FY2016	FY2017	FY2018	FY2019	FY2020	Total
Title I: Federal-Aid Highways (FAHP formula)	39,728	40,548	41,424	42,359	43,373	207,432
Nationally Significant Freight and Highway Projects (NSFH)	800	850	900	950	1,000	4,500
Transportation Infrastructure Finance and Innovation Program (TIFIA)	275	275	285	300	300	1,435
Tribal Transportation Program	465	475	485	495	505	2,425
Federal Lands Transportation Program	335	345	355	365	375	1,775
Federal Lands Access Program	250	255	260	265	270	1300
Territorial and Puerto Rico Highway Program	200	200	200	200	200	1,000
FHWA Administrative Expenses	453	460	467	474	481	2,334
Emergency Relief	100	100	100	100	100	500
Construction of Ferry Boats	80	80	80	80	80	400
Appalachian Regional Development Program [Gen. Fund]	110	110	110	110	110	550
Regional Infrastructure Accelerator Demonstration Program [Gen. Fund]	12	0	0	0	0	12
Nationally Significant Federal Lands and Tribal Projects [Gen. Fund]	100	100	100	100	100	500
Total Authorizations: Title I	42,908	43,798	44,766	45,798	46,894	224,163
Title IV: Transportation Research	415	418	418	420	420	2,090
Total Contract Authority (HTF)	43,100	44,005	44,973	46,008	47,104	225,190
Total Obligations	43,100	44,005	44,973	46,008	47,104	225,190
Total General Fund Authorizations	222	210	210	210	210	1,062
Total Authorizations	43,322	44,215	45,183	46,218	47,314	226,252

Source: Federal Highway Administration, *FAST Act: Funding Tables*, Washington, DC, 2015, http://www.fhwa.dot.gov/fastact/estfy20162020auth.pdf. For breakout of formula programs, see Table 2.

Notes: Total obligations are the annual obligation limitations plus exempt obligations. Totals do not include funding for the safety operations of the National Highway Traffic Safety Administration or the Federal Motor Carrier Safety Administration. The obligation limitation plus exempt obligation amounts are equal to the total contract authority under the FAST Act. The total contract authority figure does not reflect the $7.569 billion rescission scheduled for July 1, 2020.

After several years of flat funding in terms of nominal dollars, the FAST Act provides highway funding increases of 4.2% above previous law adjusted for expected future inflation (see Figure 1 and Table 1). The Federal-Aid Highway and research titles authorize an average of $45 billion annually for FY2016-FY2020. Of this, an average of $41 billion is provided annually for Federal-Aid Highway programs. The act includes no new congressional earmarks for highway projects.

A major focus of the FAST Act is the movement of freight. This is reflected in a new formula freight program, the National Highway Freight Program (NHFP), and a new competitive discretionary grant program, the Nationally Significant Freight and Highway Projects Program (NSFHP). The freight policy aspects of the FAST Act are discussed together in a separate section of this chapter (see "Freight Policy").

Formulas and Apportionments

The apportioned programs—those whose funds are distributed by formula—include the five "core" programs plus the Metropolitan Planning Program. The FAST Act does not use separate formulas to calculate each state's apportionments under each core program. Instead, the act first provides for a single gross apportionment for each of the states. Each state's apportionment total is then divided among the separate programs based on a series of set-asides and percentage formulas.

Table 2 shows the dollar amounts of the aggregate programmatic split.[15]

Although each core program has specific objectives, the core programs also have many areas of overlapping eligibility to increase states' ability to use the funds as they prefer. The federal share for most FAHP projects is generally either 80% or 90%.

[15] Federal Highway Administration, *Fixing America's Surface Transportation Act or FAST Act Funding Tables*, Federal Highway Administration, Washington, DC, 2015, http://www.fhwa.dot.gov/fastact/funding.cfm. This site includes tables that set forth the authorizations as well as the estimated apportionments on a state-by-state basis over the life of the FAST Act.

Table 2. Apportioned Programs (Contract Authority) (millions of dollars)

Program	FY2016	FY2017	FY2018	FY2019	FY2020	Total
National Highway Performance Program (NHPP)	22,332	22,828	23,262	23,741	24,236	116,399
Surface Transportation Block Grant Program (STBG)	11,163	11,424	11,668	11,876	12,137	58,268
Highway Safety Improvement Program (HSIP)	2,226	2,275	2,318	2,360	2,407	11,585
Safety-related programs (HSIP set- aside)	3.5	3.5	3.5	3.5	3.5	17.5
Railway-highway crossings (HSIP set- aside)	225	230	235	240	245	1,175
National Highway Freight Program (NHFP)	1,140	1,091	1,190	1,339	1,487	6,247
Congestion Mitigation & Air Quality Improvement Program (CMAQ)	2,309	2,360	2,405	2,449	2,499	12,023
Metropolitan Transportation Planning	329	336	343	350	359	1,718
Total	39,728	40,548	41,424	42,359	43,373	207,432

Source: Federal Highway Administration. STBG amounts include the transportation alternatives annual set-aside of $751 million. Totals may not add due to rounding. NHFP figures represent net amounts after a portion is applied to the Metropolitan Planning Program under Section 1104 (b)(6). Total apportioned programs figure represents gross authorizations. State-by-state apportionments are available at http://www.fhwa.dot.gov/fastact/estfy20162020apports.pdf.

States may transfer up to 50% of any apportionment to any other apportioned program. However, no transfers are permitted of funds that are suballocated to areas by population (such as a portion of STBG funds) or of Metropolitan Planning funds. The broad areas of eligibility overlap among the core programs under the FAST Act should make it easier for states to operate within the 50% restriction on transfers.

National Highway Performance Program (NHPP; §1106)

NHPP is the largest of the federal-aid highway programs, with annual authorizations averaging over $23 billion. The program supports improvement of the condition and performance of the National Highway System (NHS), which includes Interstate System highways and bridges as well as virtually all other major highways. The FAST Act left the existing NHPP intact but added language allowing states to use NHPP funds to pay subsidy and administrative costs under the Transportation Infrastructure

Finance and Innovation Act (TIFIA). The FAST Act also allows states to use NHPP funds on bridges not on the NHS as long as the bridge is on the Federal-Aid Highway system (i.e., not an off-system bridge). Finally, the FAST Act allows states to use NHPP funds for projects intended to reduce the risk of failure of critical infrastructure in a state.

Surface Transportation Block Grant Program (STBG; §1109)

STBG is the highway program with by far the broadest eligibility criteria. Funds can be used on any federal-aid highway, on bridge projects on any public road, on transit capital projects, on routes for nonmotorized transportation, and on bridge and tunnel inspection and inspector training. The FAST Act authorizes an annual average of almost $11.7 billion for STBG.

The Transportation Alternatives program authorized under the previous transportation authorization law, the Moving Ahead for Progress in the 21st Century Act (MAP-21; P.L. 112- 141), which funded such projects as bicycle paths and walkways, is effectively absorbed into the STBG program. The FAST Act provides that $850 million per year from the STBG apportionment be set aside for transportation alternative-like uses. States and MPOs obligating these funds are to develop a competitive process for local public entities to submit projects for funding. A portion of the set-aside is directed toward the recreational trails program, from which states may apply to opt out.

STBG funds may be used for Appalachian Development Highway System projects with no state match. Virtually any federally eligible mass transit use may receive STBG funds. Carpool projects and electronic toll collection and congestion management projects are eligible for STBG funding. Repairs to off system-bridges and bridge replacement at the same location are generally eligible for STBG funding.

Congress required that a portion of a state's STBG funding be allocated by the state's DOT to projects in specified locations based on a population formula (often referred to as "suballocation"). This assures that some STBG funding goes to projects in all parts of each state, whether urban or rural. The percentage allocated to areas in the state by population increases by one percentage point each year over the life of the FAST Act, from 51% for FY2016 to 55% for FY2020. The remainder may be spent anywhere in the state. STBG funds equal to 15% of the state's highway bridge apportionment for FY2009 are to be set aside for off-system bridges, but there is no upper percentage limit on bridge spending. Some STBG funds reserved for rural areas may be used on minor collector roads.

Highway Safety Improvement Program (HSIP; §1113)

HSIP supports projects that improve the safety of road infrastructure by correcting hazardous road locations, such as dangerous intersections, or by making road improvements such as adding rumble strips. Under the FAST Act, HSIP is funded at an annual average of $2.6 billion. The Rail-Highway Grade Crossing Program continues as an HSIP set-aside and averages $235 million per year. The FAST Act broadened the eligibility of HSIP funds to make vehicle-to-vehicle technology, median separations, and other infrastructure projects eligible.

Congestion Mitigation and Air Quality Improvement Program (CMAQ; §1114)

CMAQ was established to fund projects and programs that may reduce emissions of transportation-related pollutants. In recent years, well over $1 billion of annual CMAQ funding has been transferred to the Federal Transit Administration (FTA) for local public transportation projects.[16] Under the FAST Act, CMAQ's average annual authorization is $2.4 billion. The act expands eligibility to include port-related freight operations and projects to reduce emissions from port-related equipment within metropolitan areas that do not meet federal air-quality standards ("nonattainment" or "maintenance" areas). The installation of vehicle-to-infrastructure communication equipment has also been made CMAQ-eligible. The act also eases the requirement for CMAQ spending on

---

[16] American Public Transportation Association, *APTA Primer on Transit Funding, FY2013-FY2015*, Final Edition, Washington, DC, December 2015, p. 77, http://www.apta.com/resources/reportsandpublications/Documents/APTAPrimer-MAP-21-Funding.pdf.

projects that reduce particulate matter for areas for states with low population density.

National Highway Freight Program (NHFP; §1116)

Annual apportionments for NHFP will average about $1.2 billion annually through FY2020. This new program is to help states and MPOs remove impediments to the movement of goods. For a detailed discussion of this program, see “National Highway Freight Program (NHFP; §1116)” in the “Freight Policy” section.

Other Highway Programs[17]

Nationally Significant Freight and Highway Projects (NSFHP; §1105)

The NSFHP provides an average of $900 million per year in discretionary grants for projects of regional or national importance, as determined by the Office of the Secretary of Transportation. States, groups of states, municipal governments, special purpose districts or transportation authorities, Indian tribes, federal land agencies and other public entities may apply. Applicants may apply directly to the Secretary of Transportation, circumventing the state DOTs. This program is not administered by FHWA. See “Nationally Significant Freight and Highway Projects (NSFHP; §1105)” in the “Freight Policy” section.[18]

---

[17] The act also amends 23 U.S.C. 503(c), the Technology and Innovation Deployment Program, to establish an Advanced Transportation and Congestion Management Technologies Deployment initiative (§6004). The program, authorized at $60 million annually, will provide competitive grants (on a 50-50 matching basis) to five to 10 recipients annually for deployment of technologies that improve the efficiency, safety, or state of good repair of surface transportation systems. Eligible recipients include state and local governments, transit agencies, metropolitan planning organizations, and consortia of research or academic institutions.

[18] The Office of the Secretary of Transportation administers another discretionary transportation infrastructure program, the Transportation Investment Generating Economic Recovery (TIGER) program. This program, however, is not authorized in surface transportation authorization legislation, but is funded annually via appropriations.

Emergency Relief Program (ER; §1107)

ER funds are made available following natural disasters or catastrophic highway infrastructure failures (from an external cause) for emergency repairs, restoration of federal-aid highway facilities to pre-disaster conditions, and debris removal from roads on tribal and federal lands. The program is funded by an annual authorization of $100 million from the HTF and general fund appropriations authorized on a "such sums as necessary" basis, usually in supplemental appropriations bills. ER funds can only be used on federal-aid highways. Generally, the Federal Emergency Management Agency, not FHWA, funds debris removal after major disasters.[19] The FAST Act broadened the definition of roads "open to public travel" to clarify the eligibility for ER funds on some federally owned roads.

Territorial and Puerto Rico Highway Program (§1115)

The Territorial and Puerto Rico Highway programs are funded at $42 million and $158 million annually, respectively, through FY2020.

Appalachian Development Highway System Program (ADHS; §1435)

The ADHS is made up of designated corridors in the 13 participating Appalachian states. The ADHS program is a road-building program intended to reduce Appalachia's isolation and encourage economic development. Construction has been ongoing since the mid-1960s. The ADHS is not a freestanding federal-aid program with a separate authorization, but eligibilities for ADHS projects are incorporated into the eligibilities of NHPP and STBG. The FAST Act extended the ADHS 100% federal share to the year 2050, but also allows states to contribute a share if they wish.[20]

---

[19] CRS Report R42804, *Emergency Relief Program: Federal-Aid Highway Assistance for Disaster-Damaged Roads and Bridges*, by Robert S. Kirk, available to congressional clients upon request.

[20] Federal Highway Administration, "Appalachian Development Highway System (ADHS): Fact Sheet," http://www.fhwa.dot.gov/map21/adhs.cfm. NHPP funds are limited to construction of ADHS routes that are also on the National Highway System.

Construction of Ferry Boats and Ferry Facilities (§1112)

The Ferry Boats and Ferry Terminal Facilities Program is a formula program that includes no set-asides for specific states.[21] The FAST Act provides $80 million annually, available until expended, for the construction of ferryboats and terminal facilities. The funding is to be apportioned according to a formula weighted by passengers (40%), vehicles carried (35%), and total route miles (30%). The FAST Act requires that unused allocations be withdrawn and redistributed after four years. Ferryboats and facilities are also eligible for formula funds under the NHPP.

Federal Lands and Tribal Transportation Programs

The FAST Act makes few changes to the Federal Lands Programs, but it does provide nominal increases in funding. Funding for the Federal Lands Transportation Program is increased from $300 million in FY2015, as authorized by MAP-21, to $335 million in FY2016 up to $375 million in FY2020. Funding for the Federal Lands Access Program in FY2016 remains at the FY2015 level of $250 million, but increases thereafter to $270 million in FY2020.

Funding increases are also provided for the Tribal Transportation Program (TTP). The TTP is authorized at $465 million in FY2016, $15 million more than in FY2015. Moreover, the TTP authorization increases by $10 million per year to $505 million in FY2020. Funding for the program comes from the highway account of the HTF. The FAST Act establishes a Tribal Transportation Self-Governance Program to allow the Secretary of Transportation to more fully delegate to tribes the administration of the TTP (§1121). To be eligible, a tribe must meet certain financial and managerial criteria.

The FAST Act authorizes a new Nationally Significant Federal Lands and Tribal Projects Program (NSFLTP) at $100 million per year, with funds coming from the general fund (§1123). In addition to projects on

---

[21] The program is part of the Federal-Aid Highway Program because it is designed to permit federal participation in the construction of ferryboats and terminals where it is not feasible to build a bridge, tunnel, or other highway structure.

tribal land, eligible projects include those on land managed by federal land management agencies, such as the National Park Service, the Forest Service, and the Bureau of Land Management. This program is for projects that are estimated to cost more than $25 million. At the same time the FAST Act did not reauthorize funding for the Tribal High Priority Projects Program (THPP). The THPP was authorized in MAP-21 at $30 million per year in general funds, although no funding was appropriated.

FREIGHT POLICY

The FAST Act directs a portion of federal funds towards highway segments and other projects deemed most critical to freight movement. It does this by creating a new competitive grant program and a new formula program for distributing federal funds to states. The stated goals of these two programs are very similar: increase U.S. global economic competitiveness, reduce congestion and bottlenecks, increase the efficiency and reliability of the highway network, and reduce the environmental impact of freight movement.[22]

Nationally Significant Freight and Highway Projects Program (NSFHP; §1105)

This is a competitive grant program with funding of $800 million in FY2016 rising to $1 billion in FY2020. Public entities are eligible to apply, including states and groups of states, Metropolitan Planning Organizations (MPOs), local governments or a group of local governments, political subdivisions of states or local governments, transportation-related authorities such as port authorities, and tribal governments. Eligible uses of funds include highway projects, railway-highway grade crossing projects,

---

[22] For more information on freight issues, see CRS Report R44367, *Federal Freight Policy: In Brief*, by John Frittelli.

connections to ports and intermodal freight facilities, and elements of private freight rail projects that provide public benefits. However, grants for freight intermodal or freight rail projects are capped at $500 million over the life of the program. A grant is to provide not more than 60% of the cost of a project, but other federal assistance can be used to provide up to a total federal share of 80% (i.e., the local cost share required must be at least 20% but not more than 40%).

This grant program is designed primarily for relatively high-cost projects; each grant awarded must be at least $25 million, and the project must have eligible costs amounting to at least $100 million or a significant share of a state's highway funding apportionment the previous fiscal year (e.g., 30% in the case of a one-state project). However, 10% of grant funds are reserved for smaller projects with awarded grants of at least $5 million each. The U.S. Department of Transportation (DOT) is to consider the dispersion of projects geographically, including between rural and urban communities. Congress has 60 days to disapprove of a DOT grant approval (§1105).[23]

National Highway Freight Program (NHFP; §1116)

The NHFP is a formula program with funding of $1.1 billion in FY2016 rising to $1.5 billion in FY2020. Funds are administered through state DOTs and must be directed toward highway components designated by FHWA, state DOTs, or MPOs as especially important to freight movement. These components include a "Primary Highway Freight Network" (PHFN) designated by FHWA, "critical rural freight corridors" designated by state DOTs, and "critical urban freight corridors" designated by either state DOTs or MPOs, depending on the population size of an urban area.[24] These components, along with Interstate Highway segments

[23] The NSFHP is administered by the National Surface Transportation and Innovation Finance Bureau, not by FHWA.

[24] FHWA, "Designation of the Primary Freight Network," 78 *Federal Register* 69520, November 19, 2013.

not designated as part of the PHFN, comprise the "National Highway Freight Network" (NHFN). The FAST Act directs FHWA to issue biennial reports on the condition and performance of the NHFN.

Larger states with 2% or more of total mileage in the PHFN are required to spend their program funds on the PHFN, critical rural, or critical urban freight corridors. States with less than 2% of the mileage may spend their program funds on any part of the NHFN. Up to 10% of a state's apportionment can be directed toward projects "within the boundaries of public or private freight rail or water facilities (including ports); and that provide surface transportation infrastructure necessary to facilitate direct intermodal interchange, transfer, and access into or out of the facility" (§1116).

Other Freight-Related Provisions

In addition to these two new programs, other provisions in the FAST Act particularly relevant to freight transportation include the following:

- Land Border Infrastructure. States bordering Canada or Mexico can use up to 5% of their Surface Transportation Block Grant Program funds for highway infrastructure supporting cross-border movements (§1437).
- Railway-Highway Grade Crossings. The FAST Act increases the amount provided for grade crossing safety improvements, such as train warning devices, by $5 million each year, reaching a total program set-aside of $245 million in FY2020. The FAST Act also specifies that projects intended to mitigate hazards posed by idling trains blocking crossings are eligible for these funds (§1108 and §1412).
- Mulitmodal Freight Designation. Although no specific funding provision is tied to this designation, DOT is directed to designate a "National Multimodal Freight Network" (NMFN) in addition to the NHFN. The NMFN is to include railways, ports, inland and

coastal waterways, airports, and the roads in the NHFN. The Under Secretary of Transportation for Policy will administer the NMFN. The purpose of the designation is to guide both federal and state funding decisions. This section also directs U.S. DOT and state DOTs to take a number of steps to support and improve freight planning, including developing state freight plans, establishing state freight advisory committees, and improving federal freight transportation data (§8001).

TOLLING (§1411)

Tolling of non-Interstate federal-aid highways has been allowed since 1992. Totally new Interstate Highway routes or extensions of existing routes may be built as toll roads. Toll lanes may be added to an existing Interstate route as long as the number of "free" lanes is maintained. Under the FAST Act, public authorities may impose tolls on single-occupant vehicles using high-occupancy vehicle (HOV) lanes. This allows cities, towns, counties, or transportation authorities to exercise authority over HOV facilities where only state agencies could do so previously. This could further encourage the use of congestion pricing.

The FAST Act modifies the Interstate System Construction Toll Pilot Program, which allows for up to three toll-free Interstate Highway segments in three states to be subject to tolls when that is the only way to provide funding for rehabilitation or reconstruction. Under a new provision, if the selected states have not started construction within three years of approval, their approval lapses, and other states may apply to participate in the pilot program. The act also mandates that intercity buses have the same access to toll roads and pay the same tolls as public transportation buses. As under previous legislation, the federal government does not regulate toll rates.

FINANCING

The FAST Act cuts the direct authorization of funding for the Transportation Infrastructure Finance and Innovation Act (TIFIA) program from $1 billion in FY2015 to $275 million in both FY2016 and FY2017, $285 million in FY2018, and $300 million in both FY2019 and FY2020. Seen in isolation, this reduces DOT's capacity to issue loans by approximately $750 million in FY2016, assuming a 10% subsidy cost.[25] TIFIA loans have been important in financing major surface transportation projects such as the Tappan Zee Bridge replacement in New York State and the East Link Extension, a 14.5-mile light rail line in Seattle.

However, the FAST Act also allows funding in two other highway programs to pay for the subsidy and administrative costs of credit assistance. These two programs are the new discretionary Nationally Significant Freight and Highway Projects Program (NSFHPP) (FAST Act; §1105), authorized at $800 million in FY2016 and the existing formula National Highway Performance Program (NHPP) (FAST Act; §1106), authorized at $22.3 billion in FY2016. This has the potential for increasing TIFIA financing much above the $275 million direct authorization, but at the discretion of state DOTs.

The FAST Act also

- provides authority for a TIFIA loan to a state infrastructure bank (SIB) to capitalize a "rural project fund";
- adds transit oriented development (TOD) infrastructure as an eligible project.

---

[25] The subsidy cost is "the estimated long-term cost to the government of a direct loan or a loan guarantee, calculated on a net present value basis, excluding administrative costs," Federal Credit Reform Act of 1990 (FCRA), Title V of the Omnibus Budget Reconciliation Act of 1990 (P.L. 101-508), Section 502(5)(A)).

- TOD infrastructure is a "project to improve or construct public infrastructure that is located within walking distance of, and accessible to, a fixed guideway transit facility, passenger rail station, intercity bus station, or intermodal facility" (FAST Act; §2001);
- allows up to $2 million of TIFIA budget authority each fiscal year to pay the application fees for projects costing $75 million or less instead of requiring payment by the project sponsor;
- modifies or sets the minimum project cost thresholds for credit assistance at $10 million for TOD projects, the capitalization of a rural project fund, and local government infrastructure projects. The maximum loan for a rural project fund is $100 million;
- provides for a streamlined application process for loans of $100 million or less.

In addition to allowing an SIB to receive a TIFIA loan to capitalize a rural projects fund, the FAST Act provides authority for states to capitalize SIBs with federal highway, transit, and rail funds through FY2020. Authority to do so had lapsed at the end of FY2009.

The FAST Act (§1109(b)(14)) allows STBG funding for the creation of offices that will "assist in the design, implementation, and oversight of public-private partnerships." The law made no change to the $15 billion volume cap on tax-exempt, private activity bonds for qualified highway or surface freight transfer facilities.

The FAST Act (§9001) creates a new National Surface Transportation and Innovative Finance Bureau within DOT to administer federal transportation financing programs, specifically the TIFIA program, the SIB program, the Railroad Rehabilitation and Improvement Financing (RRIF) Program, and the allocation of authority to issue private activity bonds for "qualified highway or surface freight transfer facilities" (26 U.S.C. §142(m)). The bureau will also be responsible for establishing and promoting best practices for innovative financing and public-private partnerships (P3s), and for providing advice and technical expertise in these areas. The bureau will administer the new discretionary Nationally

Significant Freight and Highway Projects grant program and will have responsibilities related to procurement and project environmental review and permitting.

The FAST Act (§1441) also establishes a new Regional Infrastructure Accelerator Demonstration Program "to assist entities in developing improved infrastructure priorities and financing strategies for the accelerated development of a project that is eligible for funding under the TIFIA program." The program is designed to make grants to regional infrastructure accelerators that will support and promote innovative financing and public-private partnerships. The FAST Act authorizes $12 million in FY2016 from the general fund for the program.

PUBLIC TRANSPORTATION

The public transportation provisions of the FAST Act are contained in Title III of Division A, the Federal Public Transportation Act of 2015, which authorizes federal public transportation programs for FY2016 through FY2020.[26]

Funding

The FAST Act authorizes $11.8 billion for public transportation in FY2016, an amount rising to $12.6 billion in FY2020. The five-year total of public transportation funding authorized is $61.1 billion, an average of $12.2 billion per year (Table 3). Of the total amount, 80% comes from the mass transit account of the HTF, and 20% is authorized from the general fund.

[26] See CRS Report R42706, *Federal Public Transportation Program: In Brief*, by William J. Mallett.

Table 3. Public Transportation Funding Authorized by the FAST Act (millions of dollars)

	FY2016	FY2017	FY2018	FY2019	FY2020
Total	11,789	12,176	12,175	12,381	12,592
Trust Funded Programs	9,348	9,734	9,733	9,939	10,150
Urbanized Area Formula Grants	4,539	4,630	4,727	4,827	4,929
State of Good Repair Grants	2,507	2,550	2,594	2,638	2,684
Bus and Bus Facilities Grants	696	720	747	777	809
Bus and Bus Facilities Formula	428	436	446	455	465
Grants Competitive Grants	268	284	302	322	344
Formula Grants for Rural Areas	620	632	646	659	673
Growing States and High Density	536	544	553	561	570
States Formula					
Enhanced Mobility of Seniors and	263	268	274	280	286
Individuals with Disabilities					
Planning Programs	131	133	136	139	142
Public Transportation Innovation	28	28	28	28	28
Pilot Program for Transit Oriented	10	10	10	10	10
Development Planning					
Technical Assistance and	9	9	9	9	9
Workforce Development					
National Transit Database	4	4	4	4	4
Bus Testing Facility	3	3	3	3	3
Pilot Program for Enhanced Mobility	2	3	3	4	4
Positive Train Control	0	199	0	0	0
General Funded Programs	2,442	2,442	2,442	2,442	2,442
Capital Investment Grants	2,302	2,302	2,302	2,302	2,302
Administrative Expenses	115	115	115	115	115
Research, Development,	20	20	20	20	20
Demonstration, and Deployment					
Program					
Technical Assistance and	5	5	5	5	5
Workforce Development					
Emergency Relief		such sums as are necessary			

Source: Federal Transit Administration.

Program Changes

The biggest programmatic change related to public transportation is the creation of a competitive discretionary component within the Bus and Bus Facilities Grant Program.[27] This program provides funding to purchase and rehabilitate buses and to construct bus-related facilities such as maintenance depots. In FY2016, the Bus Program is authorized at $696 million, with $428 million (61%) for formula grants and $268 million (39%) for discretionary grants. Bus Program funding increases to $809 million in FY2020, with $465 million (57%) provided for formula grants and $344 million (43%) for discretionary grants. Of the discretionary amounts, $55 million per year is set aside for the acquisition of low- or no-emission buses and related facilities. Also, of the discretionary amounts, not less than 10% must be made available for rural areas, and a single grantee cannot receive more than 10% of total program funding.

Smaller transportation agencies complained that the yearly formula apportionments from the bus program under MAP-21 were too small to fund a substantial bus investment. The FAST Act seeks to facilitate infrequent bus purchases with a pilot program for the creation of voluntary state funding pools for transit agencies. The pilot program will allow formula Bus Program funds apportioned to transit agencies in urbanized areas with a population of 200,000 to 999,999 to be transferred between recipients participating in a pool. The distribution of funds to each recipient by the state funding pool over the FY2016-FY2020 period must be equal to the amount of funds that each would have received individually according to the Bus Program formula.

The Capital Investment Grant (CIG) program (commonly known as the New Starts program) is a discretionary funding program for the construction of new fixed-guideway public transportation systems and the expansion of existing systems.

---

[27] The Bus and Bus Facilities Program was wholly discretionary prior to MAP-21, which converted it to a formula program.

The FAST Act increases the general fund authorization for the New Starts Program from $1.9 billion per year to $2.3 billion per year. However, these amounts are subject to appropriation. The new law changes the definition of a Small Starts project to one that involves $100 million or less of CIG funding (up from $75 million) and costs less than $300 million (up from $250 million). Another change to the New Starts Program is the authority to fund projects that benefit both public transportation and intercity passenger rail (although the eligible costs must be attributable to the transit portions of the project). The law also creates an Expedited Project Delivery for Capital Investment Grants Pilot Program to fund quickly up to eight projects involving public-private partnerships in which the federal grant is 25% or less of the project cost.[28]

Other changes include the following:

- Increasing the set-aside from the Urbanized Area Formula Program for Small Transit Intensive Cities, small urbanized areas that provide a relatively high level of transit service, from 1.5% to 2% in FY2019 and FY2020.
- A new HTF-funded Pilot Program for Innovative Coordinated Access and Mobility at an average of $3 million a year. The pilot program will provide discretionary grants "to assist in financing innovative projects for the transportation disadvantaged that improve the coordination of transportation services and nonemergency medical transportation services" (FAST, §3005(b)).
- An increase in the Buy America requirement for rail cars and buses used in federally funded public transportation. Prior law required that at least 60% of a vehicle's value result from domestic production or assembly. The FAST Act raises that requirement to 65% in FY2018 and FY2019, and to 70% in FY2020 and later.[29]

---

[28] This pilot program replaces the Pilot Program for Expedited Project Delivery in Section 20008(b) of MAP-21.

[29] CRS Report R44266, *Effects of Buy America on Transportation Infrastructure and U.S. Manufacturing: Policy Options*, by Michaela D. Platzer and William J. Mallett.

- Authority for transit agencies to cooperatively procure rolling stock and related equipment with agencies in other states. The law establishes a pilot program for nonprofit cooperative procurement to "demonstrate the effectiveness of cooperative procurement contracts administered by eligible nonprofit entities," and requires FTA to establish a clearinghouse for information on cooperative procurement (§3019).
- Authorization of $199 million from the mass transit account of the HTF in FY2017 for costs associated with the installation of positive train control by public transportation agencies. Positive train control, a safety system, is mandated to be installed on all commuter rail lines by the end of 2018.
- Affirmation of FTA's authority to directly oversee safety improvements at public transportation agencies, clarifying an issue raised after FTA took over safety oversight of the Washington, DC, Metro system following a fatal incident in 2015.

EFFORTS TO ACCELERATE PROJECT DELIVERY

Subtitle C of the Federal-Aid Highway title includes 18 provisions identified as pertaining to "acceleration of project delivery." As in the two most recent long-run reauthorization acts, the Safe Accountable, Flexible, Efficient Transportation Equity Act: a Legacy for Users (SAFETEA; P.L. 109-59) and MAP-21, the provisions primarily involve efforts to expedite surface transportation project delivery by changing how the environmental review process is implemented.[30] For individual highway and transit projects, that process generally involves preparing documentation and analysis necessary to demonstrate that any project-related impacts to the human, natural, or cultural environment are identified; that the effects of those impacts are taken into consideration among other factors considered

[30] For information about that process, see CRS Report R42479, *The Role of the Environmental Review Process in Federally Funded Highway Projects: Background and Issues for Congress*, by Linda Luther.

during the decision-making process (e.g., economic or community benefits); and that any applicable state, tribal, or federal compliance requirements are met. Provisions in this subtitle will affect the following:

- NEPA implementation—includes changes to elements of FHWA and FTA procedures to identify and consider the environmental impacts of a proposal, as required under the National Environmental Policy Act (NEPA);[31]
- Section 4(f)[32] prohibitions—includes changes to procedures and requirements associated with the DOT's prohibition on the approval of projects that have anything more than a minor impact on historic sites;[33] and
- State DOT action to expedite federal approvals—establishes or changes existing programs that allow state DOTs to assume federal authority to implement NEPA or other federal requirements or to undertake actions intended to expedite federal approvals associated with transportation projects.[34]

Title XI of the FAST Act, Section 11503, "Efficient Environmental Review," amends Title 49 U.S.C. to require DOT to apply project development procedures applicable to federal-aid highway projects[35] to railroad projects.

---

[31] See particularly the provisions in Sections 1304,"Efficient environmental reviews for project decision-making," and 1311, "Accelerated decision-making in environmental reviews."

[32] The term "Section 4(f)" refers to the section of the Department of Transportation Act of 1966 (P.L. 89-670) under which the requirement was originally set forth. Initially codified at 49 U.S.C. §1653(f), it applies to all DOT agencies. Later that year, similar legislation was enacted at 23 U.S.C. §138 that applies only to the Federal-Aid Highway Program. The provision no longer falls under "Section 4(f)," but DOT has continued this reference. For information about the Section 4(f) process and its requirements, see FHWA's "Environmental Review Toolkit: Section 4(f) Program Overview," at https://www.environment.fhwa.dot.gov/4f/index.asp.

[33] See particularly the provisions in Sections 1301, "Satisfaction of requirements for certain historic sites," and 1303, "Treatment of certain bridges under preservation requirements."

[34] See particularly the provisions in Section 1309, "Program for eliminating duplication of environmental reviews," §1312, "Improving State and Federal agency engagement in environmental reviews," and Section 1316, "Assumption of authorities."

[35] Those provisions are established under 23 U.S.C. §139.

Until DOT interprets the directives, it is difficult to determine the extent to which the amendments will affect the environmental review process.

SAFETY PROGRAMS

The National Highway Traffic Safety Administration (NHTSA) is responsible for vehicle safety regulation and for driver safety other than for commercial drivers. The Federal Motor Carrier Safety Administration (FMCSA) is responsible for the safety of trucks and buses and for commercial driver safety.

Noncommercial Driver Safety

In addition to addressing the safety aspects of passenger vehicles (e.g., requiring seat belts, air bags, and electronic stability control), NHTSA promotes safety by addressing driver behaviors that contribute to crashes (e.g., driving while intoxicated, speeding, and distracted driving). Most of NHTSA's funding is for addressing driver behavior, and is in the form of contract authority, funded from the HTF.[36] In the FAST Act, Congress authorizes modest increases in NHTSA's driver behavior programs, rising by roughly 2% annually from FY2015 ($700 million) to FY2020 ($778 million) (see Table 4).

Driver behavior, however, is a state matter, not under federal control. Consequently, when Congress addresses driver behavior issues, it does so by encouraging the states to act. NHTSA's driver behavior programs are primarily grants to states to help pay for state actions addressing these issues.

---

[36] NHTSA's funding for vehicle safety activities, as discussed above, is appropriated from the general fund.

The FAST Act also changes NHTSA's safety grant programs. It eases eligibility requirements for states to qualify for incentive grants for efforts to prevent impaired and distracted driving, and to implement graduated driver licensing. It creates a new incentive grant program to encourage states to adopt "24-7 sobriety programs," which require an individual to totally abstain from alcohol or drugs and be subject to testing at least twice a day or continuous electronic monitoring. It also creates a grant to promote safety of nonmotorized travelers (e.g., bicyclists and pedestrians). Additionally, it directs NHTSA to study possible standards for judging when users of marijuana are too impaired to drive safely.

Table 4. NHTSA Driver Behavior Program Authorizations, FY2016-FY2020 (millions of dollars)

	2016	2017	2018	2019	2020
Grant to States					
State Formula Grants (§402)	243.5	252.3	261.2	270.4	279.8
National Safety Priorities (§405)	274.7	277.5	280.2	283	285.9
Occupant Protection	35.7	36.1	36.4	36.8	37.2
State Traffic Safety Information System	39.8	40.2	40.6	41.0	41.5
Improvements					
Impaired Driving Countermeasures	144.2	145.7	147.1	148.6	150.1
Distracted Driving	23.3	23.6	23.8	24.1	24.3
Motorcyclist Safety	4.1	4.2	4.2	4.2	4.3
State Graduated Driver Licensing Laws	13.7	13.9	14.0	14.2	14.3
Nonmotorized Safety	13.7	13.9	14.0	14.2	14.3
Subtotal—Grants to States	518.2	529.8	541.4	553.4	565.7
Highway Safety Research & Development	137.8	140.7	143.7	146.7	149.8
(§403)					
National Driver Register	5.1	5.2	5.3	5.4	5.5
High Visibility Enforcement Program	29.3	29.5	26.9	30.2	30.5
Administrative Expense	25.8	26.1	26.3	26.6	26.8
Total	716.2	731.3	743.6	762.3	778.3

Source: Estimated by CRS, based on figures in P.L. 114-94 §4001 and §4005.

Federal Motor Carrier Safety Administration (FMCSA)

In the FAST Act, Congress consolidates FMCSA's grant programs, reducing the number from nine to four. It authorizes a significant increase in funding beginning in FY2017 for grants to states for motor carrier inspections and other enforcement activities (see Table 5).

Table 5. FMCSA Program Authorizations, FY2016-FY2020 (millions of dollars)

	FY2016	FY2017	FY2018	FY2019	FY2020
Motor Carrier Safety Operations and Programs	267.4	277.2	283	284	288
Motor Carrier Safety Grants	313	367	374.8	381.8	387.8
Total	580.4	644.2	657.8	665.8	675.8

Source: P.L. 114-93, §5101 & §5103, except FY2016 from P.L. 114-113, Division L (the FY2016 Department of Transportation Appropriations Act).

The FAST Act directs FMCSA to commission a study of its central safety program, the Compliance, Safety, Accountability (CSA) program, which uses data from roadside inspections and traffic violations to evaluate the safety performance of carriers. Currently, FMCSA publishes the results of this analysis in the form of percentile rankings in several categories; the act directs that FMCSA suspend publication of the percentile rankings for carriers pending the results of the study.

In addition, Congress directs FMCSA to

- adjust the CSA program in order to reward carriers that implement certain safety measures, such as installation of advanced safety equipment or improved measures of driver fitness;
- to take steps to improve the consistency and accuracy of data used in the CSA program; and

- to review the treatment of preventable crashes (crashes that could have been prevented by a driver exercising normal judgment and taking actions that would not have risked causing some other type of mishap) in the CSA program.

Congress also adds other provisions intended to promote commercial motor vehicle safety, including statutory changes and directives to conduct studies of various issues. These include

- requiring FMCSA to complete rulemakings currently in progress before undertaking new rulemakings, and to report to Congress every six months on the status of rulemakings, including an explanation of why any rulemakings that were not completed by statutory deadlines were delayed;
- allowing the use of hair testing as an alternative to urine testing in conducting preemployment screening of, or random testing of, commercial drivers for use of controlled substances;
- allowing Department of Veterans Affairs physicians to certify the medical fitness of commercial drivers who are veterans, even if those physicians have not met the qualifications to certify the medical fitness of commercial drivers.

Vehicle Safety in the FAST Act

The FAST Act makes a number of changes to the law governing recalls of unsafe vehicles. These include

- an increase in the maximum civil fine imposed on an automaker that violates auto safety laws from $35 million to $105 million;[37]

---

[37] Some Members of Congress suggested in debate that higher penalties would increase the deterrent effect of the law. The Obama Administration had called for increasing the penalty cap to $300 million, and some Senators had advocated eliminating it altogether.

- new authority for NHTSA to enforce repair of recalled vehicles used in rental fleets. The agency will have the same authority over recalled rental cars that it currently has over auto dealers who sell new cars: recall-related repairs must be made before a vehicle is rented or sold. An effort in the Senate to require that all vehicles subject to recalls be repaired before being sold was not enacted; instead, the FAST Act requires auto dealers to inform motorists of open recalls when they bring their cars in for servicing;
- a direction for NHTSA to conduct a feasibility study to determine if new cars could be equipped with a system to inform motorists of open recalls and to establish two-year pilot programs in up to six states to determine whether recall compliance rates will improve if consumers are told of open recalls when they renew their vehicle registrations;
- new privacy standards specifying that the data retained by an event data recorder ("black box") in a vehicle are the property of the vehicle owner or lessee. Data stored by such devices can be viewed by others only under a court order; after owner consent; when the data are retrieved as part of a NHTSA investigation; if the data are needed to provide emergency medical response to a crash; or for anonymous traffic safety research;[38]
- mandates for internal NHTSA reforms recommended by the DOT Inspector General (IG). Congress provided essentially flat funding for NHTSA in FY2016 until the IG certifies that all the IG's June 2015 recommendations for agency reforms have been met.[39] At that time, NHTSA's budget authorization would increase by $45 million, as originally requested by the Obama Administration.

---

[38] For more information about event data recorders, see CRS Report R43651, *"Black Boxes" in Passenger Vehicles: Policy Issues*, by Bill Canis and David Randall Peterman.

[39] The IG report makes 17 recommendations for improving NHTSA's collection and analysis of vehicle safety data, such as implementing a method to assess early warning reporting data and developing a process to prioritize potential safety defects. Calvin Scovel III, *Inadequate Data and Analysis Undermine NHTSA's Efforts to Identify and Investigate Vehicle Safety Concerns*, U.S. Department of Transportation, Office of the Inspector General, ST-2015-063, June 18, 2015, https://www.oig.dot.gov/sites/default/files/NHTSA%20Safety-Related%20Vehicle%20Defects%20- %20Final%20Report%5E6-18-15.pdf.

NHTSA must also report regularly to Congress on progress in achieving reforms.

INTERCITY RAIL TRANSPORTATION

The FAST Act includes authorization of passenger and freight rail transportation programs, thus bringing all surface transportation modes together within a single authorization bill for the first time. The total amount authorized for all intercity rail programs, including Amtrak, increases significantly over the authorization period, with year-over-year increases of 8%-12% (see Table 6).

Table 6. Intercity Rail Authorizations in the FAST Act (millions of dollars)

	FY2016	FY2017	FY2018	FY2019	FY2020
Amtrak					
Northeast Corridor (NEC)	450	474	515	557	600
National Network	1,000	1,026	1,085	1,143	1,200
Amtrak Inspector General	20	20.5	21	21.5	22
Subtotal—Amtrak	1,470	1,520.5	1,621	1,721.5	1,822
Consolidated Rail Infrastructure and Safety	98	190	230	255	330
Improvements					
Federal-State Partnership for State of Good Repair	82	140	175	300	300
Restoration and Enhancement Grants	20	20	20	20	20
Subtotal—General Grants	200	350	425	575	650
Total Intercity Rail Authorizations	1,670	1,870.5	2,046	2,296.5	2,472

Source: P.L. 114-94, §11101-11105.

However, funding for intercity rail programs is authorized from the general fund, not from the HTF, and it is possible that appropriators will not approve the full amounts authorized. For example, while the total amount authorized for FY2016 was \$1.67 billion, the actual amount appropriated for FY2016 was \$1.465 billion, \$205 million (12%) less than the authorized total. Also, the totals are significantly less than the amount authorized for Amtrak alone in the previous intercity rail authorization act.

For FY2013, the final year of that authorization, Amtrak was authorized $2.25 billion but appropriated $1.36 billion, 40% less than the authorized amount.

Amtrak operates regular intercity passenger rail service both over infrastructure it owns (primarily the Northeast Corridor running from Washington, DC, through New York City to Boston) and over the rail network owned by freight rail companies. Some Amtrak trains are operated under contract with states, which must cover a portion of any losses on those routes. It runs an annual deficit of roughly $1 billion, on revenues of roughly $2 billion and expenses of roughly $3 billion, and receives capital and operating support from Congress to cover the deficit.

One of the continuing criticisms many have of Amtrak is that it does not cover its costs. Amtrak's passenger service in the Northeast Corridor (NEC) makes an operating profit each year, but does not cover all costs of maintaining the infrastructure owned by Amtrak. Outside the NEC, Amtrak's long-distance trains run large operating deficits, but have relatively low capital costs (since the rail infrastructure they operate over is owned by other companies). The FAST Act requires Amtrak to structure its accounts so that all costs and revenues are assigned to either the Northeast Corridor or the National Network (everything outside of the NEC) in order to clarify the receipts and outlays for each of these two groups of services.

Congress also directs Amtrak to hire an independent entity to develop methodologies for Amtrak to use in determining what routes and services it should provide, and to submit the results to Congress by December 2017.

Other provisions include

- an increase in the cap on claims against Amtrak arising from the May 12, 2015, derailment in Philadelphia, PA, to $295 million, and a provision that the general $200 million cap on claims will be adjusted based on changes in the Consumer Price Index (which will increase the statutory cap to approximately $295 million) and readjusted every five years;

- a requirement that Amtrak implement a plan to eliminate its operating loss on food and beverage service by December 2020;
- a requirement that Amtrak develop a pilot program allowing passengers to carry domesticated dogs and cats;
- a requirement that DOT convene a working group to evaluate restoration of intercity rail passenger service between New Orleans, LA, and Orlando, FL, which was disrupted by infrastructure damage caused by hurricanes in 2007;
- a requirement that DOT implement a pilot program allowing bidding for the right to operate up to three long-distance passenger routes;
- a requirement that DOT promulgate a rule requiring intercity passenger and commuter rail carriers to install inward- and outward-facing audio and image recorders to monitor train operators;
- a requirement that DOT, Amtrak, states and other stakeholders submit a study evaluating the shared use of right-of-way by passenger and freight rail systems; and
- statutory language requiring that the recipient of a high-speed rail grant for more than $1 billion must demonstrate that it has funding committed to fulfill the nonfederal share required for the grant, that it has identified nonfederal funding required for any subsequent phases of the project, and that the grant will result in a useable segment that has operational independence. This appears intended to limit future grants such as to the California high-speed rail project, which received a $2.5 billion federal grant in January 2010 but has not identified local funding for the balance of the proposed rail line between San Francisco and Los Angeles.

APPENDIX A. ESTIMATED HIGHWAY APPORTIONMENTS

Table A.1.Comparison of Actual FY2015 and Estimated FY2016-FY2020 Apportionments under the FAST Act (before post-apportionment set-asides; before penalties; before sequestration)

State	Actual FY2015	Est. FY2016	Est. FY2017	Est. FY2018	Est. FY2019	Est. FY2020	FY2016-FY2020 Total	FY2016-FY2020 Average
Alabama	732,263,043	769,571,910	785,463,731	802,438,701	820,550,261	840,202,114	4,018,226,717	803,645,343
Alaska	483,955,039	508,614,600	519,117,557	530,336,370	542,306,359	555,294,332	2,655,669,218	531,133,844
Arizona	706,182,063	742,166,445	757,492,248	773,862,621	791,329,101	810,281,016	3,875,131,431	775,026,286
Arkansas	499,714,166	525,175,061	536,020,027	547,604,161	559,963,932	573,374,836	2,742,138,017	548,427,603
California	3,542,468,412	3,723,001,547	3,799,881,396	3,882,001,196	3,969,619,475	4,064,689,233	19,439,192,847	3,887,838,569
Colorado	516,112,989	542,412,699	553,613,557	565,577,841	578,343,213	592,194,216	2,832,141,526	566,428,305
Connecticut	484,770,705	509,473,713	519,994,372	531,232,092	543,222,256	556,232,120	2,660,154,553	532,030,911
Delaware	163,267,961	171,587,491	175,130,787	178,915,587	182,953,804	187,335,451	895,923,120	179,184,624
Dist. Of Col.	154,002,708	161,850,034	165,192,253	168,762,270	172,571,324	176,704,316	845,080,197	169,016,039
Florida	1,828,689,002	1,921,860,645	1,961,547,473	2,003,939,263	2,049,169,471	2,098,246,272	10,034,763,124	2,006,952,625
Georgia	1,246,238,772	1,309,739,819	1,336,786,115	1,365,675,824	1,396,499,894	1,429,945,392	6,838,647,044	1,367,729,409
Hawaii	163,244,192	171,562,378	175,105,158	178,889,407	182,927,036	187,308,045	895,792,024	179,158,405
Idaho	276,061,294	290,127,532	296,118,707	302,518,228	309,346,239	316,754,938	1,514,865,644	302,973,129
Illinois	1,372,231,384	1,442,156,608	1,471,937,238	1,503,747,647	1,537,687,978	1,574,514,759	7,530,044,230	1,506,008,846
Indiana	919,668,926	966,529,532	986,488,498	1,007,807,822	1,030,554,618	1,055,235,912	5,046,616,382	1,009,323,276
Iowa	474,345,450	498,513,780	508,808,186	519,804,234	531,536,542	544,266,622	2,602,929,364	520,585,873
Kansas	364,737,489	383,321,318	391,236,975	399,692,143	408,713,444	418,501,959	2,001,465,839	400,293,168
Kentucky	641,292,458	673,966,719	687,884,265	702,750,398	718,611,920	735,822,382	3,519,035,684	703,807,137
Louisiana	677,413,014	711,927,496	726,628,943	742,332,405	759,087,323	777,267,157	3,717,243,324	743,448,665

Table A.1. (Continued)

State	Actual FY2015	Est. FY2016	Est. FY2017	Est. FY2018	Est. FY2019	Est. FY2020	FY2016-FY2020 Total	FY2016-FY2020 Average
Maine	178,165,560	187,243,965	191,110,574	195,240,722	199,647,412	204,428,868	977,671,541	195,534,308
Maryland	580,007,300	609,563,599	622,151,114	635,596,565	649,942,279	665,508,023	3,182,761,580	636,552,316
Massachusetts	586,191,765	616,064,316	628,786,048	642,374,865	656,873,544	672,605,261	3,216,704,034	643,340,807
Michigan	1,016,207,628	1,067,989,869	1,090,043,951	1,113,601,188	1,138,735,743	1,166,007,859	5,576,378,610	1,115,275,722
Minnesota	629,372,872	661,441,891	675,100,754	689,690,575	705,257,282	722,147,855	3,453,638,357	690,727,671
Mississippi	466,803,812	490,587,875	500,718,610	511,539,831	523,085,607	535,613,291	2,561,545,214	512,309,043
Missouri	913,719,741	960,274,903	980,104,758	1,001,286,170	1,023,885,822	1,048,407,455	5,013,959,108	1,002,791,822
Montana	396,007,464	416,184,959	424,779,247	433,959,302	443,754,023	454,381,736	2,173,059,267	434,611,853
Nebraska	278,976,662	293,191,186	299,245,632	305,712,735	312,612,854	320,099,792	1,530,862,199	306,172,440
Nevada	350,472,546	368,332,024	375,938,098	384,062,585	392,731,061	402,136,745	1,923,200,513	384,640,103
New Hampshire	159,469,843	167,595,715	171,056,584	174,753,337	178,697,613	182,977,330	875,080,579	175,016,116
New Jersey	963,682,664	1,012,792,050	1,033,706,218	1,056,045,847	1,079,881,265	1,105,743,762	5,288,169,142	1,057,633,828
New Mexico	354,439,590	372,498,916	380,191,084	388,407,532	397,174,128	406,686,276	1,944,957,936	388,991,587
New York	1,620,088,460	1,702,649,572	1,737,809,280	1,775,365,392	1,815,436,141	1,858,914,699	8,890,175,084	1,778,035,017
North Carolina	1,006,630,450	1,057,922,052	1,079,768,287	1,103,103,510	1,128,001,186	1,155,016,278	5,523,811,313	1,104,762,263
North Dakota	239,621,802	251,831,294	257,031,648	262,586,445	268,513,174	274,943,940	1,314,906,501	262,981,300
Ohio	1,293,739,008	1,359,663,237	1,387,740,399	1,417,731,235	1,449,730,162	1,484,450,429	7,099,315,462	1,419,863,092
Oklahoma	612,127,810	643,315,998	656,600,603	670,790,656	685,930,829	702,358,595	3,358,996,681	671,799,336
Oregon	482,423,497	507,004,353	517,474,070	528,657,381	540,589,488	553,536,361	2,647,261,653	529,452,331
Pennsylvania	1,583,603,275	1,664,296,550	1,698,664,445	1,735,374,776	1,774,543,112	1,817,042,511	8,689,921,394	1,737,984,279
Rhode Island	211,081,927	221,837,373	226,418,345	231,311,545	236,532,377	242,197,215	1,158,296,855	231,659,371
South Carolina	646,306,850	679,236,584	693,262,955	708,245,330	724,230,875	741,575,911	3,546,551,655	709,310,331
South Dakota	272,190,802	286,059,805	291,966,983	298,276,779	305,009,059	312,313,885	1,493,626,511	298,725,302
Tennessee	815,605,297	857,163,013	874,863,555	893,770,525	913,943,445	935,831,968	4,475,572,506	895,114,501

State	Actual FY2015	Est. FY2016	Est. FY2017	Est. FY2018	Est. FY2019	Est. FY2020	FY2016-FY2020 Total	FY2016-FY2020 Average
Texas	3,331,596,800	3,501,354,175	3,573,657,617	3,650,889,094	3,733,291,741	3,822,702,306	18,281,894,933	3,656,378,987
Utah	335,148,600	352,225,393	359,498,902	367,268,156	375,557,614	384,552,048	1,839,102,113	367,820,423
Vermont	195,886,832	205,868,282	210,119,484	214,660,438	219,505,440	224,762,485	1,074,916,129	214,983,226
Virginia	982,180,040	1,032,226,472	1,053,542,076	1,076,310,501	1,100,603,428	1,126,962,342	5,389,644,819	1,077,928,964
Washington	654,304,963	687,644,962	701,844,910	717,012,693	733,196,062	750,755,744	3,590,454,371	718,090,874
West Virginia	421,797,542	443,288,929	452,442,922	462,220,829	472,653,435	483,973,279	2,314,579,394	462,915,879
Wisconsin	726,226,908	763,229,980	778,990,803	795,825,845	813,788,109	833,277,970	3,985,112,707	797,022,541
Wyoming	247,262,623	259,861,381	265,227,558	270,959,481	277,075,196	283,711,020	1,356,834,636	271,366,927
Apportioned Total	37,798,000,000	39,724,000,000	40,544,305,000	41,420,520,075	42,355,403,696	43,369,794,311	207,414,023,082	41,482,804,616

Source: Federal Highway Administration, http://www.fhwa.dot.gov/fastact/estfy20162020apports.pdf. Note: Reflects $3,500,000 takedown for safety-related programs for each fiscal year 2016-2020.

Appendix B. Estimated Public Transportation Apportionments

Table B.1. Comparison of Actual FY2015 and Estimated FY2016-FY2020 Apportionments under the FAST Act

State/Territory	Actual FY2015	Est. FY2016	Est. FY2017	Est. FY2018	Est. FY2019	Est. FY2020	FY2016-FY2020 Total	FY2016-FY2020 Average
Alabama	52,838,746	53,895,400	54,882,913	55,938,294	56,975,799	58,082,843	279,775,249	55,955,050
Alaska	44,509,181	51,625,429	52,586,431	53,606,720	54,555,033	55,609,594	267,983,207	53,596,641
American Samoa	825,834	830,951	838,295	846,118	854,176	862,408	4,231,949	846,390
Arizona	107,526,627	109,929,569	112,124,626	114,481,119	117,005,463	119,470,089	573,010,866	114,602,173
Arkansas	30,744,551	31,650,538	32,281,902	32,956,660	33,585,909	34,292,591	164,767,599	32,953,520
California	1,253,984,980	1,317,468,210	1,343,523,066	1,371,406,841	1,399,901,100	1,428,800,364	6,861,099,581	1,372,219,916
Colorado	111,531,891	114,618,713	116,920,877	119,391,655	122,239,166	124,818,533	597,988,945	119,597,789
Connecticut	157,663,159	166,747,877	169,453,629	172,171,163	175,543,758	178,524,502	862,440,929	172,488,186
Delaware	24,593,444	25,309,286	25,701,073	26,092,624	26,603,153	27,042,819	130,748,955	26,149,791
District of Columbia	168,198,179	199,737,485	203,238,336	206,883,698	210,465,763	214,222,831	1,034,548,113	206,909,623
Florida	360,848,078	370,830,314	378,287,718	386,278,461	393,569,020	401,881,816	1,930,847,329	386,169,466
Georgia	174,055,051	183,012,059	186,581,763	190,380,254	194,509,592	198,474,317	952,957,985	190,591,597
Guam	1,353,130	1,366,494	1,385,726	1,406,210	1,427,308	1,448,864	7,034,603	1,406,921
Hawaii	41,053,996	42,177,804	43,033,630	43,960,581	45,307,477	46,277,457	220,756,949	44,151,390
Idaho	23,242,376	24,198,622	24,647,159	25,127,247	25,567,579	26,069,692	125,610,299	25,122,060
Illinois	537,023,178	574,434,635	585,480,846	597,240,902	609,101,428	621,263,354	2,987,521,165	597,504,233
Indiana	87,621,924	89,514,098	91,340,644	93,302,797	95,799,196	97,858,794	467,815,528	93,563,106
Iowa	38,625,980	39,618,960	40,423,483	41,287,628	42,829,880	43,747,990	207,907,940	41,581,588
Kansas	34,721,200	35,647,051	36,359,895	37,123,575	38,031,055	38,833,884	185,995,460	37,199,092

State/Territory	Actual FY2015	Est. FY2016	Est. FY2017	Est. FY2018	Est. FY2019	Est. FY2020	FY2016-FY2020 Total	FY2016-FY2020 Average
Kentucky	51,536,663	52,622,836	53,664,547	54,781,805	55,940,231	57,109,859	274,119,278	54,823,856
Louisiana	59,629,607	61,355,354	62,580,348	63,890,686	65,058,832	66,425,793	319,311,013	63,862,203
Maine	30,348,165	32,222,947	32,840,133	33,500,527	34,314,921	35,003,493	167,882,022	33,576,404
Maryland	230,324,429	240,125,310	244,171,732	248,283,480	252,138,184	256,597,797	1,241,316,503	248,263,301
Massachusetts	339,311,761	359,729,860	365,677,024	371,687,458	377,572,975	384,082,886	1,858,750,203	371,750,041
Michigan	131,602,215	133,673,157	136,425,114	139,382,241	142,597,929	145,691,410	697,769,851	139,553,970
Minnesota	101,583,605	106,375,143	108,481,379	110,741,154	113,535,596	115,897,694	555,030,967	111,006,193
Mississippi	28,244,679	29,251,670	29,815,340	30,417,129	31,135,281	31,769,726	152,389,146	30,477,829
Missouri	94,320,943	97,989,234	99,942,315	102,028,634	104,260,944	106,439,219	510,660,347	102,132,069
Montana	19,129,871	20,189,160	20,547,538	20,930,711	21,513,897	21,920,038	105,101,345	21,020,269
N. Mariana Islands	811,990	816,885	823,922	831,416	839,135	847,021	4,158,379	831,676
Nebraska	23,591,337	24,436,766	24,902,865	25,401,365	25,867,517	26,389,450	126,997,963	25,399,593
Nevada	57,172,866	58,568,600	59,745,130	61,010,636	62,094,164	63,408,583	304,827,113	60,965,423
New Hampshire	15,671,744	16,348,701	16,655,446	16,984,448	17,279,946	17,623,298	84,891,839	16,978,368
New Jersey	573,263,437	600,206,411	610,554,099	621,157,490	630,788,783	642,180,359	3,104,887,142	620,977,428
New Mexico	43,810,139	45,479,144	46,375,940	47,339,618	48,338,006	49,341,315	236,874,023	47,374,805
New York	1,342,157,884	1,444,263,279	1,470,596,038	1,498,180,729	1,523,909,156	1,552,716,390	7,489,665,591	1,497,933,118
North Carolina	114,759,873	116,782,034	119,136,874	121,659,719	124,046,200	126,683,975	608,308,803	121,661,761
North Dakota	13,689,174	14,500,492	14,754,249	15,025,978	15,536,147	15,826,002	75,642,867	15,128,573
Ohio	174,852,836	179,927,728	183,526,137	187,376,240	190,956,911	194,964,160	936,751,176	187,350,235
Oklahoma	47,171,865	49,690,521	50,502,207	51,368,977	52,170,951	53,079,553	256,812,209	51,362,442
Oregon	93,960,863	98,155,574	100,089,189	102,160,155	104,230,003	106,381,040	511,015,962	102,203,192
Pennsylvania	387,365,825	413,084,498	420,935,822	429,280,566	438,670,071	447,340,760	2,149,311,717	429,862,343
Puerto Rico	67,260,623	68,960,340	70,403,091	71,970,086	74,078,304	75,705,729	361,117,550	72,223,510
Rhode Island	36,370,777	37,669,483	38,224,248	38,764,678	39,263,151	39,875,752	193,797,311	38,759,462
South Carolina	46,830,050	47,871,638	48,819,578	49,830,587	50,819,486	51,881,824	249,223,114	49,844,623

Table B.1. (Continued)

State/Territory	Actual FY2015	Est. FY2016	Est. FY2017	Est. FY2018	Est. FY2019	Est. FY2020	FY2016-FY2020 Total	FY2016-FY2020 Average
South Dakota	15,500,616	16,615,357	16,877,303	17,157,454	17,499,311	17,794,271	85,943,695	17,188,739
Tennessee	85,414,174	87,455,463	89,210,411	91,091,850	92,833,519	94,795,606	455,386,849	91,077,370
Texas	415,592,412	418,547,079	427,069,295	436,204,251	444,293,604	453,806,215	2,179,920,444	435,984,089
Utah	70,692,671	72,409,921	73,855,775	75,411,205	76,951,916	78,567,470	377,196,287	75,439,257
Vermont	8,370,585	8,993,579	9,149,649	9,316,920	9,830,307	10,013,037	47,303,492	9,460,698
Virgin Islands	1,843,783	1,858,440	1,887,738	1,919,754	1,946,186	1,979,038	9,591,156	1,918,231
Virginia	161,234,228	164,111,816	167,491,647	171,144,995	175,630,030	179,443,568	857,822,056	171,564,411
Washington	231,768,948	244,940,420	249,771,733	254,951,297	261,144,863	266,532,075	1,277,340,389	255,468,078
West Virginia	24,824,408	25,763,816	26,230,110	26,729,734	27,796,756	28,331,742	134,852,159	26,970,432
Wisconsin	80,216,787	82,142,223	83,785,699	85,552,786	88,028,303	89,887,719	429,396,729	85,879,346
Wyoming	10,937,600	11,597,917	11,808,489	12,033,228	12,253,695	12,489,441	60,182,770	12,036,554
Apportioned Total	8,482,130,936	8,917,346,291	9,086,420,167	9,265,382,535	9,449,037,070	9,636,406,049	46,354,592,112	9,270,918,422

Source: Federal Transit Administration.

Note: Excludes amounts reserved for administration of FTA.

In: Transportation
Editor: Frederick Daniels
ISBN: 978-1-53615-651-5

Chapter 4

TRENDS IN PUBLIC TRANSPORTATION RIDERSHIP: IMPLICATIONS FOR FEDERAL POLICY*

William J. Mallett

SUMMARY

Despite significant investments in public transportation at the federal, state, and local levels, transit ridership has fallen in many of the top 50 transit markets. If strong gains in the New York area are excluded, ridership nationally declined by 7% over the past decade. This chapter examines the implications for federal transit policy of the current weakness and possible future changes in transit ridership.

Although there has been a lot of research into the factors that explain transit ridership, there seems to be no comprehensive explanation for the recent decline. One complication is that national trends in public transportation ridership are not necessarily reflected at the local level; thus, different areas may have different reasons for growth or decline. But at the national level, the two factors that most affect public transportation

* This is an edited, reformatted and augmented version of Congressional Research Service, Publication No. R45144, dated March 26, 2018.

ridership are competitive factors and the supply of transit service. Several competitive factors, notably the drop in the price of gasoline over the past few years and the growing popularity of bikeshare and ridesourcing services, appear to have adversely affected transit ridership. The amount of transit service supplied has generally grown over time, but average fares have risen faster than inflation, possibly deterring riders.

The future of public transportation ridership in the short to medium term is likely to depend on population growth; the public funding commitment to supplying transit; and factors that make driving more or less attractive, such as the price of parking, the extent of highway congestion, and the implementation of fuel taxes, tolls, and mileage-based user fees. Over the long term, ridership is also likely to depend on the introduction of autonomous vehicle technology, although its timing is uncertain. Fleets of driverless taxis that can be hailed with a smartphone, a plausible scenario, promise to be much cheaper than taxis and ridesourcing today. Widespread deployment of driverless taxis could reduce transit ridership, unless restrictions or fees make them an expensive alternative in some areas.

Two major federal transit policies related to these issues are the general funding of public transportation, distributed mainly by formula, and the discretionary funding of new large capital projects such as rail and bus rapid transit systems through the Capital Investment Grant (CIG) Program, also known as New Starts. One option to boost ridership without raising funding would be to tie federal formula funds to ridership or fare revenue. If the most consequential uncertainty for transit ridership is the introduction of autonomous vehicles, federal funding might focus on buses, which last about 10 years, and not new rail systems that last 30 years or more. Another option would be to redirect CIG funding from building new rail systems and lines to refurbishing rail transit in the large and dense cities where rail transit currently carries large numbers of riders. If fully autonomous ridesourcing vehicles become available, policymakers may face pressure to subsidize ridesourcing trips for disabled and elderly passengers alongside or in place of traditional transit and paratransit services.

INTRODUCTION

Many public transportation agencies across the United States are losing riders. While ridership nationally has risen about 3% over the past decade, that increase is due largely to strong gains in the New York area, which accounts for about 40% of all U.S. transit riders. Patronage has fallen in many of the other top 50 transit markets.

This downward trend, despite significant investments in light rail, streetcar, and bus rapid transit lines in many communities, has led to warnings that transit service in the United States is in crisis.[1] Some of the factors contributing to the ridership decline, such as low gasoline prices and service problems at particular transit systems, may be transitory, but others, such as the growing popularity of telework and the rise of ridesourcing companies such as Uber and Lyft, may be longer lasting. Technological changes on the horizon, such as autonomous highway vehicles, might revolutionize transportation mobility, but whether this will increase or decrease transit ridership is by no means clear.

The federal government supports public transportation by distributing general funding for capital and operating expenses, mainly by formula, and by providing grants for major capital projects on a discretionary basis. This chapter discusses the implications of recent trends in transit ridership for future federal policy.

TRENDS IN PUBLIC TRANSPORTATION RIDERSHIP

According to data from the American Public Transportation Association, annual public transportation ridership nationally declined by 3% between 2014 and 2016. Preliminary figures show a further decline in 2017.[2] However, the longer-term trend shows a small to moderate increase in ridership (Figure 1). The modest increase in national ridership over the past decade is due mainly to an increase of more than 20% in the New York City region. That region, which includes parts of New York, New Jersey, and Connecticut, accounts for about 40% of national transit

---

[1] See, for example, Rob Puentes, "Ghosts of Transit Past: What Can We Do About Declining Transit Ridership?" *Eno Transportation Weekly*, June 1, 2017, pp. 5-6.

[2] American Public Transportation Association, *Transit Ridership Report, Third Quarter 2017*, http://www.apta.com/resources/statistics/Documents/Ridership/2017-q3-ridership-APTA.pdf.

ridership. If the New York region is excluded from the data, national transit ridership decreased by 7% over the past 10 years.[3]

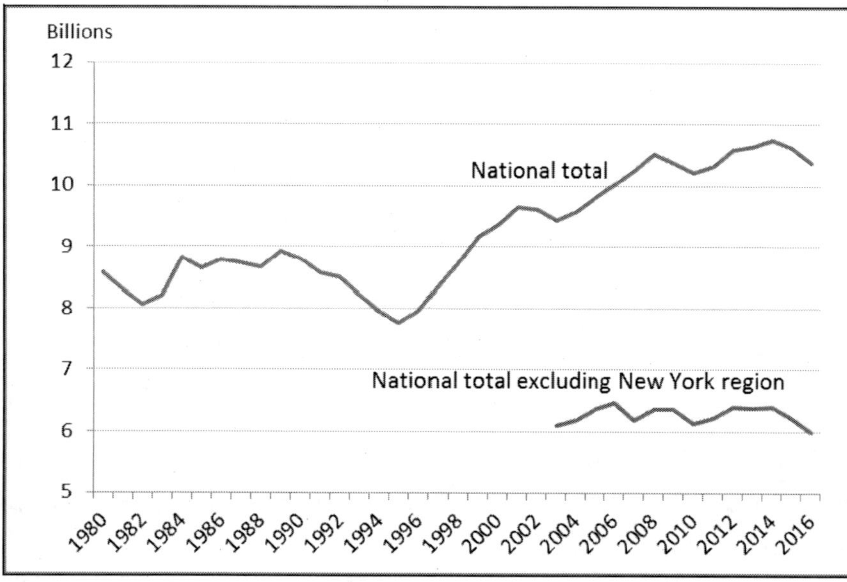

Source: American Public Transportation Association, 2016 Public Transportation Fact Book Appendix A; American Public Transportation Association, Transit Ridership Report.

Figure 1. Annual Public Transportation Ridership, 1980-2016 Unlinked Trips.

Ridership was lower in 2016 than it was in 2006 in a number of major urban areas, including Los Angeles, Washington, DC, Miami, and Atlanta, according to data from the Federal Transit Administration (FTA) (Figure 2). Over the same period, smaller urban areas were almost equally split between those gaining and those losing ridership (Figure 3).

A separate analysis of FTA data from June 2014 through June 2017 found that among the 41 urban areas with populations of 1 million or more, Los Angeles accounted for 23% of ridership losses. New York, which saw ridership declines in 2016 and 2017 after several years of increases,

[3] Throughout this report, ridership is measured in unlinked trips. An unlinked trip is counted each time a passenger boards a transit vehicle; American Public Transportation Association, *Public Transportation Ridership Report*, http://www.apta.com/resources/statistics/Pages/ridershipreport.aspx.

accounted for 14% of national ridership losses during that period, followed by Washington, DC (11%), Chicago (8%), Miami (6%), Philadelphia (5%), and Boston (4%). Six of the 41 areas gained ridership over this period.[4]

Nationally, buses were the main transit mode in 2016, providing slightly more than half of all trips in that year. Bus ridership declined between 2006 and 2016, but this was offset by higher growth in rail ridership, particularly in the New York region. Transit rail includes subways, light rail and streetcars, and commuter rail. If New York is excluded, buses provided about twice as many public transportation trips as rail services. Without New York, the decline in bus ridership is about the same between 2006 and 2016, but the increase in rail ridership is less pronounced (Figure 4).

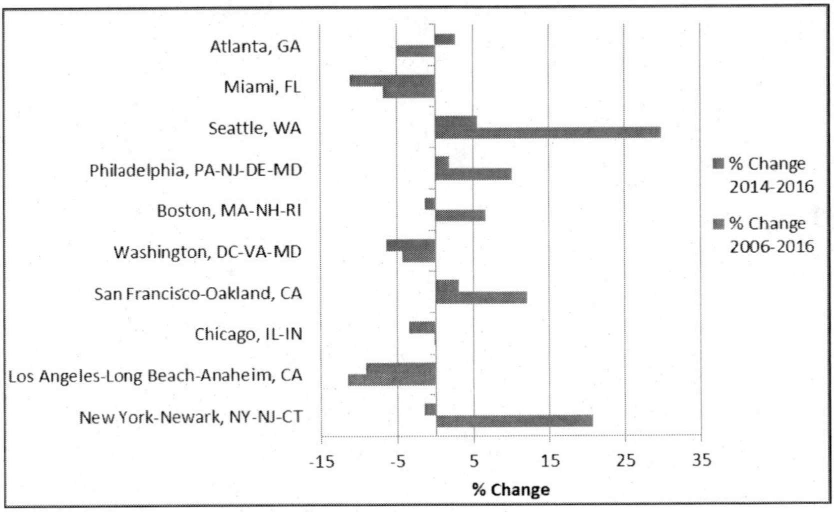

Source: Federal Transit Administration, National Transit Database.

Figure 2. Change in Public Transportation Ridership in Top 10 Transit Markets.

[4] Wendell Cox, "Los Angeles Transit Ridership Losses Lead National Decline," *New Geography*, November 15, 2017, http://www.newgeography.com/content/005800-los-angeles-transit-ridership-losses-lead-national-decline.

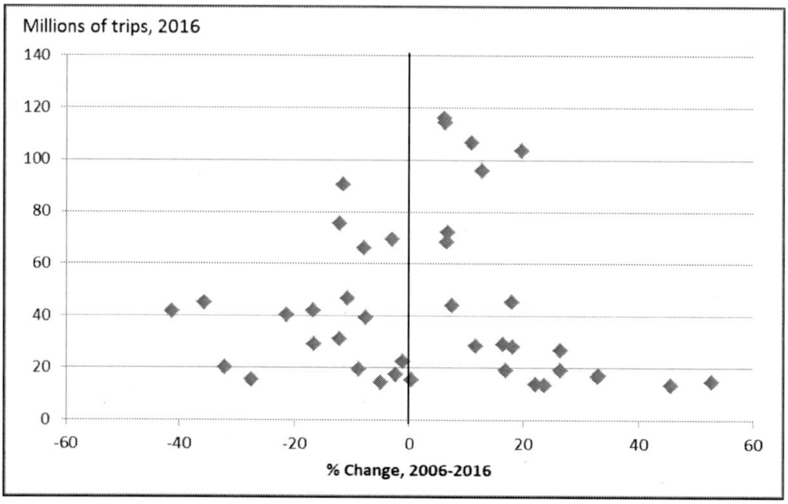

Source: Federal Transit Administration, National Transit Database.

Figure 3. Ridership Change in Smaller Transit Markets, 2006-2016 40 Largest Transit Markets Outside Top 10.

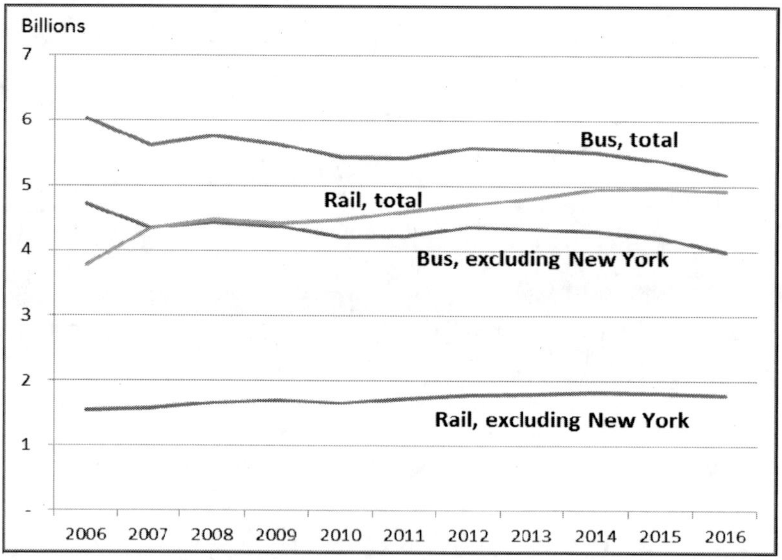

Source: American Public Transportation Association, 2016 Public Transportation Fact Book; American Public Transportation Association, Transit Ridership Report; Federal Transit Administration, National Transit Database.

Figure 4. Annual Public Transportation Ridership by Bus and Rail, 2006-2016 Unlinked Passenger Trips.

In many places, rail ridership has grown because of the opening of new rail systems and lines. These new rail lines, however, have not necessarily boosted transit ridership overall.[5] New rail service can be detrimental to an existing bus network as service overall is realigned and resources are shifted toward operating and maintaining the new rail lines. Moreover, the building of new rail systems, often in search of wealthier discretionary riders, can be to the detriment of lower-income, bus-dependent populations in areas not served by the new lines. The effect sometimes has been to turn bus riders into rail passengers with little net gain in transit patronage, and at increased cost.[6] Some have suggested that the restructuring of bus routes in response to the opening of new rail lines, along with an increase in bus fares, has contributed to lower ridership in Los Angeles.[7]

FACTORS AFFECTING PUBLIC TRANSPORTATION RIDERSHIP

There is no comprehensive explanation for the overall decline in ridership outside of New York. National trends in public transportation ridership are not necessarily reflected at the local level; thus, different areas may have different reasons for growth or decline.

---

[5] Martin Wachs, "U.S. Transit Subsidy Policy: In Need of Reform," *Science*, vol. 244 (1989), pp. 1545-1549.

[6] Jonathan Richmond, "A Whole-System Approach to Evaluating Urban Transit Investments," *Transport Reviews*, vol. 21, no. 2 (2001), pp. 141-179; Nathaniel Baum-Snow and Matthew E. Kahn, "Effects of Urban Rail Transit Expansions: Evidence from Sixteen Cities, 1970–2000," *Brookings-Wharton Papers on Urban Affairs*, 2005, pp. 147- 197; Laura J. Nelson and Dan Weikel, "Billions Spent, But Fewer People Are Using Public Transportation in Southern California," *Los Angeles Times*, March 1, 2016; Hilary Nixon et al., *Changes in Transit Use and Service and Associated Changes in Driving Near a New Light Rail Transit Line*, Mineta Transportation Institute, Report 12-44, 2015; Jeongwoo Lee et al., "Changes in Service and Associated Ridership Impacts Near a New Light Rail Transit Line," *Sustainability*, vol. 9 (2017).

[7] Laura J. Nelson, "The Metro Can Take You Farther than Ever. Here's Why Ridership Dropped—Again," *Los Angeles Times*, February 13, 2017, http://www.latimes.com/local/lanow/la-me-ln-2016-metro-ridership-decline-20170209- story.html; Thomas A. Rubin, "Is The Los Angeles Times Article 'Billions Spent, But Fewer People Are Using Public Transportation in Southern California,' Misleading?" http://demographia.com/db-rubin-la-transit.pdf, p. 4.

Probably the two most relevant factors in the current context are the attractiveness of other transportation options and transit service supply issues.

Transportation Options

Public transportation ridership is affected by other competitive or complementary transportation options, particularly the cost of owning and operating a personal vehicle. Compared with other countries, car ownership, licensing, and use, including parking, are relatively cheap in the United States. Consequently, U.S. public transportation ridership is relatively low. For example, compared with people from a number of European countries, Americans take from one-half to one-tenth the number of transit trips per year.[8]

Among the factors that account for transit ridership changes within the United States is the price of gasoline. Research shows that gasoline prices are associated with short-term changes in transit ridership, with a drop in the price of gasoline typically resulting in a drop in ridership.[9] In a study of bus demand in metropolitan areas, for example, the price of gasoline was the only factor other than service quality that predicted ridership.[10] Ridership fluctuations over the past decade seem to track changes in the average annual price of gasoline (Figure 5). Between 2014 and 2016, the price of gasoline fell from an annual average of $3.46 per gallon to $2.20 a gallon (in 2016 inflation-adjusted dollars).

---

[8] Ralph Buehler and John Pucher, "Demand for Public Transport in Germany and the USA: An Analysis of Rider Characteristics," *Transport Reviews*, vol. 32, no. 5 (September 2012), pp. 541-567.

[9] David Levinson, "On the Predictability of the Decline of Transit Ridership in the U.S.," Transportist Blog, March 20, 2017, https://transportist.org/2017/03/20/on-the-predictability-of-the-decline-of-transit-ridership-in-the-us/.

[10] Bhuiyan Alam, Hilary Nixon, and Qiong Zhang, *Investigating the Determining Factors for Transit Travel Demand by Bus Mode in US Metropolitan Statistical Areas*, Mineta Transportation Institute, MTI Report 12-30, May 2015, http://transweb.sjsu.edu/PDFs/research/1101-transit-bus-demand-factors-in-US-metro-areas.pdf.

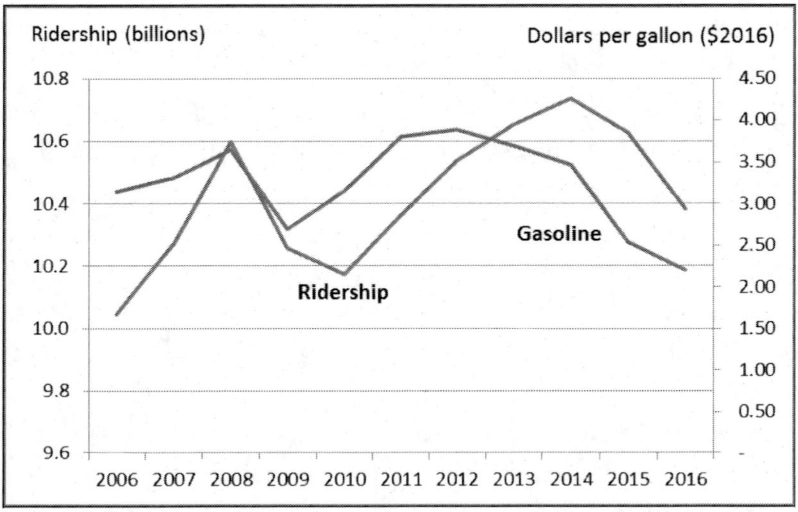

Source: American Public Transportation Association, *Transit Ridership Report;* U.S. Energy Information Administration, *Monthly Energy Review* (June 2017), Table 9.4.

Figure 5. Annual Transit Ridership and Average Gasoline Prices, 2006-2016.

Another factor that some studies have found important in explaining transit ridership is the availability of a personal vehicle.[11] A greater share of households with a vehicle, all else being equal, is likely to lead to less demand for public transportation. The share of households without a car has declined over the past few decades, and the number of vehicles available per household has increased. According to a major survey conducted by the U.S. Department of Transportation (DOT), between 1969 and 2009, the share of households without a vehicle dropped from about 21% to about 9%. Over this period, the average number of vehicles available per household increased from 1.16 to 1.86.[12] Researchers studying southern California found that vehicle access increased dramatically between 2000 and 2015, especially among groups that tend to be heavy transit users, such as foreign-born households. They argue that

[11] Brian D. Taylor et al., "Nature and/or Nurture? Analyzing the Determinants of Transit Ridership Across US Urbanized Areas," *Transportation Research Part A*, vol. 43 (2009), pp. 60-77.

[12] Federal Highway Administration, *Summary of Travel Trends: 2009 National Household Travel Survey*, Table 17, http://nhts.ornl.gov/2009/pub/stt.pdf.

while there are other factors at work, vehicle access may be the largest determinant in declining transit ridership in that region.[13]

There is some evidence that the share of households without a vehicle may have bottomed out recently or even slightly increased. DOT's survey found that the share of households without a vehicle increased between 2001 and 2009 from 8.1% to 8.7%. More recent data from the Census Bureau suggest that the share of carless households averaged 9.1% between 2011 and 2015.[14] Car ownership may be dropping, in some places, due to a drop in driver licensing among younger age groups, due in part to federal policies that promote graduated drivers licenses, and an increase in shared-use mobility, such as bikesharing, carsharing, and ridesourcing.[15]

Although ridesourcing has grown rapidly in many large cities—tripling in New York City from spring 2015 to fall 2016, for example—the effect on transit ridership is unclear. It is possible that ridesourcing could complement transit in some ways and substitute for it in others. A large share of transit trips involve journeys to work at rush hours, whereas much ridesourcing occurs at times when transit service is lacking or infrequent. Ridesourcing companies might carry passengers between outlying homes and transit stations, along routes that are inefficient for transit agencies to serve, or between places poorly served by transit entirely.

A survey of ridesouring users in San Francisco found that ridesourcing substituted for transit about one-third of the time. However, there was some evidence that ridesourcing also provided first mile/last mile service for transit users and allowed people to live car-free. As the authors note, "the survey provides evidence that ridesourcing both complements and

[13] Michael Manville, Brian D. Taylor, and Evelyn Blumenberg, *Falling Transit Ridership: California and Southern California*, UCLA Institute of Transportation Studies, January 2018, http://www.scag.ca.gov/Documents/ ITS_SCAG_Transit_Ridership.pdf.

[14] Census Bureau, "Selected Housing Characteristics, 2011-2015 American Community Survey 5-year Estimates," https://qz.com/873704/no-car-households-are-becoming-more-common-in-the-us-after-decades-of-decline/.

[15] Michael Sivak and Brandon Schoettle, "Recent Decreases in the Proportion of Persons with a Driver's License across All Age Groups," University of Michigan, Transportation Research Institute, UMTRI-2016-4, January 2016, http://umich.edu/~umtriswt/PDF/UMTRI-2016-4.pdf.

competes with public transit."[16] A separate survey of Boston, Chicago, Los Angeles, New York, San Francisco, Seattle, and Washington, DC, found that among those who began using ridesourcing, on average, transit use dropped 6%.[17] A separate survey sponsored by the American Public Transportation Association found that ridesourcing complements transit use by providing trips at times and places not well-served by transit and allowing urban dwellers to live without a personal vehicle.[18] A study of ridesourcing in New York City notes that after a period of rapid growth in trip making by transit, the city has shifted over the past few years to rapid growth in trip making by ridesourcing.[19] Similar changes have been noted in Philadelphia.[20]

Some transit ridership losses could be the result of people working from home. One survey found that 37% of workers say they telecommuted in 2015, up from 32% in 2006 and 9% in 1995.[21] This affects all modes of transportation, not just public transportation, but the incentives for working from home may be greatest in major urban areas where transit mode commuting shares are the largest.

Another recent change in travel behavior has been the rise of public bikesharing schemes in many cities and the growth of private bicycling as a result of better on-road and off-road infrastructure, such as bike lanes and bike paths. While bikesharing may lead some individuals to take a short bike trip instead of a short transit trip, it also provides a way for people to

---

[16] Lisa Rayle et al., "Just a Better Taxi? A Survey-based Comparison of Taxis, Transit, and Ridesourcing Services in San Francisco," *Transport Policy*, vol. 45 (2016), p. 176.

[17] Regina R. Clewlow and Gouri Shankar Mishra, "Disruptive Transportation: The Adoption, Utilization, and Impacts of Ride-Hailing in the United States," University of California, Davis, Institute of Transportation Studies, Research Report UCD-ITS-RR-17-07, October 2017.

[18] American Public Transportation Association, *Shared Mobility and the Transformation of Public Transit*, March 2016, https://www.apta.com/resources/reportsandpublications/Documents/APTA-Shared-Mobility.pdf.

[19] Bruce Schaller, *Unsustainable? The Growth of App-Based Ride Services and Traffic, Travel and the Future of New York City*, February 27, 2017, Schaller Consulting, http://schallerconsult.com/rideservices/unsustainable.htm.

[20] Inga Saffron, "Ride-hailing Apps Are Killing Taxis. Is Public Transit Next?" *Philadelphia Inquirer*, March 23, 2017, http://www.philly.com/philly/living/Ride-hailing-apps-Lyft-Uber-taxis-public-transit-next-saffron-SEPTA.html.

[21] Jeffrey M. Jones, "In U.S., Telecommuting for Work Climbs to 37%," *Gallup News*, August 19, 2015, http://www.gallup.com/poll/184649/telecommuting-work-climbs.aspx.

get to and from transit stations and stops. One study in the United States and Canada found that bikeshare users were, on balance, less likely to use public transit after they started using the service. However, in one of the cities surveyed, Minneapolis, bikeshare users were more likely to use public transit.[22] Many transit systems now equip buses with bicycle racks, allowing customers the option of a multimodal commute by bike and bus.

Public Transportation Service Supply

Among the factors that affect public transportation ridership, service supply variables are typically some of the most important. These include factors such as fares, hours of service, service frequency, safety, and geographic coverage. One study has noted that "the greater the supply, the greater the demand for transit."[23]

Both access to transit, such as distance to a transit stop, and hours of service and service frequency (the time between trains or buses) are associated with how much someone will use it. But some efforts to improve transit usage have found the best way to attract riders is to reduce travel times by increasing service frequencies rather than by improving access to stations and stops.[24] Fares are also an important supply factor. Higher-income residents typically will weigh the fare against the cost of other travel options, whereas lower-income residents typically will not travel if the price is too high, or will choose a slower mode, such as buses, if travel by subway or commuter rail is more expensive.

---

[22] Susan A. Shaheen et al., *Public Bikesharing in North America: Early Operator and User Understanding*, San Jose State University, Mineta Transportation Institute, Report 11-26, June 2012, http://transweb.sjsu.edu/PDFs/research/ 1029-public-bikesharing-understanding-early-operators-users.pdf.

[23] Bhuiyan Alam, Hilary Nixon, and Qiong Zhang, *Investigating the Determining Factors for Transit Travel Demand by Bus Mode in U.S. Metropolitan Statistical Areas*, San Jose State University, Mineta Transportation Institute, Report 12-30, May 2015, http://transweb.sjsu.edu/PDFs/research/1101-transit-bus-demand-factors-in-US-metro-areas.pdf.

[24] Tom Reinhold, "More Passengers and Reduced Costs—The Optimization of the Berlin Public Transport Network," *Journal of Public Transportation*, vol. 11, no. 3 (2008), pp. 57-76, http://www.nctr.usf.edu/jpt/pdf/JPT11- 3Reinhold.pdf; TransitCenter, *Who's On Board 2016*, http://transitcenter.org/wp-content/uploads/2016/07/ TransitCenter-WOB-2016.pdf.

Table 1. Public Transportation Fares, 2004 and 2014 Average Price per Unlinked Trip (inflation-adjusted 2014 dollars)

Transit Mode	2004	2014	% change
Bus	$0.96	$1.11	15.1
Commuter rail	$4.76	$5.81	22.0
Subway	$1.29	$1.31	1.2
Light rail and streetcar	$0.82	$1.03	25.9

Source: American Public Transportation Association, *2016 Public Transportation Fact Book Appendix A;* Bureau of Economic Analysis, "Current Dollar and 'Real' GDP," https://www.bea.gov/national/index.htm#gdp.

Evidence of general problems with public transportation service supply, such as service capacity and fares, is mixed. Nationally, the amount of transit service supplied, as measured in terms of the total mileage traveled by transit vehicles adjusted for their passenger-carrying capacity, has increased over time. Between 2004 and 2014, capacity-adjusted vehicle miles for buses grew by 5% and rail by 16%. It appears that public transportation fares per unlinked trip have generally risen faster than inflation in recent years. However, it is not possible to gauge whether this increase in average fares is due to the outsized effect of fare increases by the largest transit systems (Table 1).

Although it is not clear whether service supply problems have affected ridership generally, it does appear that declines in ridership in some places are at least partly the result of service supply problems. For example, safety and operational deficiencies have resulted in service disruptions at the Washington Metropolitan Area Transit Authority, particularly its subway service. Recent notable events include a customer fatality from smoke inhalation on a train in January 2015 and weeks-long shutdowns of parts of the Metrorail system since June 2016 to address safety problems and rehabilitate aging infrastructure. This appears to have contributed to a decline in ridership of 15% from 2009 to 2016, with bus ridership declining by 6% and rail ridership declining by 20%.[25] The recent decline

[25] American Public Transportation Association, *Public Transportation Ridership Report*, Third Quarter 2009 and 2016, http://www.apta.com/resources/statistics/Pages/Ridership Archives.aspx; Faiz Siddiqui, "Ridership Losses, Exacerbated by SafeTrack, Push Metro to

in ridership in New York is probably also due in part to infrastructure-related disruptions, but train and station congestion caused by longer-term ridership growth may also play a role.[26]

The failure of transit agencies to adjust service in response to changing travel patterns has also been blamed for ridership declines. Evidence for this comes from ridership increases in places that have restructured bus routes, such as Houston and Seattle.[27]

Economics, Population, and Urban Geography

It is well established that economic activity leads to more travel as employment and income grow. The prolonged economic expansion since the end of a deep recession in June 2009 might therefore be expected to lead to higher transit ridership. However, research has shown that many individuals consider transit to be inferior to driving. Consequently, the *share* of travel taken by transit decreases as household incomes increase, unemployment falls, and the cost of buying and operating a car becomes more manageable. On balance, it appears that the decline in transit's share of trips more than offsets overall urban travel growth, leading to a drop in ridership during good economic times.[28]

There is some evidence to support the notion that residential and employment density are associated with higher transit ridership, and that

Financial Tipping Point," *Washington Post*, February 21, 2017, https://www.washingtonpost.com/local/trafficandcommuting/ridership-losses-exacerbated-by-safetrack-push-metro-tofinancial-tipping-point/2017/02/21/6ec0b7ec-f85f-11e6-9845-576c69081518_story.html?utm_term=.de084dfbcc28.

[26] Emma G. Fitzsimmons, Ford Fessenden, and K. K. Rebecca Lai, "Every New York City Subway Line Is Getting Worse. Here's Why," *New York Times*, June 28, 2017, https://www.nytimes.com/interactive/2017/06/28/nyregion/subway-delays-overcrowding.html.

[27] Angie Schmitt, "Transit Ridership Falling Everywhere—But Not in Cities With Redesigned Bus Networks," *Streetsblog USA*, February 24, 2017, http://usa.streetsblog.org/2017/02/24/transit-ridership-falling-everywhere-but-notin-cities-with-redesigned-bus-networks; TransitCenter, "Seattle: America's Next Top Transit City," http://transitcenter.org/2017/01/03/seattle-americas-next-top-transit-city/.

[28] Brian D. Taylor et al., "Nature and/or Nurture? Analyzing the Determinants of Transit Ridership Across US Urbanized Areas," *Transportation Research Part A*, vol. 43, pp. 60-77, 2009.

the long-term growth of low-density suburban and exurban areas has been a major impediment to gaining transit riders. Some communities, encouraged by federal policy, have therefore promoted transit-oriented development as a way to support transit ridership.[29] Whether such urban design policies work or not, urban density changes slowly and thus is not likely to reverse the recent decline of transit ridership in the near term. In addition, the relationship between density and transit use or the longer-term increase in transit ridership is complicated by other related variables such as growth of household income, vehicle availability, and the availability of free parking.

Although there is some evidence of a "back to the city" movement led by millennials and empty-nester baby boomers, this trend appears to have brought significant inner-city population growth in only a few metropolitan areas, such as New York, Washington, DC, and San Francisco. Cities grew faster than their suburbs between 2010 and 2015, reversing a long-term trend, but Census data for 2016 show this may have now ended.[30] In terms of jobs, cities grew faster than suburbs for the first time in decades between 2007 and 2011, but it is unclear whether this trend will be sustained. Between 2011 and 2014, suburbs once again grew slightly faster than cities.[31]

Population characteristics such as race and ethnicity, age, and immigrant status are another set of factors that have been examined in terms of transit ridership. Of these factors, immigration trends seem to

---

[29] Federal Transit Administration, "Transit-Oriented Development," https://www.transit.dot.gov/TOD.

[30] William H. Frey, "City Growth Dips Below Suburban Growth, Census Shows," May 30, 2017, https://www.brookings.edu/blog/the-avenue/2017/05/30/city-growth-dips-below-suburban-growth-census-shows/; Jed Kolko, "Americans' Shift to the Suburbs Sped Up Last Year," *FiveThirtyEight*, March 23, 2017, https://fivethirtyeight.com/features/americans-shift-to-the-suburbs-sped-up-last-year/.

[31] Daniel Hertz, "City Center Job Growth Continues Strength; Suburbs Rebounding from Recession," City Observatory, May 24, 2016, http://cityobservatory.org/city-center-job-growth-continues/; Wendell Cox, "Suburbs (Continue to) Dominate Jobs and Job Growth," *NewGeography*, May 25, 2016, http://www.newgeography.com/ content/005264-suburbs-continue-dominate-jobs-and-job-growth; Elizabeth Kneebone, *Job Sprawl Stalls: The Great Recession and Metropolitan Employment Location*, Brookings Institution, April 2013, https://www.brookings.edu/wpcontent/uploads/2016/06/Srvy_JobSprawl.pdf.

have received the most attention recently.[32] Recent immigrants typically travel much more by transit than the native born, but this difference declines the longer an immigrant lives in the country. This longevity effect has been posited as a reason for the decline in transit ridership in Los Angeles and may also apply nationwide.[33] Nationally, the number of new lawful permanent residents has generally declined between 2006 and 2015. Moreover, according to one estimate, the number of unauthorized immigrants was also lower in 2016 than it was in 2007, falling from 12.2 million to 11.3 million over this period.[34] These changes may be associated with declining use of public transportation.

THE FUTURE OF PUBLIC TRANSPORTATION RIDERSHIP

In the short to medium term, roughly 10 to 20 years, transit demand is likely to be determined by population growth and the public commitment to supplying transit. Ridership is likely to increase and decrease as gas prices rise and fall, and as other factors make driving more or less attractive. These include the extent, duration, and intensity of highway congestion; the price of parking; and the implementation of fuel taxes, tolls, and mileage-based user fees. However, the most important factors are likely to be the attractiveness of public transportation in terms of fares, speed, reliability, and coverage. For this, public transportation providers will rely heavily on federal, state, and local funding. Success will depend,

---

[32] Brian D. Taylor et al., "Nature and/or Nurture? Analyzing the Determinants of Transit Ridership Across US Urbanized Areas," *Transportation Research Part A*, vol. 43 (2009), pp. 60-77.

[33] Steven A. Camarota and Karen Zeigler, "Immigrants in the United States: A Profile of the Foreign-born Using 2014 and 2015 Census Bureau Data," Center for Immigration Studies, October 2016, https://cis.org/sites/cis.org/files/ immigrant-profile_0.pdf; Laura J. Nelson, "The Metro Can Take You Farther than Ever. Here's Why Ridership Dropped—Again," *Los Angeles Times*, February 13, 2017, http://www.latimes.com/local/lanow/la-me-ln-2016-metroridership-decline-20170209-story.html.

[34] Jeffrey S. Passel and D'Vera Cohn, "As Mexican Share Declined, U.S. Unauthorized Immigrant Population Fell in 2015 Below Recession Level," Pew Research Center, April 25, 2017, http://www.pewresearch.org/fact-tank/2017/04/ 25/as-mexican-share-declined-u-s-unauthorized-immigrant-population-fell-in-2015-below-recession-level/.

to some extent, on how much of this funding goes to service improvements.

Service improvements can be made by changes that are not necessarily dependent on funding increases. Some transit agencies have recently sought to reconfigure antiquated bus routes to better serve current demand, despite local political pressure to protect the status quo.[35] In some instances, this involves increasing bus frequency with fewer stops on less circuitous routes. It can also involve making bus travel faster by designing streets with dedicated bus lanes and priority for buses at traffic signals and by using technology to enable riders to pay their fares before boarding.[36]

According to the Census Bureau, the U.S. resident population is expected to increase by about 26 million in the next 10 years (an 8% increase) and about 48 million in the next 20 years (a 15% increase).[37] Southern and western cities such as Atlanta, Dallas, Houston, and Phoenix are likely to move up the rankings of the largest urban areas over the coming years, but the fastest-growing urban areas are likely to be small and medium-sized places in the South and West where transit use is relatively low.[38] There is some evidence that in larger metropolitan areas major employers are seeking out locations that are well served by transit, but the general trend remains job dispersion across suburbs with low employment density. The combination of relatively low-density residential growth and low-density employment growth may limit the extent to which population growth brings higher transit ridership.

Although ridesourcing seems likely to depress overall demand for transit, that outcome is not a foregone conclusion. Ridesourcing companies

---

[35] Daniel Vock, "Buses, Yes Buses, Are 'the Hottest Trend in Transit,'" *Governing*, September 18, 2017, http://www.governing.com/topics/transportation-infrastructure/gov-big-city-bus-systems.html.

[36] TransitCenter, *Turnaround: Fixing New York City's Buses*, 2016, http://transitcenter.org/publications/turnaroundfixing-new-york-citys-buses/#download-the-report.

[37] U.S. Census Bureau, "2014 National Population Projections Tables," Table 1, https://www.census.gov/data/tables/ 2014/demo/popproj/2014-summary-tables.html.

[38] The United States Conference of Mayors, *U.S. Metro Economies: Past and Future Employment Levels*, May 2017, http://www.usmayors.org/wp-content/uploads/2017/05/Metro-Economies-Past-and-Future-Employment-12.pdf; Wendell Cox, "UN Projects 2030 U.S. Urban Area Population," Figure 3, http://www.newgeography.com/content/004464-un-projects-2030-us-urban-area-populations.

appear to be subsidizing their service, such that the total amount paid by riders from 2012 through the first half of 2016 may have been only 60% of the cost of providing the service.[39] If the cost of ridesourced trips were to increase to at least a breakeven proposition, ridesourcing may become a less attractive alternative to public transportation. While some transit agencies have begun cooperating with ridesourcing companies to provide the first mile/last mile of a transit trip,[40] decisions about transit service supply made on the assumption that these types of service will always be available at the current price might cause problems in the future.

The introduction of driverless vehicle technology is perhaps the biggest unknown, but potentially the most disruptive factor for future public transportation ridership. Estimates of when fully autonomous vehicles will be in use in urban environments vary wildly from a few years to a few decades.[41] Based on the introduction of past vehicle technology, it is likely that even if fully autonomous vehicles are available in a few years, it will take decades for them to become ubiquitous.[42]

Fleets of driverless taxis that can be hailed with a smartphone could potentially offer service much more cheaply than taxis and ridesourcing do

---

[39] Riley McDermid, "Uber is Losing $2 Billion a Year, New Report Says, With Passengers Paying for Only 41% of Each Ride," *San Francisco Business Times*, December 2, 2016, https://www.bizjournals.com/sanfrancisco/news/2016/ 12/02/uber-losses.html; Jarrett Walker, "Sounding the Alarm about Uber's Impacts on Transit, and on Cities," Human Transit Blog, December 15, 2016, http://humantransit.org/2016/12/sounding-the-alarm-about-ubers-impacts-ontransit.html. Some of the reported costs may involve one-time expenditures that will not recur. See also Heather Somerville, "True Price of an Uber Ride in Question as Investors Assess Firm's Value," Reuters, August 23, 2017, https://www.reuters.com/article/us-uber-profitability/true-price-of-an-uber-ride-in-question-as-investors-assess-firmsvalue-idUSKCN1B3103.

[40] "Some Cities Are Subsidizing Uber Rides to Cut Public Transportation Costs," *Business Insider*, December 15, 2016, http://www.businessinsider.com/some-cities-are-subsidizing-uber-rides-to-cut-public-transportation-costs-2016-12; Henry Grabar, "They Can Just Take an Uber: Cities Across the Country are Cutting Public Transportation Because They Think Ride-hailing Services Will Fill the Gap. They'll Regret It." *Slate*, December 14, 2016, http://www.slate.com/articles/business/metropolis/2016/12/ cities_are_cutting_transportation_service_because_they_think_uber_will_fill.html.

[41] Sarah Kessler, "A Timeline of When Self-driving Cars Will Be on the Road, According to the People Making Them," *Quartz*, March 29, 2017, https://qz.com/943899/a-timeline-of-when-self-driving-cars-will-be-on-the-roadaccording-to-the-people-making-them/; CRS Report R44940, *Issues in Autonomous Vehicle Deployment*, by Bill Canis.

[42] Todd Litman, *Autonomous Vehicle Implementation Predictions: Implications for Transport Planning*, Victoria Transport Policy Institute, September 8, 2017, p. 13, http://www.vtpi.org/avip.pdf.

today, as labor, which makes up about half of the cost of such a trip, would no longer be a significant factor.[43] Autonomous vehicles may provide a new option for those currently unable to drive, such as children, the elderly, and the disabled. Widespread deployment of autonomous vehicles and driverless taxis, therefore, could lead to a greater number of vehicle trips and a decline in traditional transit ridership.

Although autonomous vehicles may use road space more efficiently and cause fewer crashes than human-driven vehicles, it is possible that their widespread use would increase traffic congestion in the largest cities, thereby creating a need for some form of shared-ride service. Traditional transit buses may be able to adopt the same driverless technology to cut costs, but in many places this is likely to be on-demand service provided by small buses, vans, and other types of "microtransit."[44] Some microtransit pilot projects along these lines, with drivers, are being run by transit agencies in Los Angeles; Austin, TX; Kansas City, MO; Santa Clara County, CA; and the Alameda-Contra Costa Transit District near San Francisco.[45] Ridesourcing companies are experimenting with shared-ride services as well.

Because road space is severely limited in the largest and most dense cities, rail transit service will likely remain important in those places. Autonomous vehicles may even provide a relatively cheap and easy way to access rail service. However, in general, autonomous vehicles will significantly reduce the costs of traveling by automobile, shifting demand

---

[43] Timothy B. Lee, "Uber Lost $2.8 Billion in 2016. Will it Ever Become Profitable?" *Vox*, April 15, 2017, https://www.vox.com/new-money/2017/1/9/14194202/uber-lost-22-billion-9-months.

[44] Robert Cervero, "Mobility Niches: Jitneys to Robo-Taxis," *Journal of the American Planning Association*, vol. 83, no. 4 (Autumn 2017), pp. 404-412; Johanna Zmud et al., *Strategies to Advance Automated and Connected Vehicles*, Transportation Research Board, 2017, https://www.nap.edu/catalog/24873/strategies-to-advance-automated-andconnected-vehicles.

[45] Austin's pilot project is known as Pickup (see https://www.capmetro.org/pickup/); for Los Angeles Metro's microtransit pilot, see https://www.metro.net/projects/microtransit/; Eno Center for Transportation, *UpRouted: Exploring Microtransit in the United States*, January 2018, https://www.enotrans.org/etl-material/uprouted-exploringmicrotransit-united-states/.

to road from rail.[46] It is possible that travel time will become less of a concern to motorists, as fully autonomous vehicles will allow riders to engage in other activities while traveling, such as working, eating, and sleeping. Consequently, autonomous vehicles could make it more attractive, at least in transportation terms, to live in low-density places that are distant from other activity centers. Transit, particularly rail transit, is unlikely to thrive in such places.

Implications for Federal Policy

The federal government is involved in the provision of public transportation in two main ways. First, it provides about 18%, on average, of the capital and operating funds spent by public transportation agencies throughout the country. Fares and other revenues make up about 26%, local funding about 34%, and state funding about 22%.[47] Second, through the Capital Investment Grant (CIG) program (also known as the New Starts program), the federal government plays a significant role in the building of new transit rail and bus rapid transit systems and the extension and expansion of existing systems.[48] The future of public transportation ridership has implications for both general funding and CIG program funding.

Federal Public Transportation Funding

Incentive Funding

National transit ridership is somewhat dependent on the level of federal funding. Less federal funding would likely lead to less total

[46] Joel Hazan et al., *Will Autonomous Vehicles Derail Trains?* Boston Consulting Group, September 30, 2016, https://www.bcg.com/publications/2016/transportation-travel-tourism-automotive-will-autonomous-vehicles-derailtrains.aspx.

[47] American Public Transportation Association, *2016 Public Transportation Fact Book Appendix A*, Table 95.

[48] CRS Report R42706, *Federal Public Transportation Program: In Brief*, by William J. Mallett.

spending on public transportation, at least for a time as state and local governments adjust, and thus would likely lead to less service and lower ridership. Conversely, more federal outlays in the short term would likely provide for ridership at a higher level than it otherwise would be, unless they result in state and local governments cutting back on their own spending for transit purposes.

Currently, more than three-quarters of federal public transportation funding is distributed by a set of formulas that are tenuously related to ridership. For example, about 6% of funding under the Urbanized Area Formula Program[49] is distributed on the basis of passenger miles through what are known as "incentive tiers" (49 U.S.C. §5336(b)(2)(B) and 49 U.S.C. §5336(c)(2)).[50]

An alternative approach might tie federal funding to changes in ridership, such as the number of revenue passengers, or to productivity, such as the average number of passengers per bus-mile. Such an approach would provide transit agencies an incentive to improve their performance while allowing them to innovate by redesigning their bus networks, introducing technology to speed up boarding, or adjusting service levels. A possible downside is that encouraging transit agencies to focus exclusively on ridership may discourage them from serving isolated areas with transit-dependent populations.

Funding for Operations

Although small transit agencies frequently receive federal operating assistance, most transit operators in urbanized areas with populations above 200,000 or with more than 100 buses can use federal funds only for capital expenses or maintenance. Greater federal support for transit operations could increase the quantity of transit service offered by local transit agencies, potentially expanding ridership.

---

[49] 49 U.S.C. §5307.

[50] A fraction of an additional 1.5% is distributed to Small Intensive Transit Cities based on passenger miles and passengers; American Public Transportation Association, *APTA Primer on Transit Funding: The Fixing America's Surface Transportation Act and Other Related Laws, FY 2016 Through FY 2020*, April 2016, p. 56, https://www.apta.com/resources/reportsandpublications/Documents/APTA-Primer-FAST-Act.pdf.

There are three main issues with federal operating support: its effects on service, productivity, and asset condition. Research on the rapid expansion of operating support in the 1970s generally concluded that it allowed transit agencies to maintain a higher level of transit service than would have prevailed without it, but that such support also caused productivity to decline. Much of the decline was related to the increased supply-side cost of providing service, particularly in wages and fringe benefits.[51] Some productivity decline comes from the problem of providing service in places with less demand, a problem that might be mitigated with a focus on incentives funding.

The effects of operating support on asset condition are much less clear. It is possible that greater flexibility in the use of federal funding for operating expenses may be associated with a more rapid decline in the condition of capital assets, as some transit agencies focus on pressing day-to-day needs rather than asset renewal. However, existing flexibility to use capital funds for maintenance may help agencies to preserve equipment and facilities.

Bus Funding versus Rail Funding

Uncertainty about the introduction of autonomous vehicles has increased the difficulty of forecasting the ridership of rail systems that are designed to operate for many decades. It is imaginable that autonomous vehicles could be widely used to shuttle passengers to and from rail transit stations in areas with low residential or employment density, potentially increasing demand for rail transit. However, it is also imaginable that autonomous vehicles could make it more attractive for people living or working in high-density areas to travel considerable distances by car and without parking concerns, reducing demand for rail transit. Which outcome occurs may depend, in part, on whether state and local governments seek to

---

[51] Douglass B. Lee, *Evaluation of Federal Transit Operating Subsidies, Staff Study* (Cambridge, MA: Department of Transportation, Transportation Systems Center, September 1987); John Pucher, Anders Markstedt, and Ira Hirshman, "Impacts of Subsidies on the Costs of Urban Public Transport," *Journal of Transport Economics and Policy* (May 1983), pp. 155-176.

restrain use of autonomous vehicles through road user charges or other measures.

This uncertainty poses challenges for transit systems considering long-term capital investments and for the federal programs that fund such investments. The main federal program supporting capital expenditures by transit agencies, the CIG program, was originally developed to fund construction of new rail transit and commuter rail projects, but in recent years a growing proportion of its outlays have gone for bus rapid transit projects. A key policy issue is whether future federal funding should focus on buses, which last about 10 years and can be redeployed as demand changes, rather than on rail systems that last 30 years or more and are inflexible but are far more efficient at transporting large numbers of passengers in dense corridors.

Funding for Shared-Ride Services

If demand for traditional transit service declines, there may be demand for other types of shared-ride service. In that case, there may be pressure to shift public subsidies from traditional transit services, such as buses, to on-demand shared autonomous vehicle services, whether operated publicly or privately. This could mitigate the congestion and emissions of individually owned autonomous vehicles. It might be possible to subsidize autonomous vehicle services for particular groups with limited mobility, such as disabled, elderly, and low-income populations, reducing the need for distinct transit services, such as paratransit, which tend to be expensive to provide.[52]

While federal funding of on-demand shared-ride service provided publicly is not necessarily prohibited, it could raise issues of competition with private providers, access by disadvantaged groups, and the provision of operating support. Federal support of privately operated shared-mobility

[52] Johanna Zmud et al., *Advancing Automated and Connected Vehicles: Policy and Planning Strategies for State and Local Transportation Agencies*, Transportation Research Board, NCHRP Research Report 845, 2017, p. 41, http://www.trb.org/Main/Blurbs/176418.aspx.

services is currently permissible in certain limited circumstances.[53] It might make sense to broaden the circumstances where federal funds can be used to support these types of services. Another possibility would be to allow tax-subsidized commuter benefits to cover on-demand shared autonomous vehicle services.[54]

Capital Investment Grant Program

The CIG program provides funding to support the construction of new fixed-guideway transit systems and to add to existing systems. Funding is also permitted for investments in existing fixed-guideway systems that increase the capacity of a corridor by at least 10%. Fixed-guideway services include transit rail, bus rapid transit, and ferry systems. Funding for the program is authorized from the general fund of the U.S. Treasury.

The CIG program has not been without controversy. FTA contends the program "is needed because it allows transit agencies to undertake major capital projects that would otherwise be infeasible for local governments and transit agencies to finance alone."[55] Supporters insist that growing demand for CIG funds is evidence of its success.[56] Critics, however, have contended that CIG funding encourages communities to build expensive fixed-guideway infrastructure rather than invest lesser sums in improving bus service.[57]

No comprehensive benefit-cost studies of completed CIG projects have been conducted to evaluate the CIG program as federal policy. Research

---

53 Federal Transit Administration, "Shared Mobility FAQs: Eligibility Under FTA Grant Programs," https://www.transit.dot.gov/regulations-and-guidance/shared-mobility-faqs-eligibility-under-fta-grant-programs.

54 Zmud et al., pp. 45-49.

55 Federal Transit Administration, *Budget Estimates FY2017*, CIG-10, https://www.transportation.gov/sites/dot.gov/ files/docs/FTA-FY-2017-CJ.pdf.

56 American Public Transportation Association, *APTA Recommendations on Federal Public Transportation Authorizing Law*, December 2013, http://www.apta.com/gap/legissues/authorization/Documents/APTA%20Authorizing%20Law%20Recommendations_FINAL_adopted%206Dec2013.pdf.

57 Nathaniel Baum-Snow and Matthew E. Kahn, "Effects of Urban Rail Transit Expansions: Evidence from Sixteen Cities, 1970–2000," *Brookings-Wharton Papers on Urban Affairs*, Brookings Institution Press, 2005, pp. 147-197, https://muse.jhu.edu/article/192572/pdf.

has shown that some rail transit lines built at great cost with federal support have low ridership, but there are significant differences in benefit/cost ratios among systems. According to one study, two of the systems with the largest net benefits include the subway systems in San Francisco and New York City, while the rail system in Buffalo and those operated by New Jersey Transit in Newark, Jersey City, and Trenton have some of the largest net costs.[58]

If the full promise of autonomous vehicles is realized, the benefits of rail in all but the largest and most dense cities are likely to decline dramatically. In this situation, one policy option would be to eliminate the CIG program and redirect the funding through the formula programs, possibly using formulas that have been changed to encourage ridership. Another option would be to redirect CIG funding from building rail and perhaps even bus rapid transit in relatively small and dispersed urban areas to the large and dense cities where rail transit currently carries very large numbers of riders, such as New York, Chicago, and Washington, DC. With new funds to refurbish old infrastructure and to add new capacity in congested areas, it might be possible to substantially increase national transit ridership in the short to medium term.[59]

Raising User Fees on Automobiles

The cost of car ownership and use is low in the United States compared with most other highly developed countries, a contributing factor for the major differences in transit use. For example, according to the Federal Highway Administration, the average tax per gallon on gasoline in

---

[58] Robert Cervero and Erick Guerra, "To T or Not to T: A Ballpark Assessment of the Costs and Benefits of Urban Rail Transportation," *Public Works Management & Policy*, vol. 16, no. 2 (2011), pp. 111-128. For a more critical assessment, see Peter Gordon and Paige Elise Kolesar, "A Note on Rail Transit Cost—Benefit Analysis: Do Nonuser Benefits Make a Difference?" *Public Works Management & Policy*, vol. 16, no. 2 (2011), pp. 100-110; and Lisa Schweitzer, "Benefit-Cost Analysis of Rail Projects: A Commentary," *Public Works Management & Policy*, vol. 16, no. 2 (2011), pp. 129-131.

[59] Aaron Renn, "Does America Need More Urban Rail Transit?" Manhattan Institute, May 3, 2017, https://www.manhattan-institute.org/sites/default/files/IB-AR-0517.pdf.

this country was $0.43 in December 2014, including federal and state taxes, compared with $2.22 in Japan, $4.19 in Germany, and $4.83 in Italy.[60]

Highway user fees, including fuels tax, tolls, and vehicle registration fees, cover about 60% of the cost of highway infrastructure in 2012, with the other 40% coming from, among other things, general funds, property taxes, and bond issuance.[61] As a share of highway expenditures, user fees have generally declined over the past decade.[62] Additionally, many economists note that there are external costs of driving, such as congestion, air pollution, and publicly borne costs of crashes.[63]

Raising user fees on automobiles would make transit comparatively more attractive. Many fees, such as vehicle registration fees and parking charges, are controlled at the state and local level. Options at the federal level include raising the federal fuels tax, implementing a mileage-based user charge at a level above today's fuels tax, and encouraging greater use of tolling, including congestion pricing.[64]

---

[60] FHWA, Highway Statistics, Table IN-1, https://www.fhwa.dot.gov/policyinformation/statistics/2015/in1.cfm.

[61] This calculation includes highway user revenue diverted to nonhighway uses. Federal Highway Administration, *Highway Statistics 2015*, Table HF-10, https://www.fhwa.dot.gov/policyinformation/statistics/2015/hf10.cfm.

[62] Department of Transportation, *2015 Status of the Nation's Highways, Bridges, and Transit: Conditions and Performance*, January 2017, Chapter 6, https://www.fhwa.dot.gov/policy/2015cpr/pdfs/chap6.pdf.

[63] Todd Litman, *Socially Optimal Transport Prices and Markets*, Victoria Transport Policy Institute, July 18, 2017, http://www.vtpi.org/sotpm.pdf.

[64] CRS Report R44674, *Funding and Financing Highways and Public Transportation*, by Robert S. Kirk and William J. Mallett.

In: Transportation
Editor: Frederick Daniels

ISBN: 978-1-53615-651-5

Chapter 5

THE RAILROAD REHABILITATION AND IMPROVEMENT FINANCING (RRIF) PROGRAM (UPDATED)*

David Randall Peterman

SUMMARY

Congress created the Railroad Rehabilitation and Improvement Financing (RRIF) program to offer long-term, low-cost loans to railroad operators, with particular attention to small freight railroads, to help them finance improvements to infrastructure and investments in equipment. The program is intended to operate at no cost to the government, and it does not receive an annual appropriation. Since 2000, the RRIF program has made 37 loans totaling $5.4 billion (valued at $5.9 billion in 2018 dollars). The program, which is administered by the Build America Bureau within the Office of the Secretary of Transportation, has approved only four loans since 2012.

* This is an edited, reformatted and augmented version of Congressional Research Service Publication No. R44028, Updated January 31, 2018.

Congress has authorized $35 billion in loan authority for the RRIF program and repeatedly has urged the Department of Transportation (DOT) to increase the number of loans the program makes. Reports suggest the uncertain length and outcome of the RRIF loan application process and the up-front costs to prospective borrowers are among the elements of the program that have reduced its appeal compared with other financing options available to railroads.

By statute, the Build America Bureau has 90 days from the time a completed application is submitted to render a decision on the application. This timeline becomes uncertain due to the Bureau's discretion in determining when a loan application is "complete." A 2014 audit indicated that some loan applications had been in process for more than a year.

Unlike DOT's other prominent loan assistance program, the Transportation Infrastructure Finance and Innovation Act (TIFIA) program, RRIF requires loan recipients to pay a credit risk premium, which is intended to offset the risk of a default on their loan. The credit risk premium helps the program comply with a congressional requirement that federal loan assistance programs operate at no cost to the federal government. However, it may make RRIF loans less attractive to borrowers than other types of federal, state, or private financing.

Several RRIF loans have been made to government-run intercity passenger rail projects. A number of private companies seeking to build intercity passenger rail lines also have expressed interest in RRIF loans. Changes made by Congress in the Fixing America's Surface Transportation Act (P.L. 114-94), enacted in December 2015, may lead to even greater use of the RRIF program by sponsors of passenger rail and transit-related projects, as opposed to small freight railroads. Such loans likely would be quite large relative to those RRIF typically extends to small freight railroads, raising questions about the risk to the federal government if the projects are not completed or if they fail to generate sufficient revenue to service the loans.

INTRODUCTION

The Railroad Rehabilitation and Improvement Financing (RRIF) program offers long-term, low-interest loans to railroad operators for improving rail infrastructure. The program is intended to operate at no cost to the government and does not receive an annual appropriation.

Congress has authorized $35 billion in loan authority for the program, but freight railroads have been relatively unenthusiastic. Since 2000, RRIF has made 37 loans to 29 operators for a total of $5.4 billion, representing $5.9 billion in 2018 dollars. From 2000 through 2015, private railroads' total investment in structures and equipment was approximately $154 billion ($174 billion in 2016 dollars).[1] RRIF supplied less than 1% of freight railroads' capital expenditures for track and other structures over that period.

In recent years, sponsors of intercity passenger rail projects have shown increasing interest in the program. About 85% of the RRIF program's nominal loan amount has gone to government-controlled entities for passenger rail projects rather than to freight operators; loans to Amtrak, the national intercity passenger rail provider, alone represent almost 60% of the total nominal loan amount. Part of this activity may be explained by a growing interest in passenger rail services at the state and local level and the scarcity of other funding assistance for such projects, which tend to be extremely costly.

The Fixing America's Surface Transportation Act (FAST Act; P.L. 114-94), enacted in December 2015, included changes intended to make the RRIF program more attractive to potential applicants, though one change—elimination of the requirement that the U.S. Department of Transportation (DOT), which administers the program, refund borrowers' credit risk premiums— may make the program less attractive. Some of the changes may make the program more useful for funding passenger rail and transit-related projects. The prospect of large loans for private intercity passenger rail and transit-related projects raises questions about potential risks to the RRIF program, because such projects may have no source of earnings until and unless they are completed and, even then, may not be able to generate sufficient revenue to service their loans.

---

[1] Association of American Railroads, *Railroad Facts*, annual, 2015 & 2016 editions, "Capital Expenditures," p. 46. Figures inflated using the Chained GDP column from Table 10.1, "Gross Domestic Product and Deflators Used in the Historical Tables," from the "Historical Tables" volume of the annual *Budget of the United States*.

RAILROAD INDUSTRY BACKGROUND

The railroad industry has changed significantly since Congress created a forerunner of RRIF in 1976. At that time, the nation's railroads were in great financial difficulty, investment in infrastructure and equipment had lagged, and there were questions about the future viability of the industry. Subsequently, Congress significantly deregulated the railroad industry, making it easier for carriers to consolidate and to shed less profitable routes. Since that time, mergers have reduced a large number of regional railroads to a handful of companies that operate across many states (known as Class I carriers).

Deregulation allowed the large railroads to focus their construction and maintenance efforts on heavily trafficked main lines and to stop service on routes that were not profitable. Some of this lightly used trackage was sold to smaller operators, which believed they could build business by working closely with shippers that used or might use the line. These smaller railroads, collectively known as short line railroads, are classified by the Federal Railroad Administration (FRA) as Class II and Class III carriers.[2] Although there are now only seven Class I railroads operating in the United States,[3] there are more than 560 short line railroads.[4]

The Class I freight railroads—large, profitable commercial entities—are able to finance improvements out of their considerable revenues, as well as by issuing stock and by borrowing in the commercial market. Class II and Class III railroads have fewer financing options. Their revenues are smaller, their lines of business typically are more limited than those of the Class I railroads, and their creditworthiness generally is lower. However, nearly half of the nation's short line railroads have come under the control

---

[2] The classification of a railroad as being in Class I, II, or III is based on the company's annual revenue; the threshold amounts are adjusted for inflation each year and are roughly $450 million and above for a Class I, between $40 and $450 million for a Class II, and below $40 million for a Class III.

[3] The seven Class I railroads are freight rail companies; Amtrak is not included in the category.

[4] U.S. Department of Transportation, Federal Railroad Administration, *Summary of Class II and Class III Railroad Capital Needs and Funding Sources: A Report to Congress*, October 2014, p. iv, at https://www.fra.dot.gov/Elib/Document/14131.

of 27 holding companies,[5] potentially offering them easier access to private financing. In addition, a number of short line railroads are terminal switching, port, or harbor rail lines that have a relationship with a Class I railroad, which may help them obtain financing, and some short line railroads are owned by states. These entities typically have easier access to the financial markets than do stand-alone short line railroads.[6]

Amtrak operates at a loss and relies on federal grants appropriated annually to continue operations. Amtrak's primary service corridor is the Northeast Corridor (NEC), a rail line running from Washington, DC, through New York City to Boston. This line also is used heavily by commuter rail operations and also hosts freight service. There is an estimated backlog of $38 billion in capital investment needed to restore the aging NEC infrastructure to a state of good repair.[7] In July 2017 DOT published a proposal for expanded and faster service on the NEC, with a capital cost estimate of $121-$153 billion.[8]

RRIF PROGRAM

Congress created the RRIF program in 1998[9] and revised it in 2005,[10] 2008,[11] and 2015.[12] The program allows DOT to provide credit assistance for rail infrastructure by making low-cost direct loans or providing loan

---

[5] For example, Genesee & Wyoming Inc. owns 113 short line and regional freight railroads in the United States and another seven outside the United States; it would qualify as a Class I railroad if its U.S. operations were considered as a single rail operator.

[6] U.S. Department of Transportation, Federal Railroad Administration, *Summary of Class II and Class III Railroad Capital Needs and Funding Sources: A Report to Congress*, October 2014, p. v, at https://www.fra.dot.gov/Elib/ Document/14131.

[7] Northeast Corridor Commission, *Northeast Corridor Capital Investment Plan, Fiscal Years 2018-2022*, p. 8, http://www.nec-commission.com/capital-investment-plan/plan/NEC-Capital-Investment-Plan-18-22.pdf.

[8] U.S. Department of Transportation, Federal Railroad Administration, *Record of Decision* for *A Rail Investment Plan for the Northeast Corridor, Tier 1 Final Environmental Impact Statement*, July 2017, http://www.necfuture.com/.

[9] P.L. 105-178, Transportation Equity Act for the 21st Century, §7203.

[10] P.L. 109-59, Safe, Accountable, Flexible and Efficient Transportation Equity Act: A Legacy for Users, §9003.

[11] P.L. 110-432, Rail Safety Improvement Act of 2008, Division A, §701(e).

[12] P.L. 114-94, Fixing America's Surface Transportation Act, Title XI, Subtitle F.

guarantees to project sponsors. Eligible recipients of this assistance include railroads, state and local governments, government-sponsored corporations, and joint ventures that include at least one railroad.

The RRIF program replaced a railroad financing program that Congress created in 1976.[13] The original program allowed DOT to provide financial assistance for rail infrastructure by purchasing preference shares or issuing loan guarantees. The authorization to purchase preference shares expired in 1996.

In the 1998 revision that renamed the program, Congress authorized DOT to make direct loans as well as loan guarantees, set an overall cap of $3.5 billion on the total amount of outstanding debt that the program could have at any one time, and reserved almost 30% of that ($1 billion) for projects benefiting short line railroads. In 2005, Congress increased the limit on outstanding debt to $35 billion and increased the amount reserved for smaller freight railroads to $7 billion. The increase was not due to demand for the program—the program had issued a total of less than $1 billion in loans at that point—but in hopes of boosting interest in the program. In 2012, Congress provided that applicants could use future dedicated revenues as security for a RRIF loan. In 2015, it added new types of security that applicants could use to reduce the amount of their credit risk premium, and moved the administration of the program from the FRA to a newly created Build America Bureau.

Projects eligible for RRIF assistance include acquiring, improving, and rehabilitating track, bridges, rail yards, buildings, and shops (or refinancing existing debt that was incurred for these purposes); preconstruction activities; positive train control; transit-oriented development projects; and new rail or intermodal facilities. Loans can be for up to 100% of the project cost, with repayment periods up to 35 years.

[13] P.L. 94-210, the Railroad Revitalization and Regulatory Reform Act of 1976, Title V.

The RRIF program is designed to operate at no cost to the government. Applicants are charged a fee of 0.5% of the amount requested to cover the cost of processing their applications. Borrowers are charged another fee (the credit risk premium) at the time a loan is issued to cover the potential cost to the government of the loan not being repaid. The amount of the credit risk premium is based on several factors, including the financial condition of the applicant and the amount of collateral securing the loan.

This no-cost-to-the-government structure is why it was not controversial for Congress to raise the maximum outstanding loan amount from $3.5 billion to $35 billion in 2005. But the up-front costs of a RRIF loan may deter would-be applicants. By contrast, the other major DOT credit assistance program, established in the Transportation Infrastructure Finance and Innovation Act (TIFIA), covers the cost of the credit risk premium for loan recipients (known as TIFIA's subsidy cost). For private loans, the processing costs and credit risk premium typically are folded into the loan repayment schedule rather than being charged up front.

Program Overview

The RRIF program is one of four credit programs run by DOT.[14] RRIF loan applications are reviewed by the Build America Bureau, independent financial analysts hired by the Bureau, and DOT's Office of Credit and Finance.[15] The Secretary Of Transportation has final authority over loan approval.

---

[14] The other three are the TIFIA Program, the Maritime Guaranteed Loan (Title XI) Program, and the Minority Business Resource Center (MBRC) Short-Term Lending Program. These programs all must conform to the requirements of the Federal Credit Reform Act of 1990.

[15] The Office of Credit and Finance consists of eight to 11 DOT officials, including the Deputy Secretary of Transportation (the chair) and the administrators of several DOT operating agencies.

The appeal of the RRIF program is that the recipient is able to borrow money at the lowest rate available (that paid by the federal government itself)[16] and for a longer period of time than most other types of loans would permit. RRIF borrowers can also ask to defer loan repayment for a period of six years (though interest accrues during this period). Alternatively, the Build America Bureau can guarantee a private loan extended at a rate DOT determines to be reasonable; to date, no loan guarantees have been provided through the program.

Congress has imposed certain other restrictions on the program. For example, for FY2017, as in previous years, appropriations legislation prohibited the use of any federal funds to pay the credit risk premium on a RRIF loan.[17]

Congress has specified[18] that in evaluating RRIF applications, the Build America Bureau should favor projects that

- enhance public safety (including installation of positive train control);
- promote economic development;
- enhance the environment;
- enable U.S. companies to be more competitive in international markets;
- are endorsed by the plans prepared under Section 135 of Title 23 by the state or states in which they are located;[19]
- improve railroad stations and passenger facilities and increase transit-oriented development;
- preserve or enhance rail or intermodal service to small communities or rural areas;
- enhance service and capacity in the national rail system; and

---

[16] The interest rate on a RRIF loan is equal to the rate paid by the U.S. Treasury to borrow for a similar period of time as of the date the loan is approved.

[17] P.L. 115-31, the Consolidated Appropriations Act, 2017, Division K, Title I.

[18] In 45 U.S.C. §822(c).

[19] This refers to state transportation plans and state transportation improvement programs, which indicate the transportation projects states plan to undertake in the near future.

- materially alleviate rail capacity problems that degrade the provision of service to shippers and fulfill a need in the national transportation system.

Program Performance

The RRIF program has used relatively little of its lending authority. RRIF may have a maximum of $35 billion of outstanding loans and loan guarantees. It currently has about 11% of this amount committed. From its inception through January 2018, the RRIF program issued 37 loans for a total amount of $5.4 billion (see *Table 1*).[20]

Table 1. RRIF Executed Loans

Fiscal Year	Recipient	Amount
2002	Amtrak	$100,000,000
2002	Mount Hood Railroad	2,070,000
2003	Arkansas & Missouri Railroad	11,000,000
2003	Nashville and Western Railroad	2,300,000
2003	Dakota Minnesota & Eastern Railroad	233,601,000
2004	Stillwater Central Railroad	4,675,250
2004	Wheeling & Lake Erie Railway	25,000,000
2005	Great Smoky Mountains Railroad	7,500,000
2005	Riverport Railroad	5,514,774
2005	Montreal Maine & Atlantic Railwaya	34,000,000
2005	Tex-Mex Railroad	50,000,000
2005	Iowa Interstate Railroad	32,732,533
2006	Virginia Railway Express	72,500,000
2006	Wheeling & Lake Erie Railway	14,000,000
2006	Iowa Interstate Railroad	9,350,000
2007	RJ Corman Railway	11,768,274
2007	RJ Corman Railway	47,131,726
2007	Nashville and Eastern Railroad	4,000,000
2007	Nashville and Eastern Railroad	600,000

[20] U.S. Department of Transportation, Build America Bureau, "Railroad Rehabilitation & Improvement Financing (RRIF)," "Executed Loan Agreements," at https://www.transportation.gov/buildamerica/programs-services/rrif.

Table 1. (Continued)

Fiscal Year	Recipient	Amount
2007	Columbia Basin Railroad	3,000,000
2007	Great Western Railway	4,030,000
2007	Dakota Minnesota & Eastern Railroad	48,320,000
2007	Iowa Northern Railroad	25,500,000
2009	Georgia & Florida Railways	8,100,000
2009	Permian Basin Railways, Inc	64,400,000
2009	Iowa Interstate Railroad	31,000,000
2010	Denver Union Station Project Authority	155,000,000
2010	Great Lakes Central Railroad	17,000,000
2011	Northwestern Pacific Railroad Company and North Coast Railroad Authority	3,180,000
2011	Amtrak	562,900,000
2011	C&J Railroad	56,204
2012	Alameda Corridor Transportation Authority	83,710,000
2012	Kansas City Southern Railway Company	54,648,000
2015	New York City Metropolitan Transportation Administration	967,100,000
2015	The Arkansas and Missouri Railroad Company	6,809,000
2016	Amtrak	2,450,000,000
2018	Massachusetts Bay Transit Authority	220,000,000
Total		$5,372,496,761

Source: U.S. Department of Transportation, Build America Bureau, "Railroad Rehabilitation & Improvement Financing (RRIF)," Executed Loan Agreements, at https://www.transportation.gov/buildamerica/programsservices/rrif.

Notes: Loan amounts are not adjusted for inflation. Loans in bold have been repaid. A total of 21 loans have been repaid. The total amount of loans that have been made is $5.9 billion in 2018 dollars (nominal dollar values adjusted to 2018 dollars using the Total Non-defense column from Table 10.1: Gross Domestic Product and Deflators Used in the Historical Tables: 1940-2022, published in Executive Office of the President of the United States, Office of Management and Budget, Fiscal Year 2018 Historical Tables, Budget of the United States Government, available at https://www.whitehouse.gov/omb/historical-tables/).

[a] Montreal Maine & Atlantic (MMA) was responsible for the July 2013 derailment and explosion of oil transport cars in Lac-Megantic, Canada, which resulted in extensive damage and the deaths of 47 people. MMA entered bankruptcy in August 2013; its loan is in default, with $27.5 million outstanding.

The loans ranged in amounts from $53,000 to $2.45 billion. Twenty-one of the 37 loans have been repaid in full. One loan is in default. The total amount of RRIF loans outstanding as of January 2018 was $4.02

billion. Of the 37 loans made, two-thirds were executed prior to 2008; four have been approved since 2012 (see *Figure 1*). The Build America Bureau reports that as of January 2018 it was evaluating five applications totaling $5.5 billion.[21] (By comparison, FRA was evaluating 13 applications totaling $10 billion in February 2014, suggesting that several applications were withdrawn between 2014 and 2018).[22] DOT may approve a loan for less than the amount requested; in the case of a 2007 loan, the Dakota, Minnesota & Eastern Railroad applied for $2.5 billion and received a loan of $48 million.[23]

Public-sector entities have emerged as the largest borrowers under the RRIF program, representing some 85% of the amount loaned. Most loans to public-sector entities have been intended for passenger rail projects. However, one, an $83.7 million loan to the Alameda Corridor Transportation Authority in 2012, was to support a freight project.

RRIF Program Issues and Options

Need for Program

The policy rationales for the RRIF program are that railroad companies, especially short line companies too small to raise money in the bond market, need better access to long-term, low-cost financing to

[21] As directed in the FAST Act (codified at 45 U.S.C. 822(i)(5)), DOT now posts a monthly report on its website providing summary information about each loan application under consideration; see https://www.transportation.gov/ buildamerica/programs-and-services/rrif/railroad-rehabilitation-and-improvement-financing-rrif-program-dashboard.

[22] U.S. Department of Transportation, Federal Railroad Administration, *FY2015 Budget Estimate*, February 2014, p. 128, at http://www.dot.gov/sites/dot.gov/files/docs/FRA-FY2015-Budget-Estimates.pdf.

[23] The loan request was part of a $6.5 billion plan to expand access to coal fields in Wyoming and Montana. Dakota, Minnesota & Eastern subsequently was acquired by a Class I railroad (Canadian Pacific) in 2008, and the loan (along with an earlier RRIF loan) was repaid. U.S. Department of Transportation, Federal Railroad Administration, *Dakota, Minnesota & Eastern Railroad Powder River Basin Expansion Project Environmental Impact Statement and Section 4(f)/303 Statement*, at https://www.fra.dot.gov/Page/P0234; Greg Gormick, "Steady As She Goes," *Railway Age*, November 2008, p. 32; personal communication from FRA.

maintain and expand their networks, and that the safety and efficiency of their networks is a public concern.[24] However, it is not clear that railroads, even short line railroads, have significant difficulty financing the maintenance and expansion of their networks. FRA looked at the safety record of short line railroads, taking accident rates as a proxy for the condition of the infrastructure (that is, if the infrastructure were deteriorating, the accident rate likely would increase). FRA found that the number of infrastructure-related accidents per million train-miles on short line railroads declined significantly between 2001 and 2013, from more than eight accidents per million train-miles to fewer than four accidents per million train-miles. FRA stated that "the positive trend, illustrated by a decreasing accident rate, suggests improving maintenance and investment.... "[25]

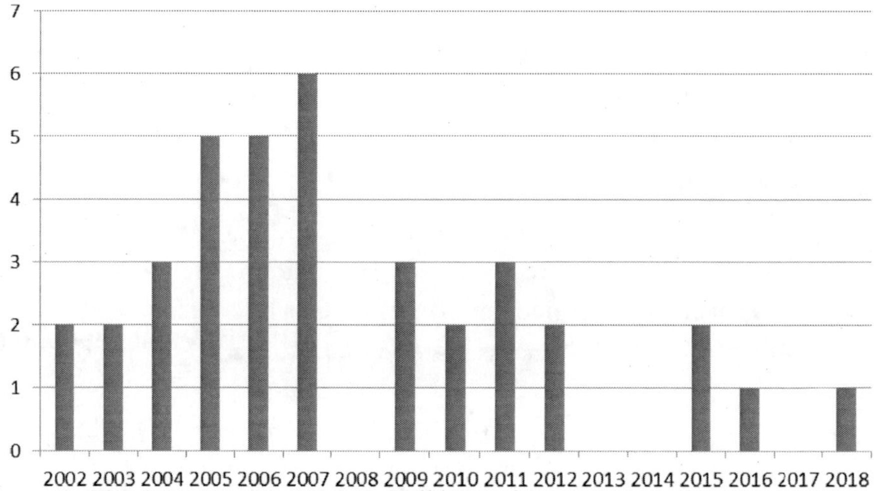

Sources: CRS, based on data from the Build America Bureau's Railroad Rehabilitation and Improvement Financing program website.

Note: First loans made in 2002.

Figure 1. RRIF Loans Executed by Year. (fiscal years through January 2018)

---

[24] U.S. Department of Transportation, Federal Railroad Administration, *FY2016 Budget Estimate*, p. 122, at http://www.dot.gov/sites/dot.gov/files/docs/FY2016-BudgetEstimate-FRA.pdf.

[25] U.S. Department of Transportation, Federal Railroad Administration, *Summary of Class II and Class III Railroad Capital Needs and Funding Sources: A Report to Congress*, October 2014, p. 4, at https://www.fra.dot.gov/Elib/Document/14131.

Another measure of the condition of short line railroad infrastructure is its capability to handle 286,000-pound rail cars. Since the late 1980s, Class I railroads have moved from maximum car weights of 263,000 pounds to 286,000 pounds. Track and bridges must be strengthened to handle these heavier loads. According to the Association of Short Line Railroads, 39% of short line route-miles were able to handle the 286,000-pound cars in 2002, whereas 57% of a larger number of total route-miles could handle the heavier cars in 2010. FRA stated, after examining both the safety and capacity numbers, that "these data points and trends illustrate that these carriers in aggregate are maintaining their systems and enhancing infrastructure to meet their customer needs."[26]

On the basis of a 2013 survey of Class II and Class III railroads' estimated spending requirements for infrastructure and equipment, FRA estimated that the total investment needs of short line railroads would be $6.9 billion over the five-year period from 2013 to 2017. The survey respondents anticipated that they would be able to cover about 70% to 75% of their estimated spending needs for infrastructure and equipment during that period, with most of the funding coming from their revenues; they expected about a quarter of the funding to come from other sources, chiefly state (9%) and federal (8%) grants and loans.[27] The survey results suggested an estimated gap of around $265 million per year between the available funding and the amount short lines felt was needed.[28]

Alternatives to RRIF

RRIF is only one of several federal and state programs available to reduce the cost of railroads' investment in infrastructure. Others include the following.

---

[26] Ibid., pp. 5-6.

[27] Ibid., pp. 22-24.

[28] FRA extrapolated Class II and III investment needs from 2013 to 2017 to be $5.3 billion (ibid., p. 23); respondents anticipated that they would be able to cover around 70% (pp. 22-23) to 75% of their investment needs (ibid., p. 24), leaving a shortfall of around one-fourth of the estimated $5.3 billion, or $1.3 billion over five years, around $265 million annually.

Section 45G Tax Credit

This tax credit, first enacted in 2004, allows Class II and Class III railroads to reduce their taxes by 50% of the cost of track maintenance expenses incurred in a year, up to a limit established by multiplying the railroad's track mileage by $3,500. The cost to the federal government in forgone tax revenue is estimated at $165 million to $202 million per year, which represents investments of roughly $300-$400 million annually.[29] In contrast to the RRIF program, this tax credit is targeted exclusively to short line railroads. It does not require the recipient to undertake an uncertain loan application process, with its attendant costs, or to comply with requirements for RRIF loans, such as the National Environmental Policy Act (NEPA) and the RRIF program's Buy America policy.[30] The tax credit expired on December 31, 2016. Legislation to extend the credit has been introduced in the 115th Congress (H.R. 721; S. 407; S. 2256).

TIGER Grant Program

Congress created a National Infrastructure Investment discretionary grant program within the Office of the Secretary of Transportation in 2009. This program, popularly known as the Transportation Investment Generating Economic Recovery (TIGER) grant program, made over $5 billion in grants through FY2017. Grants require a 20% match in urbanized areas; in rural areas, no local match is required. Although only governmental entities are eligible to receive grants, applications may represent public-private partnerships. Passenger and freight rail infrastructure projects are eligible uses of TIGER funds. Freight rail projects (including port improvement projects with a rail component) have received nearly $810 million in grants; short line railroad improvement

---

[29] American Short Line and Regional Railroad Association, "The 45G Short Line Railroad Tax Credit," at http://www.aslrra.org/legislative/Short_Line_Tax_Credit_Extension.

[30] U.S. Department of Transportation, Office of Inspector General, *Audit Report: Process Inefficiencies and Costs Discourage Participation in FRA's RRIF Program*, June 10, 2014, CR-2014-054, Exhibit E, pp. 19-20, at https://www.oig.dot.gov/sites/default/files/RRIF%20final.pdf.

projects have received more than $270 million.[31] The program is very competitive, with several times as much funding requested each year as the $500 million typically available for grants.

TIFIA Loan Program

The TIFIA loan program, like the RRIF program, was authorized by Congress in 1998. As of the end of calendar year 2016, the program had assisted 56 projects with a total value of over $82 billion; the federal value of credit assistance provided was more than $20 billion, at a direct cost of more than $1 billion (representing the cost of the credit risk premium and the administrative costs of processing applications).[32] Eligible projects include "rail projects involving the design and construction of intercity passenger rail facilities or the procurement of intercity passenger rail vehicles" and "intermodal freight transfer facilities."[33] Although five intermodal projects involving rail freight have received assistance, no TIFIA loans have been approved for pure rail projects. Congress appropriates funding to cover the credit risk premium cost of TIFIA loans, reducing the cost of loans to recipients. See *Table 2* for a summary of differences between the RRIF and TIFIA programs.

In the FAST Act, the 2015 surface transportation authorization legislation, Congress authorized $1.435 billion through FY2020 to administer the program and cover the credit risk premium. Since DOT assumes a loss ratio of around 10%, the $1.435 billion available after administrative costs gave it the capacity to provide about $14 billion in TIFIA loans or loan guarantees from FY2016 through FY2020.[34]

---

[31] U.S. Department of Transportation, Federal Railroad Administration, *Summary of Class II and Class III Railroad Capital Needs and Funding Sources: A Report to Congress*, October 2014, p. 16, at https://www.fra.dot.gov/Elib/ Document/14131.

[32] U.S. Department of Transportation, *TIFIA 2016 Report to Congress*, August 11, 2016, https://cms.dot.gov/policyinitiatives/tifia/2016-tifia-report-congress.

[33] U.S. Department of Transportation, Federal Highway Administration, *TIFIA Program Guide*, December 2009, p. 3-1, at http://www.fhwa.dot.gov/ipd/pdfs/tifia/tifia_program_guide.pdf.

[34] U.S. Department of Transportation, *TIFIA 2016 Report to Congress*, August 11, 2016, at https://cms.dot.gov/sites/dot.gov/files/docs/TIFIA%20Report%20to%20Congress%202016.pdf.

Table 2. Comparison of RRIF and TIFIA Programs

	RRIF	TIFIA
Limit on Total Value of Outstanding Loans	$35 billion	—[a]
Number of Loans/Loan Guarantees Provided	36	56
Average Assistance Value	$143 million	$384 million
Loan Amount as % of Eligible Project Costs	Up to 100%	Up to 49%, typically no more than 33%
Loan Term	Up to 35 years	Up to 35 years
Up-Front Cost	Up to 0.5% of loan amount for processing, plus the credit risk premium	$400,000 to $500,000 for loan processing

Sources: CRS, based on information from U.S. Department of Transportation, Build America Bureau, Railroad Rehabilitation & Improvement Financing RRIF, https://www.transportation.gov/buildamerica/programs-services/rrif; U.S. Department of Transportation, TIFIA 2016 Report to Congress, August 11, 2016, at https://cms.dot.gov/sites/dot.gov/files/docs/TIFIA%20Report%20to%20Cong ress%202016.pdf.

Note: These programs are not mutually exclusive; at least one project, the redevelopment of Denver Union Station as a multimodal center, received loans from both RRIF and TIFIA.

[a] The amount of TIFIA loans is limited by the funding available to the program to cover the subsidy cost of the loans.

State Programs

A number of states have established grant, loan, and tax benefit programs to help short line railroads finance infrastructure or equipment purchases. In its report on Class II and Class III railroad capital needs and funding sources, FRA reported that, in a survey of how short line railroads expected to fund their needs in the near future, respondents expected to get a greater percentage of funding for infrastructure and equipment investments from state programs (9%) than from federal programs (8%).[35]

Supportive Policy Options

The primary competition for short line and regional railroads is the trucking industry. The degree of competition is affected by the extent of regulation and taxation on the rail and truck sectors. Trucks operate over

---

[35] U.S. Department of Transportation, Federal Railroad Administration, *Summary of Class II and Class III Railroad Capital Needs and Funding Sources: A Report to Congress*, October 2014, pp. 23-24 and Figure 3, at https://www.fra.dot.gov/Elib/Document/14131.

publicly provided infrastructure (the highway network), whereas railroads are financially responsible for their own infrastructure. Although federal and state taxes on diesel fuel contribute to maintaining the highway infrastructure, studies indicate that heavy trucks cause much more damage to highways than they pay in fuel taxes. This problem is exacerbated by exemptions Congress has provided to limits on truck weights, which raise the productivity of trucking vis-à-vis railroads while increasing the amount of damage the trucks cause to the highway infrastructure.

Congress could aid the short line and regional railroads by, for example, increasing the amount of fuel tax paid by heavy trucks to a level commensurate with the damage they cause to the highway infrastructure and limiting exemptions to truck weight restrictions. Such changes also would benefit the Class I railroads. However, these changes could increase the cost of shipping goods by truck, adversely affecting trucking industry employment. In addition, higher truck rates could affect rail shippers by giving railroads room to raise their own rates.

Program Effectiveness

There are many possible ways of evaluating the effectiveness of the RRIF program. By one measure on which Congress has focused—the extent to which railroads have made use of RRIF loans—the program has not been very effective, considering that less than $6 billion of the $35 billion in loan authority has been used. However, the $35 billion limit appears to have been set somewhat arbitrarily, rather than reflecting an analysis of railroad investment needs that could not be met by other means. The fact that the RRIF program has lent far less than the amount Congress authorized, particularly to private-sector borrowers, may indicate that freight railroads' ability to finance their investment needs without recourse to government support is greater than Congress believed.

Congress has expressed a desire that the program be used more heavily, especially by short line railroads, and has identified two aspects of the program that may be reducing its attractiveness: the uncertain length of the loan review process and the cost to the applicant of the loan. A third aspect that may be reducing the program's attractiveness is the requirement that loan recipients comply with the requirements of the National Environmental Protection Act, various "Buy America" requirements, and federal prevailing wage and employee protection requirements.

Length of Review Process

By statute, a RRIF loan application is supposed to be approved or disapproved within 90 days. But that 90-day clock does not begin until a loan application is considered complete. In a 2014 audit of the program, the DOT Office of Inspector General found that unclear program information resulted in incomplete loan applications that required FRA to work with applicants on completing the applications. The Inspector General determined that due to the extensive loan review process, which involved FRA, outside reviewers, DOT's Office of Credit Oversight and Risk Management, and its Credit Council, the loan application process took a long time and had an uncertain outcome, discouraging potential applicants.[36]

Management of the program was subsequently transferred to the Build America Bureau. The Bureau published a guide to its credit programs (covering both RRIF and TIFIA) in January 2017.[37] The Bureau had five loan applications under review as of January 1, 2018; all were draft applications (after review, an applicant may or may not be invited to submit a final application). The length of time since the draft applications had been submitted was 19 months, 14 months, 10 months, 8 months, and 5 months, suggesting that in spite of the publication of the program guide

---

[36] To cite some extreme cases, the DOT Inspector General's audit found that four RRIF loan applications were still in pending status after more than two years. U.S. Department of Transportation, Office of the Inspector General, *Audit Report: Process Inefficiencies and Costs Discourage Participation in FRA's RRIF Program*, CR-2014-054, June 10, 2014, p. 18, at https://www.oig.dot.gov/sites/default/files/RRIF%20final.pdf.

[37] Available at https://cms.dot.gov/sites/dot.gov/files/docs/ Bureau%20Credit%20Programs%20 Guide_January_2017.pdf.

and other changes made to shorten the review process, it may still be quite lengthy.[38]

Loan Costs

Federal law requires that federal credit programs operate at no cost to the government. The government faces two primary costs for loan assistance and guarantee programs: that of administering the program, including evaluating applicants, and that of a borrower failing to repay its loan.

To cover the cost of administering the program (including evaluating loan applications), the RRIF program charges loan applicants a nonrefundable fee of up to 0.5% of the loan amount. To protect against the possibility of defaults, federal law requires that loan programs keep enough money in reserve to cover the estimated cost to the government of defaults on the loans made. This reserve amount, which in the case of the RRIF program is paid by the borrower, is referred to as a credit risk premium. A credit risk premium is calculated for each loan, based primarily on the financial soundness of the borrower and the amount of collateral pledged by the borrower. Credit risk premiums for the RRIF program generally have been between 0% and 5% of the loan amount.[39] For example, Amtrak paid a 4.424% credit risk premium for its 2011 RRIF loan and 5.8% for its 2016 RRIF loan.[40] If collateral of sufficient value is pledged, no credit risk premium may be required.

The 2014 audit of the RRIF program noted that some short line railroads had pointed to the credit risk premium as discouraging them from applying to the program. In response, FRA stated that it has no discretion

---

[38] See Build America Bureau, *Railroad Rehabilitation and Improvement Financing (RRIF) Program Dashboard, January 1, 2018*, https://www.transportation.gov/buildamerica/programs-and-services/rrif/railroad-rehabilitation-andimprovement-financing-rrif-program-dashboard.

[39] .S. Department of Transportation, Office of the Inspector General, *Audit Report: Process Inefficiencies and Costs Discourage Participation in FRA's RRIF Program*, CR-2014-054, June 10, 2014, p. 20, at https://www.oig.dot.gov/ sites/default/files/RRIF%20final.pdf.

[40] National Railroad Passenger Corporation, *Consolidated Financial Statements, Years Ended September 30, 2016 and 2015, with Report of Independent Auditors*, at https://www.amtrak.com/ccurl/736/320/Audited-Consolidated-FinancialStatements-FY2016.pdf, p. 24.

to subsidize the credit risk premium for applicants. Such a step would require congressional action. As noted above, for several years Congress has included in DOT appropriations bills a provision barring the use of federal funds to pay the credit risk premium.

Prior to the FAST Act, DOT was required to refund the credit risk premium to borrowers after all the loans in their cohort of loans had been repaid. DOT had originally been instructed to establish cohorts of loans for this purpose, with the intent of both maintaining "sufficient balances of credit risk premiums to adequately protect the Federal Government from risk of default, while minimizing the length of time the Government retains possession of those balances."[41] However, as of January 2018, DOT has not issued a formal definition of a "cohort of loans." As a result, while 21 RRIF loans have been repaid, DOT has not yet returned any credit risk premiums to their borrowers.

In Section 11607 of the FAST Act (P.L. 114-94), Congress repealed the language requiring DOT to repay the credit risk premium for future loans, leaving the decision about repayment to the discretion of DOT. DOT has reportedly decided that credit risk premiums paid for loans made after enactment of the FAST Act will not be repaid.[42]

With respect to loans made prior to passage of the FAST Act, the conference committee report accompanying the FAST Act directed DOT to refund credit risk premiums to borrowers that had repaid their RRIF loans, "regardless of whether the loan is or was included in a cohort. The intent of this provision is for the Secretary to pay back such credit risk premium, with interest, as soon as feasible but not later than three months after the date of enactment."[43] As noted, more than two years after adoption of this chapter DOT has yet to repay any credit risk premiums to borrowers that have repaid their loans.

---

[41] 45 U.S.C. 822(f)(4). This passage was repealed by the FAST Act.

[42] The Build America Bureau's Credit Programs Guide, published in March 2017, does not address the issue of what happens to a borrower's credit risk premium after a loan is repaid. However, the Government Accountability Office (GAO) reports that FRA officials said credit risk premiums paid after passage of the FAST Act are not refundable; see https://www.gao.gov/assets/680/678388.pdf, p. 9.

[43] From the conference report on H.R. 22, the Surface Transportation Reauthorization and Reform Act of 2015, published in the *Congressional Record*, December 1, 2015, p. H8809.

Project Requirements

To qualify for a loan, an applicant must comply with a variety of federal laws, including NEPA, various "Buy America" requirements, and federal prevailing wage and employee protection requirements.[44] NEPA requires that FRA review a project's environmental impact.[45] The Buy America Act requires that a project receiving a government loan use steel, iron, and other manufactured goods produced in the United States, unless the project sponsor receives a waiver from FRA.[46]

Loans to Passenger Rail Projects

Growth in Lending to Passenger Rail Projects

The RRIF program was created primarily to support freight rail service, particularly that of small ("short line") railroads. But a significant portion of RRIF assistance has gone to passenger rail service, especially since 2008. The recipients of the greatest amount of assistance have been Amtrak (three loans totaling $3.1 billion) and the New York City Metropolitan Transportation Administration (one loan for $967 million). As of January 2018, just over four-fifths of the total assistance provided by the program has gone to passenger rail projects (see *Table 3*).

One cause of much larger loan amounts for passenger projects is that the short line railroads that borrow from RRIF typically have small and thus relatively inexpensive projects; the Class I railroads that might be undertaking larger projects have not made use of RRIF funding. Another cause may be the lack of alternative funding sources for intercity passenger rail projects.

---

[44] These requirements apply to both the RRIF and TIFIA program. U.S. Department of Transportation, Build America Bureau, *Credit Programs Guide*, March 2017, Section 3-3.

[45] Section 11504 of the FAST Act directed DOT to propose a regulation exempting railroad rights-of-way from NEPA review, similar to an existing exemption for interstate highways; this would greatly reduce any NEPA compliance burden for most RRIF loan applicants. This regulation is in progress.

[46] See CRS Report R44266, *Effects of Buy America on Transportation Infrastructure and U.S. Manufacturing: Policy Options*, by Michaela D. Platzer and William J. Mallett.

Table 3. RRIF Executed Loans by Category (millions of 2018 dollars)

Category	Number of Loans	Total Amount of Loans	Average Loan Amount
Freight	30	$1,038	$35
Passenger	7	$4,840	$691
Total	37	$5,878	$159

Source: CRS, based on RRIF grant information. Nominal dollar values adjusted to 2018 dollars using the Total Non-defense column from Table 10.1: Gross Domestic Product and Deflators Used in the Historical Tables: 1940-2022, published in Executive Office of the President of the United States, Office of Management and Budget, Fiscal Year 2018 Historical Tables, Budget of the United States Government, available at https://www.whitehouse.gov/omb/ historical-tables/.

In calendar year 2009, Congress appropriated $10.5 billion (later reduced to $10.1 billion through a rescission of appropriated funding) for grants for high-speed and intercity passenger rail projects.[47] The availability of that funding generated significant interest on the part of states to establish or expand passenger rail service; FRA reported receiving applications for a total of more than $75 billion.[48] Congress provided virtually no funding for intercity passenger rail service expansion from 2010 until 2017, so organizations interested in passenger rail services may have turned to RRIF as an alternative or supplemental source of funding.

Unique Risks

Lending to intercity passenger rail projects creates some unique challenges for RRIF. Passenger rail projects often fail to make an operating profit, and few of them anywhere in the world generate sufficient operating profit to cover their capital costs.

Amtrak, the federally owned intercity passenger railroad operator, has received more than half of all funds loaned by the RRIF program. Amtrak has repaid two of the loans; it does not have to begin repaying the 2016 loan until 2022. Amtrak states that it will service this loan with revenue

[47] Congress appropriated $8 billion in P.L. 111-5, the American Recovery and Reinvestment Act of 2009 (ARRA; also known as the economic stimulus act), and $2.5 billion in P.L. 111-117, the Consolidated Appropriations Act. Congress rescinded $400 million of this funding in 2010 (in P.L. 112-10 §2222).

[48] U.S. Department of Transportation, Federal Railroad Administration, "High Speed Intercity Passenger Rail (HSIPR) Program," at http://www.fra.dot.gov/Page/P0134.

from its Northeast Corridor operations. However, while Amtrak earns an operating profit on its Northeast Corridor operations, it loses money overall and relies on an annual appropriation of approximately $1.4 billion from Congress to continue operating. Thus, the railroad's ability to repay its RRIF loan depends on the receipt of other federal funds.

In 2010, RRIF extended a $155 million loan to the Denver Union Station Project Authority for the reconstruction of Denver Union Station as an intermodal passenger station. The loan was serviced from the proceeds of tax-increment revenue from development around the station, with a backstop commitment from the City and County of Denver.[49] The project repaid both its RRIF and TIFIA loans in February 2017.[50]

Several private entities seeking to build and operate passenger rail projects have expressed interest in RRIF loans in recent years. Privately owned companies operate passenger rail services in many countries, but they typically pay only a portion of the cost of building and maintaining rail infrastructure, which usually receives some form of government support.

One entity that began operating passenger rail service in 2018, All Aboard Florida (which has branded its trains as Brightline), reportedly applied for a $1.87 billion RRIF loan to develop 110-mile per hour passenger service between Miami and Orlando.[51] The company later told the press it was seeking other financing instead of a RRIF loan, and was issued $1.75 billion in private activity bonds by the Florida Development Finance Corporation. The company is using $600 million to pay for upgrades to the line between Miami and West Palm Beach (Phase I), and

---

[49] Regional Transportation District, *Denver Union Station,* at http://onlinepubs.trb.org/onlinepubs/conferences/2014/ Finance/14.Lien,Marla.pdf, pp. 10-11; Fitch Ratings, "Fitch Affirms Denver Union Station Project Authority's (CO) 2010 Senior Notes at 'A,'" press release, December 5, 2014, at http://www.reuters.com/article/ 2014/12/05/ny-fitch-ratings-denver-idUSnBw055872a+100+BSW20141205.

[50] City of Denver, Department of Finance, "Denver Union Station revenues exceeding projections, positioning City and RTD [Regional Transportation District] to save money with new refinancing agreement," February 3, 2017, at https://www.denvergov.org/content/denvergov/en/denver-department-of-finance/newsroom/news-releases/2017/denver-union-station-revenues-exceeding-projections—positioning.html.

[51] Lidia Dinkova, "All Aboard Florida on line for government aid," *Miami Today*, October 22, 2014, at http://www.miamitodaynews.com/2014/10/22/aboard-florida-line-government-aid/.

$1.15 billion to pay for the new high-speed line from its coastal line (at West Palm Beach) to Orlando.[52]

XpressWest, a proposed privately funded high-speed rail line between Las Vegas and Southern California, reportedly applied for a $5.5 billion RRIF loan in December 2010.[53] The chairs of the House and Senate Budget Committees sent a letter to the Secretary of DOT on March 6, 2013, opposing the loan as being too risky;[54] on June 28, 2013, DOT issued a letter saying it had suspended review of the XpressWest loan application due to the applicant's difficulties in satisfying Buy America requirements and providing documentation for the loan request.[55] A subsequent venture with a Chinese rail company to build the line was terminated, reportedly also due to difficulties in satisfying the Buy America requirements of the RRIF program.[56] The Texas Central Railway, a private group proposing to build a high-speed line between Dallas and Houston, has said that it is considering seeking a loan from the RRIF or TIFIA programs but that it presently is not eligible to apply.[57] To date, FRA has approved no RRIF loans to private passenger rail operators.

---

[52] Kim Miller, "All Aboard Florida seeks private financing to replace or augment federal loan request," *Palm Beach Post*, October 7, 2014, at http://realtime.blog.palmbeachpost.com/2014/10/07/all-aboard-florida-seeks-privatefinancing-to-replace-or-augment-federal-loan-request/; Lis Broadt, "Brightline's $600 million of bonds approved by Florida Development Finance Corp.," *TC Palm*, October 30, 2017, https://www.tcpalm.com/story/news/local/shaping-our-future/2017/10/30/brightline-all-aboard-florida-finance-development-corporation-care-fl-east-coast-railway-fortress/815335001/.

[53] Richard N. Velotta, "High-speed rail project waiting on $5.5 billion government loan," *VegasINC*, February 12, 2013, at http://www.vegasinc.com/business/2013/feb/12/high-speed-rail-project-waiting-55-billion-governm/.

[54] Letter from Representative Paul Ryan, Chairman of the House Budget Committee, and Senator Jeff Sessions, Ranking Member of the Senate Budget Committee, to Ray H. LaHood, Secretary of Transportation, March 6, 2013, at https://www.budget.senate.gov/chairman/newsroom/press/sessions-ryan-call-for-halt-on-taxpayer-funding-for-riskyhigh-speed-rail-project.

[55] Natalie Rodriguez, "Feds halt Review of $5.5B Loan For Vegas Rail Plan," *Law360*, July 18, 2013, at http://www.law360.com/articles/458185/feds-halt-review-of-5-5b-loan-for-vegas-rail-plan.

[56] Julie Makinen, "China will not build L.A.-to-Vegas rail line—U.S. company calls the deal off," *Los Angeles Times*, June 8, 2016, http://www.latimes.com/world/asia/la-fg-xpresswest-rail-line-20160608-snap-story.html.

[57] Texas Central Railway, "Answers to your Questions: Taxpayer Funding," at http://texascentral.com/answers-to-yourquestions/, accessed May 9, 2017. That page is no longer available; as of January 30, 2018, another page says "the project will explore all forms of capital available to private companies to finance debt for the project, including federal loan

If such loans are extended, they are likely to be quite large relative to the loans RRIF has extended for freight projects and may pose different risks. RRIF loans for freight projects typically are for the purpose of improving an operating railroad that already generates revenue from customers. Those existing facilities may serve as collateral for the loans. Some of the private passenger rail projects now under development, by contrast, involve provision of new services on trackage that has yet to be built, potentially leaving the RRIF program with a significant risk of loss if the project is not completed.

---

programs like RRIF and TIFIA." https://www.texascentral.com/rumors-vs-reality/project-financing/.

In: Transportation
Editor: Frederick Daniels
ISBN: 978-1-53615-651-5

Chapter 6

Rail Transit: Federal Transit Administration Can Strengthen Safety Oversight by Improving Guidance to States*

United States Government Accountability Office

Abbreviations

DOT	Department of Transportation
FAST Act	Fixing America's Surface Transportation Act
FRA	Federal Railroad Administration
FTA	Federal Transit Administration
MAP-21	Moving Ahead for Progress in the 21st Century Act
NTSB	National Transportation Safety Board

* This is an edited, reformatted and augmented version of the United States Government Accountability Office Report to Congressional Requesters, Publication No. GAO-18-310, dated March 2018.

OECD	Organisation for Economic Co-operation and Development
OIG	Office of Inspector General
OMB	Office of Management and Budget
TCRP	Transit Cooperative Research Program
WMATA	Washington Metropolitan Area Transit Authority

WHY GAO DID THIS STUDY

In 2012 and 2015, DOT was provided with additional authority to oversee the safety of rail transit. Within DOT, FTA is now implementing this authority. The DOT's Office of Inspector General has reported, though, that FTA faces challenges in carrying out its enhanced safety oversight. FRA, also in DOT, has long carried out safety oversight of freight, intercity passenger, and commuter railroads.

GAO was asked to review various rail safety and oversight issues, including the differences between FRA's and FTA's rail safety oversight programs. This chapter examines (1) key characteristics of FRA's and FTA's rail safety oversight programs and (2) strengths and limitations of FRA's and FTA's rail safety oversight programs. GAO assessed FRA's and FTA's information about rail safety oversight activities against guidance from the Office of Management and Budget, leading practices developed by the transit industry, and federal standards for internal control. GAO also interviewed stakeholders, including rail operators chosen based on mode, size, and location.

WHAT GAO RECOMMENDS

GAO recommends that FTA (1) create a plan, with timeline, for developing risk-based inspection guidance for state safety agencies, and (2) develop and communicate a method for how FTA will monitor whether state safety agencies' enforcement practices are effective. DOT agreed with our recommendations. DOT, NTSB, and WMATA provided technical comments that we incorporated as appropriate.

WHAT GAO FOUND

The Department of Transportation's (DOT) Federal Railroad Administration (FRA) and Federal Transit Administration (FTA) carry out different approaches to rail safety oversight. FRA has a more centralized safety oversight program for railroads, while FTA's program for oversight of rail transit safety largely relies on state safety agencies to monitor and enforce rail transit safety, as established in federal statute. Key characteristics of both programs include: (1) safety regulations, (2) inspections and other oversight activities, and (3) enforcement mechanisms to ensure that safety deficiencies are addressed (see figure).

There are strengths and limitations to FRA's and FTA's approaches to their safety oversight missions, including how the two agencies develop safety regulations, conduct inspections, and carry out enforcement. The National Transportation Safety Board has reported, and stakeholders GAO spoke with generally agreed, that strengths of FRA's rail safety oversight program include its safety regulations, its risk-based inspection program, and its enforcement authorities. FRA also has potential limitations in its oversight framework, though, such as difficulty evaluating the effectiveness of its enforcement mechanisms. FTA has made some progress implementing changes to the rail transit safety program. However, FTA has not provided all the necessary guidance and support to states' safety agencies to ensure they develop appropriate and effective rail transit safety inspection programs. In particular, FTA has not provided states with guidance on how to develop and implement risk-based inspection programs. Though FTA has said that it will develop such guidance, it does not have a plan or timeline to do so. Without guidance from FTA on how to develop and carry out risk-based inspections, state safety agencies may not allocate their limited resources efficiently, and important safety issues may go undetected. In addition, FTA has not developed a process or methodology to evaluate whether state safety agency enforcement authorities and practices are effective. Without clear evidence that state safety agencies' enforcement is effective, states and FTA may not be able to compel rail transit operators to remedy safety deficiencies. As a result, deficiencies may remain for long periods, potentially contributing to safety incidents.

March 20, 2018

The Honorable Trey Gowdy
Chairman

The Honorable Elijah E. Cummings
Ranking Member
Committee on Oversight and Government Reform
House of Representatives

The Honorable Mark Meadows
Chairman

The Honorable Gerald E. Connolly
Ranking Member
Subcommittee on Government Operations
Committee on Oversight and Government Reform
House of Representatives

The Honorable Tammy Duckworth
United States Senate

Until recent years, safety oversight of public transportation systems has been largely the responsibility of state entities. In 2012, the Moving Ahead for Progress in the 21st Century Act (MAP-21) provided the United States Department of Transportation (DOT) with additional authority and responsibilities to oversee the safety of the nation's rail public transportation systems.[1] Within DOT, the Federal Transit Administration (FTA) is now implementing this authority.[2] In 2015, the Fixing America's Surface Transportation Act (FAST Act) further enhanced federal safety oversight authority by, among other things, explicitly allowing FTA to assume direct safety oversight of a state's rail transit systems. While federal oversight authority of rail transit safety has recently been expanded, the Federal Railroad Administration (FRA), also in DOT, has long carried out safety oversight of freight, intercity passenger, and commuter railroads in the U.S. that operate on what is known as the general railroad system of transportation (general system).[3]

Following high-profile accidents on the Washington Metropolitan Area Transit Authority (WMATA) Metrorail system in June 2009 and January 2015, FTA assumed temporary direct oversight of WMATA's rail system in October 2015. As a result of its review of a January 2015 WMATA Metrorail accident, the National Transportation Safety Board (NTSB) recommended in that same year that DOT seek legal authority for FRA to assume safety oversight over WMATA's rail system.[4] According to NTSB, which is an independent federal agency that seeks to advance transportation safety primarily through accident investigations, FRA is better suited to providing safety oversight for WMATA's rail system because FRA has uniform safety regulations, an experienced inspection staff, and the ability to assess civil penalties for safety violations. DOT

---

[1] The term "public transportation" is defined as regular, continuing shared-ride surface transportation services that are open to the general public or open to a segment of the general public defined by age, disability, or low income. 49 U.S.C. § 5302(14). This report is specifically concerned with rail fixed guideway public transportation systems, which is defined as any fixed guideway system that uses rail, is operated for public transportation, is within the jurisdiction of a state, and is not subject to the jurisdiction of the Federal Railroad Administration, or any such system in engineering or construction. Throughout this report, we refer to these rail fixed guideway systems as "rail transit."

[2] The additional authority and responsibilities were granted to the Secretary of Transportation, who has delegated them to FTA. Throughout the rest of this report we refer to those authorities as FTA's.

[3] Throughout this report, we refer to freight, intercity passenger, and commuter railroads under the jurisdiction of FRA as "railroads."

[4] NTSB, Safety Recommendation, R-15-31 and -32 (Urgent), September 30, 2015. NTSB officials told us that this recommendation could possibly apply to other rail transit systems given their overall concerns about rail transit safety.

disagreed with NTSB that the most urgent and effective solution was to transfer safety oversight of WMATA's rail system to FRA. The DOT Office of Inspector General (OIG) also issued a report in 2016 about FTA's challenges in carrying out its enhanced safety oversight, including challenges addressing its safety oversight personnel and resource needs and establishing robust safety performance criteria and enforceable standards.[5] We have also reported that FRA has faced its own challenges in recent years, such as ensuring that it has enough inspectors for its safety oversight workload.[6]

In light of these issues and NTSB's recommendation, you asked us to review various safety and oversight issues at WMATA Metrorail and FTA, as well as differences between FRA's and FTA's rail safety oversight programs. In consultation with your office and to assist efforts to ensure effective rail transit safety oversight of WMATA and other rail transit providers, we focused this review on examining (1) key characteristics of FRA's and FTA's rail safety oversight programs and (2) strengths and limitations of FRA's and FTA's rail safety oversight programs.

In addressing the research objectives, we focused on three characteristics of DOT's rail safety oversight, as implemented by FRA and FTA: (1) developing safety regulations, (2) conducting inspections and oversight, and (3) using enforcement mechanisms. We focused on these aspects of rail safety oversight because they are the areas highlighted by NTSB as strengths of FRA's safety oversight program.

To address our research objectives, we gathered information about FRA's and FTA's rail safety oversight activities and assessed it against guidance and leading practices. We reviewed recent statutes that establish DOT's rail safety oversight authority as well as applicable implementing regulations. We also reviewed FRA's and FTA's documentation regarding safety oversight policies and practices. We also interviewed officials from FRA and FTA about their rail safety oversight activities. We assessed the

---

[5] DOT OIG, *Improvements in FTA's Safety Oversight Policies and Procedures Could Strength Program Implementation and Address Persistent Challenges*, ST-2017-004 (Washington, D.C.: Nov. 2, 2016).

[6] GAO, *Rail Safety: Improved Human Capital Planning Could Address Emerging Safety Oversight Challenges*, GAO-14-85 (Washington, D.C.: Dec. 9, 2013).

information on safety regulations gathered from agency documents and interviews against official federal government guidance, issued by the Office of Management and Budget (OMB), about the development of federal regulations.[7] We also assessed the information gathered from agency documents and interviews about inspections against leading practices developed by the Organisation for Economic Co-operation and Development (OECD)[8] and the Transportation Research Board's Transit Cooperative Research Program (TCRP).[9] For the OECD, which has played a leading role in the international community to promote regulatory reform and the implementation of sound regulatory practices, we identified reports specifically about regulatory enforcement and inspections. For the TCRP, which serves as one of the principal means by which the transit industry can develop innovative near-term solutions, we identified the reports specifically about rail safety and rail oversight. We also assessed the information gathered from agency documents and interviews about inspections and enforcement against federal internal control standards about risk assessments as well as agency information and communication.[10]

To further examine FRA and FTA rail safety oversight activities, we identified and summarized the strengths and limitations of FRA's and FTA's current safety oversight programs as identified in past studies. Specifically, we assessed the findings from our past work[11] as well as from DOT OIG[12] and NTSB reports.[13]

---

[7] OMB, Circular A-119: Federal Participation in the Development and Use of Voluntary Consensus Standards and in Conformity Assessment Activities (Washington, D.C.: Jan. 27, 2016). OMB, Circular A-4: Regulatory Analysis (Washington, D.C.: Sept. 17, 2003). We also examined the guidance provided about using performance-based regulations in Executive Order 12866 of September 30, 1993.

[8] OECD, Best Practice Principles for Regulatory Policy: Regulatory Enforcement and Inspections (Paris: OECD Publishing, 2014).

[9] TCRP, Report 149: Improving Safety-Related Rules Compliance in the Public Transportation Industry (Washington, D.C.: 2011). TCRP, Report 174: Improving Safety Culture in Public Transportation (Washington, D.C.: 2015).

[10] GAO, *Standards for Internal Control in the Federal Government*, GAO-14-704G (Washington, D.C.: September 2014).

[11] GAO, *Rail Transit: Additional Federal Leadership Would Enhance FTA's State Safety Oversight Program*, GAO-06-821 (Washington, D.C.: July 26, 2006); GAO, *Rail Safety: The Federal Railroad Administration Is Taking Steps to Better Target Its Oversight, but*

To further examine FRA's safety oversight activities specifically, we assessed the statistical model used as part of FRA's National Inspection Plan. The National Inspection Plan uses safety risk information, including as part of a quantitative model, to help target FRA inspection resources to areas of higher risk. We assessed the model based on FRA documentation and interviews with FRA officials as well as findings from our previous work.[14]

Finally, we interviewed a variety of stakeholders, including rail operators and organizations, about the strengths and limitations of FRA's and FTA's rail safety oversight activities.[15] Specifically, we interviewed railroad officials from Amtrak, BNSF Railway, Long Island Rail Road, Metro-North Commuter Railroad, New Jersey Transit, Port Authority Trans Hudson, and Union Pacific Railroad. We also interviewed rail transit officials from Dallas Area Rapid Transit, Los Angeles County Metropolitan Transportation Authority, New York City Transit, San Francisco Municipal Railway, and WMATA. We selected these railroads

---

Assessment of Results Is Needed to Determine Impact, GAO-07-149 (Washington, D.C.: Jan. 26, 2007); and GAO-14-85.

[12] DOT OIG, *Challenges to Improving Oversight of Rail Transit Safety and Implementing an Enhanced Federal Role, MH-2012-048* (Washington, D.C.: Jan. 31, 2012). DOT OIG, *FRA is Nearing Completion of Rules required by the Rail Safety Improvement Act, but Needs to Improve Oversight*, CR-2013-070 (Washington, D.C.: Apr. 17, 2013). DOT OIG, ST-2017-004.

[13] NTSB, *Organizational Factors in Metro-North Railroad Accidents*, Special Investigation Report NTSB/SIR-14/04 (Washington, D.C.: Nov. 19, 2014). NTSB, *Derailment of Amtrak Passenger Train 188, Philadelphia, Pennsylvania, May 12, 2015*, Accident Report NTSB/RAR-16/02 (Washington, D.C.: May 17, 2016). NTSB, *Washington Metropolitan Area Transit Authority L'Enfant Plaza Station Electrical Arcing and Smoke Accident, Washington, D.C., January 12, 2015*, Accident Report NTSB/RAR-16/01 (Washington, D.C.: May 3, 2016). NTSB, *Safety Recommendation Report: Rail Transit Vehicle Safe Braking*, Recommendation No.: R-17-04 (Washington, D.C., May 1, 2017).

[14] See in particular the discussion of statistical modeling in GAO, *Motor Carriers: Better Information Needed to Assess Effectiveness and Efficiency of Safety Interventions*, GAO-17-49 (Washington, D.C.: Oct. 27, 2016); GAO, *Drinking Water: Additional Data and Statistical Analysis May Enhance EPA's Oversight of the Lead and Copper Rule*, GAO-17-424 (Washington, D.C.: Sept. 1, 2017); and GAO, *Agricultural Conservation: USDA Should Improve Its Process for Allocating Funds to States for the Environmental Quality Incentives Program*, GAO-06-969 (Washington, D.C.: Sept. 22, 2006).

[15] Throughout this report, we refer to both rail transit entities and railroads collectively as "rail operators."

and rail transit operators based on their modes of operation,[16] systems' size and age, and geographic location. Though we believe these railroads and rail transit operators provided relevant and diverse perspectives on rail safety oversight, the information gathered from these entities is not generalizable to all rail operators. To further understand and assess rail transit safety oversight specifically, we also interviewed officials from state safety agencies that oversee the rail transit operators interviewed. Finally, we interviewed officials from stakeholder organizations, including the Association of American Railroads, American Association of State Highway and Transportation Officials, American Federation of Labor and Congress of Industrial Organizations, American Public Transportation Association, and National Association of Railroad Passengers.

We conducted this performance audit from April 2017 to March 2018 in accordance with generally accepted government auditing standards. Those standards require that we plan and perform the audit to obtain sufficient, appropriate evidence to provide a reasonable basis for our findings and conclusions based on our audit objectives. We believe that the evidence obtained provides a reasonable basis for our findings and conclusions based on our audit objectives.

BACKGROUND

In the United States, both FRA and FTA regulate rail transportation safety. FRA oversees safety of railroads operating on what is known as the general system, a network of standard gage track over which goods may be transported and passengers may travel. This system includes freight railroads, which typically own their own tracks and locomotives, transporting products among states and regions. FRA also oversees safety of intercity passenger and commuter railroads that operate over tracks owned by freight railroads and other entities. FTA oversees safety of rail transit systems that typically serve individual metropolitan areas, using

[16] Among railroads, we selected entities operating freight or passenger service. Among rail transit, we selected entities operating heavy rail, light rail, and cable cars.

track not shared with freight and other passenger trains. Rail transit includes a variety of modes, such as heavy and light rail,[17] streetcars,[18] automated guideways,[19] cable cars,[20] and others.

Rail Transit

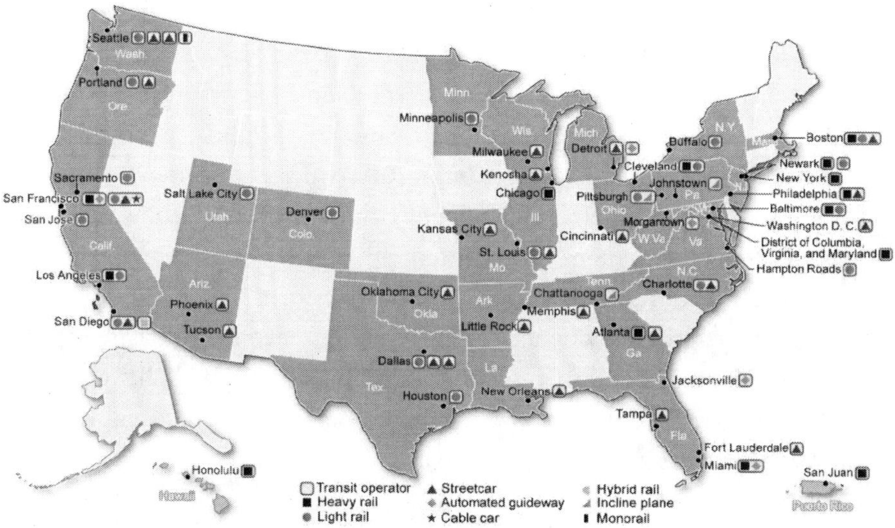

Source: GAO analysis and Map Resources. | GAO-18-310.

Figure 1. Rail Transit Systems Overseen by State Safety Agencies.

---

[17] "Heavy rail" is a transit mode that uses an electric railway with the capacity for a heavy volume of traffic. It is characterized by high speed and rapid acceleration passenger rail cars operating singly or in multi-car trains, on fixed rails, and usually a separate rights-of-way from which all other vehicular and foot traffic are excluded. "Light rail" is a transit mode that typically uses an electric railway with a light volume traffic capacity compared to heavy rail. It is characterized by rail cars operating singly (or in short trains) on fixed rails in shared or exclusive right-of-way.

[18] Streetcars are a transit mode operating entire routes predominantly on streets in mixed-traffic. This service typically operates with single-car trains powered by overhead wires or cables providing electrical power.

[19] Automated guideways are an electrically-powered mode of transit operating in an exclusive guideway or over relatively short distances. The service is characterized by either monorail systems with human-operated vehicles straddling a single guideway or by people-mover systems with automated operation.

[20] Cable cars are a transit mode that is an electric railway with individually controlled transit vehicles attached to a moving cable located below the street surface and powered by engines or motors not onboard the vehicle.

Rail transit is an important component of the nation's transportation network, particularly in large metropolitan areas. Rail transit systems provided over 4.4 billion passenger trips in 2016. "Heavy rail" systems in large cities account for much of the total rail transit activity, including 88 percent of passenger trips in 2016. According to FTA, 61 rail transit systems within 28 states, the District of Columbia, and Puerto Rico are subject to safety oversight by one of the 31 agencies in FTA's state safety oversight program (see fig. 1).

The states have long played a central role in conducting safety oversight of rail transit systems.[21] The Intermodal Surface Transportation Efficiency Act of 1991 required, among other things, that states with rail transit operators designate an agency to oversee the safety of those systems, known as a state safety oversight agency.[22] In overseeing state safety agencies, FTA designed the program as one in which FTA, states, and rail transit operators collaborate to ensure the safety and security of rail transit systems.

However, limitations have been identified in the state safety oversight program. In 2006, we reported on some state safety agency challenges in overseeing rail transit safety.[23] Specifically, we found many of the state safety agencies lacked enough qualified staff and adequate levels of training to meet their responsibilities. In a 2009 hearing before the Subcommittee on Highways and Transit of the House Committee on Transportation and Infrastructure, then Secretary Ray LaHood of the Department of Transportation discussed some of the weaknesses under the current state safety oversight program and introduced a public transportation safety legislative proposal.

---

[21] According to FTA, from the inception of the U.S. DOT's federal financial assistance program for state and local agencies until the enactment of MAP-21, FTA and its predecessor agency, the Urban Mass Transportation Administration, were prohibited from regulating any aspect of the day-to-day operations of grant recipients, including establishing national mandatory standards for transit safety.

[22] Pub. L. No. 102-240, § 3029, 105 Stat. 1914, 2116 (Dec. 18, 1991) (codified as amended at 49 U.S.C. § 5330). Throughout this report we refer to state safety oversight agencies as "state safety agencies."

[23] GAO-06-821.

In 2010, various bills were introduced in both houses of Congress that would have provided FTA with various enforcement mechanisms and with the authority to issue safety regulations. Additionally, the bills would have required the Secretary to establish a federal certification program for employees and contractors who carry out a state public transportation safety program. In the 112th Congress, the Senate amended a House bill to include a public transportation safety provision, which eventually became section 20021 of MAP-21, the federal public transportation safety program.

MAP-21 enhanced FTA's authority to oversee the safety of rail transit, potentially addressing some of the weaknesses identified by various stakeholders. Specifically, MAP-21 established a comprehensive Public Transportation Safety Program,[24] which continues to rely on state safety agencies to monitor rail transit systems' safety operations. MAP-21 required that, within 3 years of the effective date of a final state safety oversight program rule,[25] each eligible state have in place a state safety oversight program certified by FTA.[26] An eligible state must, among other things, establish a state safety agency and determine, in consultation with FTA, an appropriate staffing level for this state agency that is commensurate with the number, size, and complexity of the rail transit systems within the state.

---

[24] Pub. L. No. 112-141, § 20021, 126 Stat. 405, 709 (July 6, 2012). The Public Transportation Safety Program is comprised of five main elements—(1) a national public transportation safety plan; (2) a safety certification training program for federal, state, and local transportation agency employees with safety oversight responsibilities; (3) public transportation agency safety plans; (4) a strengthened state safety oversight program for rail transit; and (5) a new framework for federal oversight and enforcement. *See* 49 U.S.C. § 5329.

[25] FTA issued the final state safety oversight rule on March 16, 2016, with an effective date of April 15, 2016. 81 Fed. Reg. 14,230 (Mar. 16, 2016) (codified at 49 C.F.R. pt. 674).

[26] An eligible state is one that has a rail transit system within the jurisdiction of the state that is not subject to regulation by the FRA, or a rail transit system in the engineering or construction phase of development within the jurisdiction of the state that will not be subject to regulation by FRA.

Additionally, a state safety agency must be financially and legally independent from any rail transit system it oversees and have investigative and enforcement authority with respect to the safety for its rail transit systems, among other things. Each eligible state has until April 15, 2019, to receive FTA approval of its state safety oversight program, or else FTA will be prohibited from obligating certain federal financial assistance to any entity in the state that is otherwise eligible to receive that federal financial assistance.[27]

After that approval, state safety agencies will be evaluated for continued compliance with FTA regulations a minimum of once every 3 years through a triennial review process. According to FTA, these requirements represent a dramatic increase in federal expectations for state safety oversight and for the rail transit industry. MAP-21 also established a state safety oversight grant program, offering federal funding to states for their state safety activities. FTA's Office of Transit Safety and Oversight administers the state safety oversight program.

Railroads

Freight and passenger railroads have played a transformational role in the development of America and continue to be an important part of the economy. The general railroad system consists of a vast network of operations (see fig. 2). The $60 billion freight rail industry is operated by seven Class I, and hundreds of smaller, railroads.[28] In addition, about 40 railroads move passengers, which carry greater than 670 million passengers per year.

[27] Four of the 31 state safety oversight programs have been certified as of February 22, 2018.

[28] Railroads are classified based on their annual carrier operating revenues. According to the Surface Transportation Board, Class I railroads are the largest, with annual carrier operating revenue of about $447 million or more.

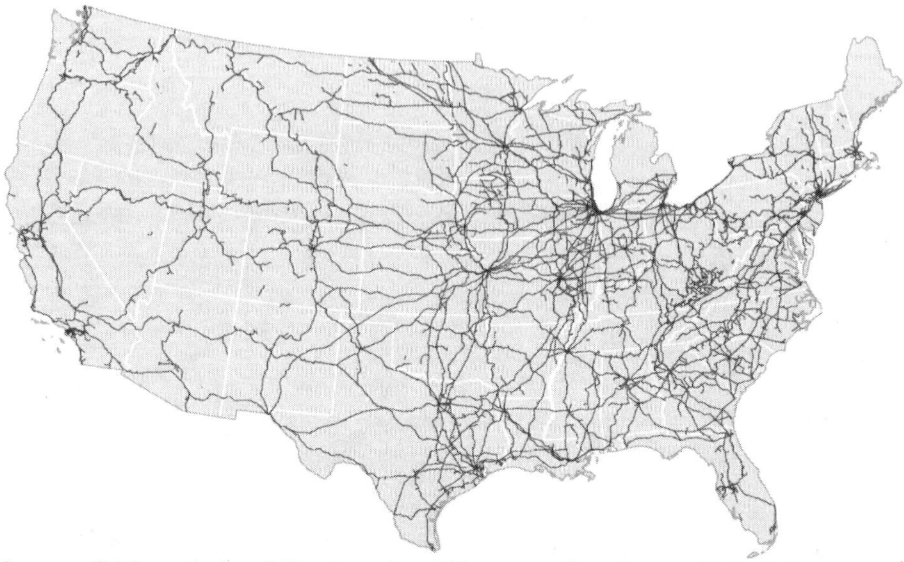

Source: GAO analysis of Department of Transportation data and MapInfo (map). | GAO-18-310.

Figure 2. United States General Railroad System.

The federal government has long provided regulatory oversight of railroad safety, both passenger and freight, that operate on the general system. The Interstate Commerce Commission, the first federal regulatory commission in U.S. history, was established in 1887 to regulate interstate commerce by rail.[29] The Commission's safety functions were transferred to FRA, which was created by the Department of Transportation Act in 1966. In its role as federal regulator and overseer of railroad safety, FRA prescribes and enforces railroad safety regulations and conducts research and development in support of improved railroad safety and rail transportation policy. FRA utilizes safety inspectors and specialists, primarily covering five safety disciplines, to review and enforce compliance with these regulations. FRA's safety disciplines are track, signal, and train control; motive power and equipment; operating practices; and hazardous materials.

[29] U.S. Senate Historical Office.

Following several fatal rail accidents between 2002 and 2008, the Rail Safety Improvement Act of 2008 was enacted, the first authorization of FRA's safety programs since 1994. This act directed FRA to, among other things, issue new safety regulations for different aspects of railroad safety, such as hours of service requirements for passenger railroad workers, positive train control implementation,[30] track inspection rules, and safety at highway-rail grade crossings. FRA's Office of Railroad Safety administers the agency's safety program.

Rail Accidents and Incidents

Rail transportation is a relatively safe way to transport people and products though serious incidents continue to occur on railroads and rail transit. According to an analysis of DOT's Bureau of Transportation Statistics data by the American Public Transportation Association, travel by rail transit is far safer than automobile travel.[31] From 2000-2014, for instance, there were 6.53 and 0.33 fatalities per billion passenger-miles traveled in cars or light trucks and rail transit, respectively. Within rail travel, the fatality rates on both railroads and rail transit operators have remained similar in recent years. Further, the rate of accidents and incidents—including collisions and derailments—also do not appear to differ substantially between railroads and rail transit in recent years.[32]

---

[30] Positive train control is a communications-based system designed to prevent certain types of rail accidents caused by human factors, including train-to-train collisions, trains entering established work zones—which could cause roadway worker casualties or equipment damage—and derailments caused by exceeding safe speeds. For example, positive train control can automatically slow or stop a train that is not being operated safely due to operator errors.

[31] American Public Transportation Association, *The Hidden Traffic Safety Solution: Public Transportation*, September 2016.

[32] See FRA, Ten Year Accident / Incident Oversight safety data, and FTA, National Transit Database, Safety and Security Time Series Data. Railroad accidents here include train accidents and highway-rail crossing incidents, as well as other accidents or incidents that cause physical harm to persons. Train accidents include railroad track, equipment and/or structures that have sustained damage in excess of FRA's accident reporting threshold. A highway-rail grade crossing incident typically involves on-track railroad equipment striking a highway user or a highway user striking on-track equipment at a highway-rail crossing.

Nevertheless, serious incidents continue to occur on railroads and rail transit, posing safety risks to passengers, railroad employees, and the public. For example, in June 2009, two WMATA trains collided, resulting in 52 injuries and 9 deaths. A smoke incident on WMATA's Metrorail system in January 2015 also resulted in the death of 1 person and injured over 90. In a 10-month period from May 2013 to March 2014, the Metro-North commuter railroad, which serves New York and Connecticut, was involved in five accidents that resulted in the death of 6 people and 126 injured. In June 2016, two BNSF Railway freight trains collided near Panhandle, Texas, resulting in the death of three crew members. Incidents such as these have prompted investigations into both the causes and contributing factors of the specific accidents as well as broader rail safety oversight.

FRA Has a Centralized Safety Oversight Framework While FTA Is Implementing a State-Based Approach

FRA has a more centralized safety oversight program for railroads, while FTA is implementing changes to the rail transit oversight program, established in federal statute, which relies on states to monitor and enforce safety. Key characteristics of both programs include: (1) the establishment of safety regulations,[33] (2) inspections and other oversight activities, such as audits and investigations, based on those regulations, and (3)

Rail transit accidents here include collisions (with motor vehicles, people, fixed objects, rail vehicles, bus vehicles, and other items), train derailments, and fires.

[33] We define "regulations" in this report as agencies' statements of general applicability and future effect, which establish legally binding requirements for regulated entities and are codified in the Code of Federal Regulations (CFR). In the context of FRA and FTA rail safety oversight, we refer to "safety regulations" as mandatory minimum safety performance requirements for regulated entities. We define "standard" in this report as conditions, guidelines, or characteristics of industry policies and practices that do not have the force and effect of law.

enforcement mechanisms to ensure that safety deficiencies are addressed (see fig. 3).

Agency		Safety regulations	Oversight activities	Enforcement mechanisms
FRA	Current status	Has extensive regulations covering various aspects of railroad industry	Conducts safety compliance inspections and investigations	Utilizes a variety of tools, including civil penalties, to resolve safety issues
	Future plans	Update existing regulations	Continue to use and update risk-based model to guide inspections	Enhance effectiveness of tools to improve safety, including increased penalties
Federal Transit Administration	Current status	Has regulations implementing statutory changes to safety program	Relies on states to conduct safety oversight activities, though it now has inspection authorities	Relies on state safety agencies to enforce safety and monitors these agencies for compliance
	Future plans	Assess specific areas to determine need for safety regulations	Recommend that state safety agencies develop risk-based inspection programs	Require that state safety agencies develop stronger enforcement mechanisms

Source: GAO analysis of FRA and FTA information. | GAO-18-310.

Figure 3. Key Characteristics of the Federal Railroad Administration's (FRA) and Federal Transit Administration's (FTA) Rail Safety Oversight Programs.

Safety Regulations

FRA has developed extensive railroad safety regulations over decades. FRA's railroad safety regulations include requirements governing track design and inspection, grade crossings, signal and train control, mechanical equipment including locomotives, and railroad-operating practices including worker protection rules. For example, FRA's regulations for track and equipment include detailed, prescriptive minimum requirements, such as formulas that determine the maximum allowable speeds on curved track. Many of FRA's rail safety regulations establish minimum safety requirements, though railroads can apply for waivers.[34]

As FRA updates its safety regulations, it has proposed more performance-based regulations in recent years. Many of FRA's current safety regulations specify the behavior or manner of compliance that railroads must adopt, such as inspecting each locomotive at least every 92 days. Performance-based regulations, however, specify a desired outcome

[34] Waiver petitions generally seek an exception from compliance with an FRA regulation that the petitioner believes is unnecessary or excessively burdensome under the specific circumstances (sometimes because the petitioners' practices exceed the regulatory requirements, according to FRA officials). Although certain statutorily mandated requirements cannot be waived, FRA may generally issue a waiver when it is in the public interest and consistent with railroad safety.

rather than a behavior or manner of compliance. For example, FRA's recent rulemaking to amend its passenger equipment safety regulations proposes performance-based crashworthiness and occupant protection requirements, rather than explicit targets or tolerances.[35] According to FRA, establishing performance requirements in these areas would allow a more open rail market that incorporates recent technologies.

FTA is currently assessing the need for rail transit safety regulations, having been provided the authority to issue safety regulations in 2012.[36] Since MAP-21 was enacted, FTA has finalized regulations implementing the public transportation safety program authorized by statute. These include regulations that establish rules for FTA's administration of a comprehensive safety program to improve rail transit safety as well as updated regulations governing state safety oversight of rail transit.[37] In addition to its public transportation safety program regulations, FTA also has regulations governing its drug and alcohol testing program.[38] MAP-21 also authorized FTA, for the first time, to issue rail transit safety regulations, which would establish minimum safety performance requirements for rail transit operators, as part of its requirement to develop a National Public Transportation Safety Plan.[39] FTA initiated a regulatory development effort after the passage of MAP-21, which included a

---

[35] Passenger Equipment Safety Standards; Standards for Alternative Compliance and High-Speed Trainsets, 81 Fed. Reg. 88006 (Dec. 6, 2016).

[36] According to FTA, the agency and its predecessor agency, the Urban Mass Transportation Administration, were previously prohibited from regulating any aspect of the day-to-day operations of grant recipients, including establishing national mandatory standards for transit safety. However, according to FTA, it has been responsible for monitoring the many state agencies that exercised direct safety oversight of rail transit operations, and providing technical assistance to those state agencies.

[37] See 49 C.F.R. pts. 670 and 674.

[38] See 49 C.F.R. pt. 655. The purpose of this part is to establish programs to be implemented by employers that receive financial assistance from FTA, and by contractors of those employers, that are designed to help prevent accidents, injuries, and fatalities resulting from the misuse of alcohol and use of prohibited drugs by employees who perform safety-sensitive functions.

[39] FTA issued the final National Public Transportation Safety Plan in January 2017. 82 Fed. Reg. 5628 (Jan. 18, 2017). According to FTA, it will periodically issue a National Public Transportation Safety Plan to improve the safety of all public transportation systems that receive funding under Chapter 53 of Title 49 of the U.S. Code. The National Public Transportation Safety Plan includes, among other things, safety performance criteria, voluntary minimum safety performance standards for vehicles in revenue operations, safety advisories, and best practices.

compilation and evaluation of existing transit safety standards, guidance, and best practices from the federal government, states, industry, and other sources. After the evaluation, FTA issued a report that concluded there was limited documentation or evidence of the effectiveness of these existing rail transit safety standards.[40] The report included recommendations that are intended to enable FTA to undertake further data-driven, risk-based analysis of rail transit safety performance and the applicability and effectiveness of the identified safety standards. FTA is also currently analyzing specific focus areas to determine any areas that should be addressed by federal safety regulations. For example, FTA is studying the need for regulations related to rail transit vehicle crashworthiness.

Since no federal rail transit safety regulations that establish minimum safety performance requirements for rail transit operators currently exist, rail transit operators are subject to different safety standards,[41] depending largely on what voluntary standards they have chosen to adopt, according to American Public Transportation Association officials we spoke with.[42] The American Public Transportation Association, for instance, has issued a variety of rail transit safety standards, addressing various aspects of the industry including operations, training, and inspections. In addition, states vary in the extent to which they have regulations for rail transit operators. For example, officials from the California Public Utilities Commission noted that it has issued a variety of safety regulations applicable to rail transit operators within the state of California to improve safety of rail operations.

Both FRA and FTA have mechanisms to gather the input of stakeholders—including rail operators, labor unions, industry associations, and others—when considering development of safety regulations. In developing most of its safety regulations, FRA seeks input from stakeholders through its Railroad Safety Advisory Committee. In 1996,

---

[40] FTA, *Review and Evaluation of Public Transportation Safety Standards*, FTA Report No. 0103, Prepared by Center for Urban Transportation Research, January 2017.

[41] According to FTA, its regulations on the prevention of alcohol misuse and prohibited drug use in transit operations can be considered "safety regulations. *See* 49 C.F.R. pt. 655.

[42] Industry standards also exist for railroads, developed by such organizations as the Association of American Railroads.

FRA established this committee to develop new regulations through a collaborative process, with the rail community working together to create mutually satisfactory solutions to safety issues. FTA is collaborating with stakeholders as it assesses the need for rail transit safety regulations. More specifically, FTA's research partner, the Center for Urban Transportation Research, established a working group to collaborate with industry stakeholders to inform the safety regulations development process. FTA also solicited comments from industry stakeholders on its compilation of existing rail transit safety standards. More broadly, FTA also has a Transit Advisory Committee for Safety, which provides information, advice, and recommendations to FTA on safety matters.

Oversight Activities

FRA fulfills its mission, in part, through safety compliance audits and inspections, and investigations. FRA ensures compliance with its safety regulations through inspections, using a staff of railroad safety experts, inspectors, and other professionals assigned to eight regional offices across the nation. For example, to determine a railroad's compliance with FRA safety regulations, inspectors examine track, equipment, signal devices, employee actions, and procedures and review maintenance and accident records. Additionally, 31 states have rail safety programs that partner with FRA.[43] Under this approach, FRA enters into agreements with states to allow state inspectors to participate in investigative and surveillance activities concerning federal railroad safety laws. State inspectors who participate in this program submit inspection reports to FRA. More broadly, FRA's inspections are guided by a risk-based model.[44] Under this

---

[43] *See* 49 U.S.C. § 20105; 49 C.F.R. pt. 212.

[44] FRA's risk-based model is a risk assessment tool, which we have defined as a process of qualitatively or quantitatively determining the probability of an adverse event and the severity of its impact on an asset. It is a function of threat, vulnerability, and consequence. A risk assessment provides the basis for the rank ordering of risks (in FRA's situation, railroad accidents) and for establishing priorities for applying countermeasures (in FRA's situation, safety inspections). See GAO, *Risk Management: Further Refinements Needed to*

approach, FRA focuses its inspections on locations that, according to the data-driven model, are likely to have safety problems. Like other operating administrations within DOT, FRA has relatively few resources for overseeing railroads, compared with the size of the general system. The risk-based model is designed to help FRA target the greatest safety risks. FRA has begun utilizing automated inspections as well. In particular, according to FRA, new imaging technologies have the potential to better inspect track for cracks in the rail that could lead to breakage as well as measure the track's geometry to ensure that rails are positioned to meet standards. To further promote safety in railroad operations, FRA conducts accident investigations. Separate from investigations conducted by NTSB, FRA investigates select railroad accidents to determine root causation, and any contributing factors, so that railroad properties can implement corrective actions to prevent similar incidents in the future.

Resources for railroad safety oversight activities have increased in recent years. FRA was appropriated about $218 million in fiscal year 2017, an increase over the approximately $187 million it received in fiscal year 2015, for safety and operations, which funds FRA's personnel, including inspectors, and safety programs. According to FRA, Congress provided FRA with increased funding in recent years for the purpose of increasing staffing related to specific safety issues, such as trespasser prevention and passenger rail safety.[45] As part of this effort, FRA has hired additional inspectors, going from 347 inspectors in fiscal year 2013 to over 360 currently, out of the nearly 930 total full-time equivalent staff. FRA officials told us, as we have reported in the past,[46] that it can be difficult to recruit, train, and certify qualified inspectors in a timely manner, especially in certain areas of expertise. Further, according to FRA, its inspectors have the ability to inspect less than 1 percent of the general system annually.

Though FTA now has more robust inspection authorities, states will continue to conduct front-line rail transit safety oversight activities. MAP-

---

Assess Risks and Prioritize Protective Measures at Ports and Other Critical Infrastructure, GAO-06-91 (Washington, D.C.: Dec. 15, 2005).

[45] FRA, Budget Estimates, Fiscal Year 2018.

[46] GAO-14-85.

21 provided FTA with new authorities to inspect, audit, and investigate practices at rail transit agencies, including safety practices, while also preserving the role of state safety agencies to monitor rail transit systems' safety operations. According to FTA officials, any federal inspections of rail transit operators are intended to supplement a state safety agency's oversight activities, except where FTA assumes temporary, direct oversight of a rail transit system from an inadequate state safety agency. FTA officials told us that establishing a nationwide safety inspection program at the federal level is inconsistent with the statutory framework of the state safety oversight program and with congressional intent, which contemplates preserving the primary role of state safety agencies in providing direct safety oversight of rail transit systems. The officials also noted that the state-based approach to rail transit safety oversight is valuable because states are generally closer to, and more familiar with, rail transit operators. To date, FTA has utilized its new inspection authorities only on WMATA's rail system.[47] As part of oversight activities, some state safety agencies have conducted inspections of the rail transit systems they oversee, though they were not required to do so, according to FTA officials we spoke with. To strengthen states' abilities to conduct oversight activities, FTA has recommended that state safety agencies develop risk-based inspection programs. Further, to ensure the independence of state safety agencies, these agencies cannot receive funding from the rail transit entities they oversee.[48]

Resources for FTA's rail transit safety oversight administrative expenses have remained relatively stable in recent years, though more are needed, according to FTA. Since fiscal year 2012, FTA's appropriations for administrative expenses, which funds FTA personnel and support

[47] FTA has conducted many inspections of the WMATA rail system's track infrastructure and internal inspection program to inform their direct oversight of the rail system.

[48] U.S.C. § 5329(e)(4)(A)(i). As noted above, FTA has also implemented a grant program, established in MAP-21, which provides funding for state safety oversight programs. Lack of resources, and independence from the entities they oversee, have historically been weaknesses of state safety oversight, according to stakeholders we spoke with. Two state safety agencies we spoke with said that they are using the new grant funds to hire inspectors, though similar to FRA, they noted that it can be difficult to recruit and retain qualified inspectors given the demand for these employees and the pay they are able to offer.

activities including the Office of Transit Safety and Oversight, has increased $14 million, to about $113 million in fiscal year 2017, according to FTA. However, for several years, FTA has averaged about 508 total full-time equivalent staff agency-wide, and a little over 30 safety staff in the Office of Transit Safety and Oversight. According to FTA, the Office of Transit Safety and Oversight has been under-resourced since it was established in response to new safety authority provided in MAP-21.[49] For fiscal year 2018, FTA requested in their submission for the President's Budget proposal funding to hire up to an additional 20 positions for various lines of safety work.

FRA's and FTA's oversight activities also include regular audits of, and communication with, the rail operators under their oversight.[50] Given finite resources and large rail networks, FRA and FTA audit rail operators' own inspections rather than conducting comprehensive federal inspections. More specifically, FRA inspectors, and state safety agencies in FTA's oversight program, regularly examine records of rail operators' internal inspections to identify safety deficiencies.[51] Officials from FRA, FTA, and five rail stakeholders we spoke with told us that FRA and FTA rail safety oversight programs also rely on collaboration and communication between rail operators and regulators to ensure safety. For example, regular meetings between FRA and railroad staff to discuss safety trends and industry developments are important to ensuring safety, according to officials we spoke with from FRA and the railroads. FRA specialists and inspectors participate, with representatives of railroad labor and management, in the implementation of voluntary safety programs. For example, FRA sponsors the Confidential Close Call Reporting System, a voluntary, confidential program allowing railroads and their employees to report accident and incident "close calls." According to FRA officials, voluntary programs such as this increase industry awareness of railroad

[49] FTA, Budget Estimates, Fiscal Year 2018.

[50] FTA officials emphasized to us that while FRA directly audits and communicates with the railroads it oversees, under FTA's program, FTA will generally oversee the state safety agencies and the state safety agencies will directly oversee the rail transit operators.

[51] According to FRA, it also routinely conducts focused, comprehensive inspections on particular safety issues involving individual railroads.

safety and engagement with it. FTA also collaborates with state safety agencies as rail transit safety issues arise, according to FTA officials, using federal oversight and enforcement authorities as a "back-stop" against the oversight of state safety agencies. Additionally, according to officials we spoke with from FTA and two rail transit operators, state safety agency staff meet with rail transit operators regularly, using knowledge of local operating conditions to help ensure safety.

Enforcement Mechanisms

FRA uses a variety of tools, including civil penalties, to resolve safety issues. While some safety issues are resolved informally through discussion and collaboration between FRA and railroads, as noted above, some defects identified during inspections are classified as violations and subject to financial penalties. More specifically, when railroads do not resolve issues in a timely manner or identified defects are serious, FRA has the authority to cite violations and assess civil penalties, against either railroads or individuals. Further, as authorized by law, FRA negotiates settlements with railroads and other entities subject to its safety jurisdiction to resolve claims for civil penalties.[52] In fiscal year 2016, FRA assessed over $11.8 million in civil penalties against railroads.

According to FRA, fiscal year 2016 was the second year in a row that it took steps to increase penalty amounts paid by railroads, as part of a continued effort to increase consequences for violations that negatively affect safety.[53]

To ensure the safety of rail transit systems, states will continue to be the primary enforcers of safety requirements, according to FTA officials, though FTA now has more enforcement tools. MAP-21 preserved the role of state safety agencies as the primary enforcement body for rail transit. FTA has now required that state safety agencies have enforcement authorities sufficient to compel action from rail transit entities to address

---

[52] 49 U.S.C. §§ 20111(a)(1), 21301(a)(3), 21302(a)(3), 21303(a)(3).

[53] FRA, Fiscal Year 2016 Enforcement Report.

safety deficiencies. Though no specific authorities are required, FTA has suggested that a variety of mechanisms could be appropriate, such as the ability to remove deficient equipment from service or assess fines. According to FTA, this requirement is designed to overcome a long-standing vulnerability in state safety oversight, which allowed safety deficiencies to remain for long periods of time. MAP-21 and the FAST Act also provided FTA with more options for enforcement when rail transit operators are found to be out of compliance with safety requirements. In particular, FTA can withhold federal funding for rail transit operators or direct a rail transit operator to use federal funding for a specific purpose.[54] Additionally, after FTA assumes temporary direct oversight of an inadequate state safety agency, FTA can withhold federal funds from the state until the state safety oversight program has been certified.[55] To date, FTA has utilized this authority only with the states responsible for safety oversight of WMATA's rail system. In February 2017, FTA announced that it would withhold 5 percent of fiscal year 2017 urbanized area formula funds from Maryland, Virginia, and the District of Columbia until a new state safety oversight program is certified for WMATA's rail system.[56] This action built upon FTA's determination that WMATA's state safety agency was ineffective at "providing adequate oversight consistent with prevention of substantial risk of death or personal injury."[57]

FRA and FTA also have the authority to directly intervene in rail operations. In particular, both FRA and FTA can suspend the service of rail operators in response to certain safety concerns.[58] Additionally, FTA can assume direct safety oversight of a rail transit operator if FTA determines

---

[54] 49 U.S.C. § 5329(g)(1)(D), (E).

[55] 49 U.S.C. § 5329(e)(8)(C)(ii).

[56] Letter from FTA Governor Hogan, Governor McAuliffe, and Mayor Bowser (Feb. 10, 2017).

[57] Letter from FTA Governor Hogan, Governor McAuliffe, and Mayor Bowser (Feb. 10, 2017).

[58] FRA's emergency order authority allows it, upon finding the existence of an unsafe condition or practice (or combination thereof) causing an emergency situation involving a hazard of death, personal injury, or significant harm to the environment, to order railroads to take immediate action to abate the emergency situation. Similarly, FTA's authority permits it to issue restrictions and prohibitions upon finding the existence of an unsafe condition or practice (or combination thereof) such that there is a substantial risk of death or personal injury.

the state safety oversight program is not adequate, among other things.[59] In response to safety incidents on WMATA's rail system, FTA assumed temporary and direct safety oversight of WMATA in October 2015, as previously noted.[60]

FRA's and FTA's Approaches to Rail Safety Oversight Have Strengths and Limitations, and FTA Can Improve Implementation of Its New Authorities

FRA and FTA's approaches to their rail safety oversight missions each have strengths and limitations, including how the agencies develop safety regulations, conduct inspections, and carry out enforcement. Compared to FRA's long-standing role in providing safety oversight over railroads, FTA is in the process of implementing significant changes to its program for rail transit safety oversight after being granted new authorities in MAP-21 and the FAST Act. With respect to regulations, FRA's extensive and well-established safety regulations are a strength. FTA has made some progress toward developing appropriate safety regulations, such as identifying subjects for potential regulatory action. With respect to inspections, FRA's use of a risk-based approach to distributing inspection resources is a strength. FTA has sought to address previously identified deficiencies in state safety oversight by recommending that state safety agencies develop

[59] 49 U.S.C. § 5329(e)(8). The FAST Act amended the public transportation safety program to allow the Secretary of Transportation to administer the state safety oversight program for a rail transit agency if the Secretary determines that the state safety oversight program is not being carried out in accordance with 49 U.S.C. § 5329, has become inadequate to ensure enforcement of federal safety regulation, or is incapable of providing adequate safety oversight consistent with the prevention of substantial risk of death or personal injury. Pub. L. No. 114-94, § 3013, 129 Stat. 1312, 1476 (Dec. 4, 2015) (codified at 49 U.S.C. § 5329(e)(8)).

[60] In 2016, DOT OIG recommended that FTA finalize and issue policies and procedures for assuming and relinquishing, direct safety oversight authority. FTA officials told us that they planned to issue such policies and procedures by the end of 2017 but have not done so as of March 1, 2018.

risk-based inspection programs. FTA, though, has not provided states guidance for these efforts. With respect to enforcement, FRA's use of its enforcement authorities is a strength. FTA is also implementing new statutory requirements that state safety agencies have enforcement authorities but does not have a process or methodology to evaluate the effectiveness of these enforcement practices.

Regulations: FRA and FTA Are Working to Improve Rail Safety Oversight by Considering Performance-based Regulations

Extensive and well-established safety regulations are a strength of FRA's safety oversight program based on studies we reviewed and discussions with rail operators and stakeholder organizations. According to NTSB, FRA's railroad safety regulations are an important and effective part of its oversight program. Our previous work reported that according to stakeholders, the Railroad Safety Advisory Committee provides a collaborative environment where stakeholders in the rail community work with FRA to identify issues and proposals for safety standards and regulations that improved the quality of railroads' safety initiatives and fostered a greater level of compliance with safety regulations.[61] This is consistent with views of stakeholders we spoke with, who characterized FRA's safety regulations as a strength. An industry association told us that FRA's regulations promote safety by helping to ensure that no operator falls below a minimum threshold for safe operations, while a rail operator told us that federal regulations help to standardize the operating environment and prevent a patchwork of various state regulations. Four stakeholders also characterized the Railroad Safety Advisory Committee, which plays a large role in crafting FRA's railroad safety regulations, as effective and inclusive.

However, based on studies we reviewed and discussions with rail operators' and stakeholders' organizations, FRA faces limitations in its

---

[61] GAO-14-85.

efforts to regulate safety across railroad systems that differ from one another and sometimes change more quickly than the federal regulatory process. Five railroad operators and an industry association told us that some of FRA's safety regulations do not account for differences in railroads or innovation in safety practices, with three railroad operators stating that this approach requires the extensive use of waivers for particular regulations. Further, two railroad operators and a rail transit operator we spoke with stated that additional federal regulations are needed to provide minimum baseline requirements in specific areas of railroad safety such as medical fitness for duty. In 2014, NTSB also found that FRA needs to do more to regulate particular safety issues including medical fitness for duty and signal protection.[62]

FRA officials acknowledged that time and resources are two of the primary challenges that the agency faces when developing safety regulations but also noted additional ways in which the agency can require railroads to adopt safety practices. FRA officials described the process of creating or significantly amending a regulation as involving years of work, even before the agency commences with the process of drafting a rule. The officials also noted that the agency has additional tools to compel railroads to adopt safety practices. For example, FRA officials discussed the use of compliance agreements, in which railroads can have fines reduced in exchange for adopting safety measures that go beyond what FRA regulations require.

FRA officials are considering the use of performance-based regulations as they update their safety regulations.[63] As noted above, FRA's proposed regulations regarding passenger equipment safety incorporates performance -based safety requirements, rather than explicit safety targets or tolerances. FRA has promulgated performance-based regulations about the implementation of positive train control, a communications-based system designed to prevent certain types of train

[62] NTSB, Special Investigation Report, SIR-14/04.

[63] Performance-based regulations specify a desired outcome rather than behavior or manner of compliance.

accidents, as well as system safety programs that set general safety parameters and thresholds by which successful performance is governed.[64]

FRA's consideration of performance-based regulations is in line with federal guidance. OMB's *Circular A-4* states that performance standards "are generally superior to engineering or design standards because performance standards give the regulated parties the flexibility to achieve regulatory objectives in the most cost-effective way."[65] Additionally, under Executive Order 12866, agencies should (to the extent permitted by law and where applicable) identify and assess alternative forms of regulation and specify performance objectives, rather than specifying the behavior or manner of compliance that regulated entities must adopt.[66]

However, as the language of OMB's *Circular A-4* and Executive Order 12866 suggest that performance-based regulations are not always feasible, studies of performance-based regulations find that as with any other form of regulation, performance-based standards have trade-offs.[67] FRA officials told us that under certain circumstances, performance-based regulations are appropriate for issues regarding design, maintenance, operation, and technology-driven safety requirements. FRA officials we spoke with did not think performance-based standards are appropriate for areas that require standardization. One example is track safety standards, where the need for different operators to use the same equipment precludes a performance-based approach that allows railroads to meet requirements through different means. FRA officials added that a key aspect of the success of performance-based regulations concerns how railroads demonstrate compliance. This concern is consistent with other studies of performance-based regulations, which find that these regulations are most

---

[64] *See* 49 C.F.R. pt. 236, subpart I; 49 C.F.R. pt. 270. The system safety program regulations have been suspended through December 4, 2018.

[65] Office of Management and Budget, *Circular A-4, Regulatory Analysis* (Sept. 2003).

[66] Exec. Order No. 12,866, 58 Fed. Reg. 51,735 (Oct. 4, 1993). A subsequent executive order reaffirmed this principle.

[67] See, for example, Coglianese, Cary, Jennifer Nash, and Todd Olmstead, "Performance-Based Regulation: Prospects and Limitations in Health, Safety, and Environmental Protection," *Regulatory Policy Program,* Report No. RPP-03 (2002); May, Peter, "Performance-Based Regulation and Regulatory Regimes: The Saga of Leaky Buildings," *Law and Policy*, vol. 25, No. 4 (2003); and Coglianese, Cary, "The Limits of Performance-Based Regulation," 50 U. Mich, *J. L. Reform* 525 (2017).

appropriate when regulators have capacity to measure and monitor performance.[68]

Though FTA has made progress assessing the state of rail transit safety standards, a limitation of FTA's rail transit safety oversight program is the lack of federal rail transit safety regulations, which may contribute to inconsistent safety practices across the rail transit industry, according to studies we reviewed and discussions with rail operators and stakeholder organizations. NTSB reported that the structure of FTA's oversight process leads to inconsistent practices, inadequate standards, and marginal effectiveness.[69] In addition, a 2016 DOT OIG report found that because FTA's safety standards are voluntary, they are unenforceable. In 2012, FTA gained the authority to issue safety regulations, though it has not done so yet, and NTSB and other stakeholders we spoke with indicated that the lack of such federal safety regulations is a weakness in federal rail transit safety oversight. Despite differences across rail transit systems, there is value in establishing federal rail transit safety regulations, according to stakeholders from all categories of those we interviewed, including a state safety agency, three rail transit operators, a railroad operator, and two industry associations. Some stakeholders identified specific areas that would benefit from federal rail transit regulations. For example, two rail transit agencies called for federal regulations to address operator fatigue. Some of these officials stated that federal rail transit safety regulations could help ensure safety by establishing clear and consistent minimum standards. Officials from a rail transit entity and an industry association stated that voluntary standards are not enough to ensure that transit entities will adopt appropriate safety measures.

According to our analysis, a past study, and stakeholders we spoke with, FTA's ability to develop and implement performance-based regulations is limited by its lack of capacity to collect and analyze rail safety performance data. In 2017, DOT OIG found that data limitations of FTA's National Transit Database results in limited safety performance

---

[68] See Coglianese (2017), 547.

[69] NTSB, *Collision of Two Washington Metropolitan Area Transit Authority Metrorail Trains Near Fort Totten Station*, Accident Report, NTSB/RAR-10/02 (Washington, D.C.: July 27, 2010).

criteria in FTA's National Public Transportation Safety Plan. Further, two rail transit entities as well as a state safety agency we spoke with stated that they face challenges in analyzing data due to either the size of their systems or their capacity.[70] FTA officials told us that they need more data to inform their decisions regarding whether to establish rail transit safety regulations, and also added that a limitation to their ongoing assessment of potential areas for rail transit safety regulation is the concern about public disclosure of safety data provided to FTA and its potential use in private litigation.[71] According to FTA officials, they need more information to do a comprehensive evaluation of efficacy of current safety standards and practices. As required by the FAST Act, FTA has entered into an agreement with the National Academies of Sciences, Engineering, and Medicine, to conduct a study to evaluate whether it is in the public interest to withhold from federal or state court proceedings any information collected by DOT through its public transportation safety program oversight activities. The National Academies of Sciences is expected to complete this study in 2018.

FTA is taking positive steps toward developing safety regulations that may address inconsistent safety practices across rail transit operators. FTA officials stated that the agency is considering issuing rail transit safety regulations and also employs additional tools to compel rail transit entities to adopt safety measures. As noted above, FTA is currently studying whether federal regulations are appropriate for specific areas of rail transit safety. Executive Order 12866 and OMB's *Circular A-4* direct federal agencies to consider performance-based regulations when developing regulations. Further, as the Transportation Research Board recently

---

[70] According to FTA, state safety agencies generally receive data from the rail transit operators they oversee. This, in some cases, is the same data rail transit operators provide to FTA's National Transit Database.

[71] According to the DOT OIG, FTA has twice sought data protection legislation that was not enacted. According to FTA officials, certain types of transit safety information that is obtained by FTA might be protected from public disclosure under a Freedom of Information Act exemption. For example, FTA may withhold from public disclosure Sensitive Security Information that was developed in the conduct of security activities, the disclosure of which the Secretary has determined would (1) be an unwarranted invasion of personal privacy; (2) reveal a trade secret or privileged or confidential commercial or financial information; or (3) be detrimental to transportation safety. *See* 49 U.S.C. § 40119; 49 C.F.R. pt. 15.

reported, any decision to use performance-based regulations "must take into account the regulator's own ability to enforce and motivate compliance (through methods such as auditing and field inspections) as well as the capacity of regulated entities to meet their obligations."[72] FTA officials noted that they are actively engaged with members of the Transportation Research Board in reviewing and discussing these recent findings related to safety regulations for high-hazards industries.[73] In January 2017, FTA issued its National Public Transportation Safety Plan, which FTA officials noted is one component of their transit safety standard development program. According to FTA officials, the plan identifies a list of issue areas that the agency is currently studying to determine whether national regulations are needed. FTA officials also stated that the plan includes "voluntary standards," which are intended to put the industry "on notice" that federal safety regulations may be proposed in those areas. FTA officials stated that they view the National Public Transportation Safety Plan as iterative and more easily updated compared with official regulations. Additional tools that FTA officials stated the agency employs in its approach to safety oversight include general directives as well as the requirements associated with FTA grants.

Inspections: FRA Utilizes a Risk-Based Model, While FTA Oversees the Development of State Safety Agencies' New Programs

Based on our assessment and studies we reviewed, a strength of FRA's safety oversight program is its risk-based approach to distributing inspection resources, which may serve as an example for FTA and state safety agencies. According to NTSB, FRA's qualified inspectors are a strength of its oversight program. To help target these inspectors to the

---

[72] Transportation Research Board, Special Report 324: Designing Safety Regulations for High-Hazard Industries (Washington, D.C.: 2018).

[73] Transportation Research Board, Special Report 324: Designing Safety Regulations for High-Hazard Industries (Washington, D.C.: 2018).

areas of highest risk, FRA developed the National Inspection Plan, which includes a quantitative model for allocating inspection resources in a way that tries to minimize railroad accidents. This model utilizes data including: (1) accident and incident data that railroads are required to report, (2) data from FRA inspection activity, and (3) information on railroad activities such as train miles and other data. Based on our assessment of FRA's model, we believe that it can be an appropriate and useful tool for directing its inspection resources based on risk because it relies on statistical methods commonly used to predict the risk of a violation for regulated entities. While we did not review FRA's entire modeling process, nor did we validate the results it generates, we do believe that FRA's approach to using these statistical models as a key part of its inspection program is appropriate.

However, a potential limitation of FRA's inspection program is the flexibility granted to individual inspectors and whether the manner and extent to which inspectors implement this discretion may be inconsistent with the risk-based National Inspection Plan. FRA's National Inspection Plan provides guidance for inspectors about how much time they should spend inspecting individual railroads. According to FRA officials, FRA inspectors have considerable flexibility to deviate from the National Inspection Plan based on their judgment regarding where to more effectively use their resources. FRA officials stated that situations arise that call for deviations in planned inspections. For example, a particular railroad may experience a serious accident and therefore require more oversight from FRA. According to FRA officials, regional offices make these decisions based on their understanding of emerging issues. Inspectors are expected to know their region and decide which locations to go to, and are in part evaluated based on these decisions. When a region's record of total inspection time spent on a particular railroad differs from the National Inspection Plan by more than 5 percent, the region's leadership submits an explanation to FRA's Office of Railroad Safety. This practice, if not monitored, could allow inspectors to deviate from the data-driven model results in ways that undermine the goal of the National Inspection Plan to deploy FRA's limited resources efficiently and based on risk. However, FRA officials told us that flexibility for individual inspectors is important, and that FRA is continuously monitoring the model's performance and making changes as appropriate. Further, OECD's *Best Practice Principles for Regulatory Policy* note that it is important to ensure "that sufficient flexibility is left to enforcement and inspection officials to adapt their response in proportion to the facts on the ground."[74]

A strength of FTA's approach to rail transit safety oversight is that it is working to overcome weaknesses in state oversight of rail transit identified in our prior work and stakeholders we spoke with. For example, FTA has noted that in the past some state safety agencies lacked sufficient oversight authorities. To now be certified by FTA, state safety agencies must demonstrate that they have authority to review, approve and oversee the implementation of rail transit operator's safety plans. Additionally, we have found, and FTA has also noted, that some state safety agencies would benefit from more training and additional staff.[75] To now be certified by FTA, state safety agencies must be capable of directly hiring and developing staff and contract support, as well as have a training plan for certain staff.

Though FTA is seeking to implement stronger safety oversight activities, a limitation of its program is that state safety agencies have not received the guidance and support necessary to develop effective inspection programs. FTA does not currently plan to conduct widespread inspections itself and recommends that state safety agencies develop risk-based inspection programs. According to FTA, states have discretion to

---

[74] OECD, 2014.

[75] GAO-06-821. We made two recommendations to FTA in this report. First, we recommended that FTA develop performance goals for the state safety oversight program. Second, we recommended that FTA develop and encourage completion of a training curriculum for state safety agency staff. FTA took action in response to both of these recommendations, establishing performance goals and a training curriculum. Additionally, MAP-21 addressed some of these concerns. Through the ongoing certification process, states determine in consultation with FTA the appropriate staffing level for their state safety agency. Further, to be certified by FTA, states must demonstrate that the employees and other personnel of the state safety agency who are responsible for the oversight of rail transit safety are qualified to perform their functions, based on appropriate training, including completion of the Public Transportation Safety Certification Training Program.

establish their inspection programs in accordance with their program standards, and are not required to actually conduct inspections as the method of verifying rail transit operators' compliance with safety rules.[76] However, direct observation, audits, and performance indicator tracking are useful methods for an oversight agency in assessing a regulated entity's safety culture.[77] Officials we spoke with from selected state safety agencies say that they have received little guidance from FTA on what their risk-based inspection programs should look like. In the materials FTA provided to states, it said that it intends to provide guidance to states on risk-based inspections but did not provide us with a plan or timeline for doing so.

Without guidance from FTA, state safety agencies may not develop effective risk-based inspection programs and thus not use their resources efficiently. Effective risk-based inspection programs are particularly important given state safety agencies' limited resources. We have reported in the past that some state safety agencies lack sufficient resources, including training and staff.[78] Officials from two rail transit operators and all four industry associations we spoke with stated that state safety agencies continue to have limited resources and capacity. Several state safety agencies we spoke with rely on contractors or employees with other responsibilities besides oversight of rail transit to meet their increased oversight responsibilities and achieve certification from FTA.

Federal standards for internal control as well as leading practices for regulatory inspections state that agency objectives, including those related to inspections and enforcement, should be clearly communicated.

Specifically, federal standards for internal control require that management communicate the necessary quality information to achieve the agency's objectives.[79] Additionally, the OECD's Best Practice Principles for Regulatory Policy recommends that governments ensure clarity of rules and processes for enforcement and inspections and clearly articulate rights

---

[76] A state safety oversight program standard must identify the processes and procedures that govern the activities of the state safety agency. Also, the program standard must identify the processes and procedures rail transit operators must have in place to comply with the standard.

[77] TCRP, 2015.

[78] TCRP, 2015.

[79] GAO-14-704G.

and obligations of officials.[80] According to OECD, the frequency of inspections and the resources employed should be proportional to the level of risk.

Enforcement: FRA Utilizes Various Mechanisms; FTA Has No Process or Methodology to Assess the Effectiveness of State Safety Agency Enforcement

A strength of FRA's safety oversight program is that the agency has and utilizes clear enforcement authority, according to NTSB and stakeholders we spoke with. As previously discussed, FRA has several enforcement tools available when inspectors find that railroads are noncompliant with applicable regulations, including civil penalties, individual liability, compliance orders, and emergency orders. According to NTSB, this array of specific enforcement tools helps ensure safety deficiencies are addressed by railroads. FRA officials also told us that the process of adjudicating civil penalties provides a forum for FRA and railroad officials to meet to discuss safety issues. Four rail operators also told us that FRA's authority to issue civil penalties is necessary to ensure railroads' compliance with regulations.

However, a potential limitation of FRA's approach to enforcement is that it is difficult to quantify the effectiveness of FRA's civil penalties. FRA has reported that it cannot determine whether observable safety improvements are directly attributable to discrete civil penalties or whether the amount of civil penalties has any effect on safety.[81] We have reported in the past about the challenges of determining the effect of penalties on compliance in tax policy, though we also noted that, despite these challenges, some analyses likely would be useful for better understanding the effect of penalties on compliance.[82] FRA also reported, though, that

---

[80] OECD, 2014.

[81] FRA, Fiscal Year 2016 Enforcement Report.

[82] GAO, Tax Administration: IRS Should Evaluate Penalties and Develop a Plan to Focus Its Efforts, GAO-09-567 (Washington, D.C.: June 5, 2009).

according to the judgments of its inspectors, issuing civil penalties yields observable improvements in safety practices and compliance with the law. Further, according to FRA, though it does not quantify the impact of civil penalties, FRA monitors railroad responses to its enforcement activity and adjusts its oversight as necessary. More broadly, civil penalties are not meant, by themselves, to ensure railroad safety. Instead, FRA reported that it uses its entire regulatory regime as a whole to try and ensure safety. FRA officials also noted that the agency has additional tools, apart from civil penalties, to compel railroads to adopt safety practices.

A strength of FTA's rail transit safety oversight is that it seeks to improve historically weak state safety agency enforcement authorities, as described in our previous report as well stakeholders we spoke with. FTA requires state safety agencies to adopt enforcement authorities that are sufficient to enable states to compel action from rail transit agencies to address identified deficiencies. FTA has also communicated to states that it is focusing its evaluation of each state's enforcement authorities in two major areas: ensuring that the state can carry out its primary responsibility for rail transit safety in response to (1) an imminent threat to public safety on the rail transit system and (2) a lack of action or noncompliance from the rail transit operator in carrying out certain safety plans. FTA has provided states with examples of the enforcement authorities and policies state safety agencies could establish to address these specific concerns. Authorities to address imminent safety threats may include the authority to suspend rail transit agencies' operations, inspect and remove deficient equipment or system infrastructure from service, or issue an order requiring the rail transit agency to correct an unsafe condition prior to placing equipment or infrastructure back into passenger service. FTA has also provided state safety agencies with examples of authorities to address a lack of action or cooperation by the rail transit operator, including the authority to withhold or redirect funds, levy civil or criminal fines or penalties, and a formal citation or ticketing program.

Though federal law requires that state safety agencies have enforcement authorities over the safety of the rail transit entities they oversee, a limitation of FTA's approach is that FTA has not developed a method to evaluate the effectiveness of states' enforcement practices. Certified state safety agencies will be evaluated for continued compliance with FTA regulations every 3 years. This triennial review process (for rail transit safety) seeks to ensure that states are effectively carrying out their responsibilities. While FTA officials told us that they will evaluate state safety agencies' enforcement during the triennial reviews, FTA has not developed a process or methodology to evaluate whether state - enforcement authorities and practices as a whole are effective. Without a method for determining the effectiveness of state safety agencies' enforcement, FTA may not have the information needed to identify ineffective safety enforcement. As a result, deficiencies may remain for long periods of time, potentially contributing to safety incidents.

Federal standards for internal control maintain that agency managers should perform a range of practices that would facilitate the establishment of a system to monitor the effectiveness of agency activities, which in the context of FTA's mission includes the effectiveness of its rail transit safety oversight. Agency managers should define objectives clearly to enable the identification of risks, establish activities to monitor performance measures and indicators, and externally communicate the necessary quality information to achieve the entity's objectives. Internal control standards further stipulate that agency managers should perform monitoring activities regarding their internal control system and evaluate the results. To do so, federal standards for internal control state that agency managers should monitor ongoing operations and effectiveness, evaluate the results of this monitoring, and identify any changes that need to be made to achieve improvement in agency operations.

The effectiveness of state safety agency enforcement is especially important because questions have been raised about the efficacy of FTA's own enforcement mechanisms, including its ability to withhold funds from and assume direct control over safety oversight for a rail transit entity. Rail transit operators and industry association representatives we spoke with stated that FTA's authority to withhold funding from states is overly punitive, and two stakeholders said the FTA needs more precise tools. Officials from an industry association added that withholding funds can be counterproductive, as most state safety agencies are already underfunded and understaffed. FTA officials pointed to examples in which the agency successfully supported state safety agencies in compelling action from rail transit agencies as evidence that the state safety oversight model, in which FTA backs up state safety agencies, is effective. Additionally, officials from numerous state safety agencies and others questioned whether FTA has the capacity to effectively assume direct safety oversight of rail transit operators. FTA has not assumed direct safety oversight of any rail transit operators outside of WMATA, and FTA officials noted that they intend to continue supporting state safety agencies in their oversight wherever possible.

CONCLUSION

The approaches to rail safety oversight utilized by FRA and FTA each have strengths and limitations. However, FTA's program is currently in transition as the agency implements new authorities and responsibilities provided in federal law. Though FTA has made progress by evaluating existing rail transit safety standards and providing some guidance to states as part of the certification process, limitations in FTA's approach may still hinder the success of the state-based rail transit safety oversight program. Given the looming 2019 deadline for state safety oversight programs to achieve FTA certification, FTA can improve its efforts to implement its new rail transit safety oversight program. In particular, without guidance from FTA on how to develop and carry out risk-based inspection programs, state safety agencies may not use limited resources efficiently, risking that important safety issues will go undetected. Further, without a method for how it will monitor the effectiveness of states safety agencies' enforcement, FTA will lack the information needed to identify ineffective state enforcement, which risks allowing safety deficiencies to remain for long periods of time. By providing this additional guidance and direction to the state safety agencies, FTA would help ensure that states are able to effectively identify and resolve rail transit safety issues.

RECOMMENDATIONS

We are making the following two recommendations to FTA:

- The Office of Transit Safety and Oversight should create a plan, with a timeline, for developing guidance for state safety agencies about how to develop and implement a risk-based inspection program. (Recommendation 1)
- The Office of Transit Safety and Oversight should develop and communicate a method for how it will monitor the effectiveness of the enforcement authorities and practices of state safety agencies. (Recommendation 2)

AGENCY COMMENTS

We provided a draft copy of this chapter to DOT, NTSB, and WMATA for review and comment.

In written comments, reproduced in appendix I, DOT agreed with both our recommendations. DOT also provided technical comments, which we incorporated as appropriate.

In e-mails, NTSB and WMATA provided technical comments, which we incorporated as appropriate. NTSB noted that we do not discuss the role of system safety initiatives, such as safety management systems, in the FRA and FTA rail safety oversight programs. We agree with NTSB that system safety concepts are increasingly influencing the FRA and FTA approaches to rail safety oversight but, as NTSB also noted, both FRA and FTA lack finalized regulations codifying their approaches to system safety initiatives. Because the extent of rail entities' implementation of these initiatives varies and is not complete we did not include an assessment of the strengths and limitations of those initiatives in our scope.

As agreed with your offices, unless you publicly announce the contents of this chapter earlier, we plan no further distribution until 30 days from the report date. At that time, we will send copies to the Secretary of Transportation, Chairman of NTSB, General Manager of WMATA, and the appropriate congressional committees.

Mark Goldstein
Director
Physical Infrastructure Issues

APPENDIX I: COMMENTS FROM THE DEPARTMENT OF TRANSPORTATION

U.S. Department of Transportation
Office of the Secretary of Transportation

Assistant Secretary for Administration

1200 New Jersey Avenue SE
Washington, DC 20590

MAR 01 2018

Mark Goldstein
Director, Physical Infrastructure Issues
U.S. Government Accountability Office (GAO)
441 G Street NW
Washington, DC 20548

Dear Mr. Goldstein:

Transportation safety is the top priority of the U.S. Department of Transportation (DOT), which remains committed to ensuring the safety of all rail passengers and employees, as well as those who interact with the rail system. Since the enactment of the Moving Ahead for Progress in the 21st Act (MAP-21) in July 2012, the Federal Transit Administration (FTA) has worked diligently to implement its new safety authority. FTA has issued five safety-related final rules, established minimum requirements for safety training, published a National Public Transportation Safety Plan, issued several safety advisories, proposed a general directive, and funded critical safety research. FTA has adopted the principles and methods of the Safety Management System (SMS) as the foundation of its safety program. Adoption of SMS by the transit industry will enable transit systems to proactively identify safety hazards and prioritize mitigating those issues that pose the greatest risk.

Since October 2015, FTA has provided direct safety oversight of the Washington Metropolitan Area Transit Authority (WMATA) Metrorail system. In this capacity, FTA has already conducted numerous inspections, audits, and accident investigations of Metrorail. FTA continues to verify WMATA's progress towards completing all required actions in their Corrective Action Plan. FTA will continue to exercise direct safety oversight of WMATA Metrorail until a new State Safety Oversight (SSO) program for Metrorail that meets Federal certification requirements is established. The lessons learned from FTA's direct oversight of Metrorail will inform the future development of guidance, technical assistance and other tools for the rail transit industry.

Upon review of the GAO's draft report, we concur with both recommendations. We will provide a detailed response to each recommendation within 60 days of the final report's issuance.

Sincerely,

Keith Nelson
Assistant Secretary for Administration

In: Transportation
Editor: Frederick Daniels
ISBN: 978-1-53615-651-5

Chapter 7

GRADE-CROSSING SAFETY: DOT SHOULD EVALUATE WHETHER PROGRAM PROVIDES STATES FLEXIBILITY TO ADDRESS ONGOING CHALLENGES*

United States Government Accountability Office

ABBREVIATIONS

DOT	Department of Transportation
FAST Act	Fixing America's Surface Transportation Act
FHWA	Federal Highway Administration
FRA	Federal Railroad Administration
HSIP	Highway Safety Improvement Program
IG	Inspector General
MAP-21	Moving Ahead for Progress in the 21st Century Act

* This is an edited, reformatted and augmented version of United States Government Accountability Office Report to Congressional Committees, Publication No. GAO-19-80, dated November 2018.

NHTSA	National Highway Traffic Safety Administration
NTSB	National Transportation Safety Board
Section 130 Program	Railway-Highway Crossings Program
state DOT	state department of transportation

Why GAO Did This Study

Crashes at highway-rail grade crossings are one of the leading causes of railroad-related deaths. According to FRA data, in 2017, there were more than 2,100 crashes resulting in 273 fatalities. Since 2009 crashes have occurred at a fairly constant rate. The federal government provides states funding to improve grade-crossing safety through FHWA's Section 130 Program. The persistence of crashes and deaths raises questions about the effectiveness of the federal grade-crossing-safety program.

GAO was asked to review federal efforts to improve grade-crossing safety. This chapter examines: (1) the focus of FRA's grade-crossing-safety research, (2) how states select and implement grade-crossing projects and what data are available from FRA to inform their decisions, and (3) the challenges states reported in implementing and assessing projects and the extent to which FHWA assesses the program's effectiveness. GAO analyzed FRA data; reviewed FRA's, FHWA's, and states' documents; reviewed a study of states' selection of projects; and interviewed FRA and FHWA headquarters and field staff, and officials from a non-generalizable sample of eight states, selected to include a mix in the number of grade crossings and crashes, and geographic diversity.

What GAO Recommends

GAO recommends that FHWA evaluate the program's requirements to determine if they allow states the flexibility to address ongoing safety issues. The Department of Transportation concurred with GAO's recommendation.

WHAT GAO FOUND

Research sponsored by the Federal Railroad Administration (FRA) has identified driver behavior as the main cause of highway-rail grade crossing crashes and that factors such as train and traffic volume can contribute to the risk of a crash. (See Figure.) Over 70 percent of fatal crashes in 2017 occurred at grade crossings with gates.

To meet the requirements of the federal grade-crossing program, states are responsible for selecting and ensuring the implementation of grade-crossing improvement projects. Most state DOT officials and other relevant transportation officials use local knowledge of grade crossings to supplement the results of models that rank grade crossings based on the risk of an accident. These states generally consider the same primary risk factors, such as vehicle and train traffic. FRA is taking steps to improve the data used in its model to help states assess risk factors at grade crossings. For example, FRA's grade-crossing inspectors will review and identify issues with railroad- and state-reported inventory data. FRA is currently developing guidelines, which it plans to finalize by the end of 2018, to implement these inspections as it has for other types of FRA inspections.

Officials we spoke with in eight states reported challenges in pursuing certain types of projects that could further enhance safety, in part because of federal requirements. While safety has improved, many crashes occur at grade crossings with gates, and officials said there could be additional ways to focus program requirements to continue improving safety. States' and the Federal Highway Administration's (FHWA) reporting focuses on the program's funding and activity, such as the number and types of projects, yet the low number of crashes makes it difficult to assess the effectiveness of projects in reducing crashes and fatalities. FHWA reports the program has been effective in reducing fatalities by about 74 percent since 1975. However, since 2009, annually there have been about 250 fatalities—almost one percent of total highway fatalities. FRA expects future crashes to grow, in part, due to the anticipated increase in rail and highway traffic. An evaluation of the program should consider whether its funding and other requirements allow states to adequately address ongoing safety issues. FHWA officials said they are not required to perform such evaluations. GAO has previously reported on the importance of program evaluations to determine the extent to which a program is meeting its objectives. An evaluation of the program could lead FHWA to identify changes that could allow states to more strategically address problem areas.

November 8, 2018

The Honorable John Thune
Chairman

The Honorable Bill Nelson
Ranking Member
Committee on Commerce, Science, and Transportation
United States Senate

The Honorable John Barrasso
Chairman
The Honorable Tom Carper
Ranking Member
Committee on Environment and Public Works
United States Senate

The Honorable Bill Shuster
Chairman

The Honorable Peter A. DeFazio
Ranking Member
Committee on Transportation and Infrastructure
House of Representatives

The U.S. railroad system consists of a vast network of operations. More than 780 railroads operate on 220,000 miles of track—including about 210,000 highway-rail at-grade crossings (hereafter "grade crossings") meaning where public or private roads intersect with the tracks at the same level as the roadway. Crashes at grade crossings are one of the leading causes of railroad-related deaths and injuries, accounting for about 30 percent of railroad-related fatalities. One recent crash—still under investigation—occurred on January 31, 2018, when a chartered Amtrak train carrying members of Congress hit a refuse truck at a grade crossing near Crozet, Virginia. According to the National Transportation Safety Board's (NTSB) preliminary report, the crossing was equipped with lights and gates to warn of a train's presence, but witnesses reported the truck drove around the gates prior to the accident.

Federal investments in grade-crossing safety improvement have noticeably reduced the number of deaths and injuries at public grade crossings.[1] According to the Federal Railroad Administration's (FRA) data, since FRA began measuring in 1975, crashes at grade crossings have declined by over 80 percent and fatalities have dropped 70 percent.[2] Crashes have leveled off in recent years, and since 2009, the number of grade-crossing crashes and fatalities has hovered at around 2,100 crashes and 250 fatalities per year. However, FRA expects future crashes to grow, in part, because of the anticipated increase in rail and highway traffic. The persistence of crashes and deaths raises questions as to whether

---

[1] Federal funds can only be used to address safety issues at public grade crossings, which account for approximately 60 percent of the grade crossings in the United States. There are approximately 80,000 private grade crossings. These crossings do not involve a public road. Access is generally determined by the railroad and the private landowner.

[2] According to FRA guidance, grade-crossing crashes can also be referred to as grade-crossing accidents, or grade-crossing accident/incidents. To be recorded as a grade-crossing accident, an accident must meet three conditions: (1) involve railroad on-track equipment, (2) involve a highway user, and (3) the accident occurs at a highway-rail grade crossing.

improvements could be made to increase the effectiveness of FRA's rail-safety oversight activities and states' use of federal grade-crossing safety improvement funds.

Within the U.S. Department of Transportation (DOT), the Federal Highway Administration (FHWA) and FRA are the two federal agencies primarily responsible for improving and overseeing safety at public grade crossings. FHWA's Railway-Highway Crossings Program (commonly referred to as the Section 130 Program) is the primary federal program for providing states, through a statutory formula, funding to address safety at grade crossings.[3] FRA oversees railroad safety, including the safety of rail operations at grade crossings. FRA also awards safety discretionary grants to states, local governments, and other public entities to address rail planning, infrastructure, and safety issues. While these grants are not specifically targeted for grade-crossing safety, they may include improvements to rail-highway crossing safety.

You requested that we review federal efforts to improve grade-crossing safety. This chapter examines:

1. What has been the focus of FRA's grade-crossing-safety research.
2. How states select and implement grade-crossing projects, and what railroad- and state-reported data are available from FRA to inform states' decisions.
3. The challenges states reported in implementing and assessing projects, and the extent to which FHWA assesses the program's effectiveness.

The scope of this work focused on the nation's more than 128,000 grade crossings where public roads cross rail tracks. We focused our work on the Section 130 Program. For each of our objectives, we reviewed pertinent statutes and FHWA and FRA regulations and documents, and interviewed FHWA and FRA program officials in headquarters as well as a non-generalizable sample of 10 stakeholders from railroads, industry and

[3] 23 U.S.C. § 130.

transportation associations, and academia, in addition to a rail safety organization and a rail safety consultant. We also interviewed federal officials from the National Transportation Safety Board and the Volpe Center. We selected these organizations based on our initial background research, prior work, and input from other stakeholders, among other things. We also selected eight states for case studies to include a mix of state experiences based on several factors. We selected half of our states from those ranked in the top 25 percent of all states for the number of grade crossings and the amount of Section 130 Program funds received. We selected the other half to include a range of these factors. We also considered geographical diversity in our selections. For these eight states, we conducted in-depth interviews with the FHWA division staff assigned to those states and the FRA regional staff assigned to the regions that included those states, as well as officials from states' departments of transportation (state DOT), public utility commissions, and other state officials involved with state use of Section 130 Program funds (referred to collectively as "state officials" in our report). We used a similar set of questions to collect information from the eight selected states on each of our objectives. Information from these state discussions cannot be generalized to other states; instead, we used the information for illustrative purposes, including when we describe the challenges interviewees reported facing. When appropriate, we indicate whether the challenges we summarize are shared by:

- "some" (two or three);
- "many" (four or five); or
- "most" (six or seven)

of the state officials, but frequency is not necessarily indicative of the relative importance of a challenge or consensus, or lack thereof.

We also conducted additional work related to each of the objectives.

- To describe the focus of FRA's grade-crossing-safety research, we examined FRA research aimed at understanding the causes of grade-crossing crashes and identifying potential safety improvements and described FRA efforts to test new approaches that could improve safety.

- To describe how states select and implement grade-crossing projects, and what FRA data are available to inform their decisions, we reviewed an academic study that included a literature review and interviews with state officials to describe how states select Section 130 Program projects.[4] We also assessed the reliability of FRA's National Highway-Rail Crossing Inventory data, which are the only source for national statistics on grade-crossing characteristics. We tested whether the data were within reasonable ranges, were internally consistent, and appeared complete. We identified data reliability issues in FRA's crossing inventory that we will discuss more fully later in this chapter.
- To determine the challenges states reported in implementing and assessing projects and the extent to which FHWA assesses the program's effectiveness, we reviewed program requirements and state project information and other components from FHWA's 2016 and 2018 Biennial Section 130 Program progress reports to Congress.[5] We also reviewed federal laws and guidance related to implementing projects and measuring performance. We interviewed state DOT officials from the eight selected states and other stakeholders on the challenges states face implementing projects and FHWA and FRA officials for their perspectives on managing the program, including how FHWA measures performance and assesses program effectiveness. We compared information collected from FHWA to federal internal control standards and criteria on program evaluation identified in our

---

[4] Benjamin R. Sperry, Bhaven Naik, Jeffrey E. Warner, *Evaluation of Grade Crossing Hazard Ranking Models,* a report prepared at the request of the Ohio Department of Transportation, May 2016.

[5] Every 2 years the Secretary of DOT sends Congress a report on the progress all the states have made in implementing projects to improve grade crossings. The report is submitted by FHWA's Office of Safety. 23 U.S.C. § 130(g).

previous work. Appendix I describes our objectives, scope, and methodology in greater detail.

We conducted this performance audit from October 2017 to November 2018 in accordance with generally accepted government auditing standards. Those standards require that we plan and perform the audit to obtain sufficient, appropriate evidence to provide a reasonable basis for our findings and conclusions based on our audit objectives. We believe that the evidence obtained provides a reasonable basis for our findings and conclusions based on our audit objectives.

BACKGROUND

Grade-Crossing-Safety Trends

Grade-crossing safety has improved significantly since 1975, but since 2009, the number of crashes and fatalities at grade crossings has plateaued (see Figure 1). The yearly number of grade-crossing crashes declined from 12,126 in 1975 to 2,117 in 2017. In that time frame, fatalities dropped from 917 to 273.

The most significant reductions in grade-crossing crashes and fatalities were achieved from 1975 to 1985, when states closed or improved the most dangerous crossings.[6] Grade-crossing safety continued to improve until the mid-2000s, though at a slower rate. Since 2009, the number of grade-crossing crashes and fatalities remains at around 2,100 crashes and 250 fatalities a year. These fatalities typically make up less than one percent of all highway-related fatalities. The decrease in crashes and fatalities occurred as the volume of train and highway traffic generally increased over the years. FRA expects the traffic volumes to continue to

---

[6] GAO, Railroad Safety: Status of Efforts to Improve Railroad Crossing Safety, GAO/RCED-95-191 (Washington, D.C.: Aug. 3, 1995).

increase and has expressed concern that grade-crossing crashes and fatalities may also increase.[7]

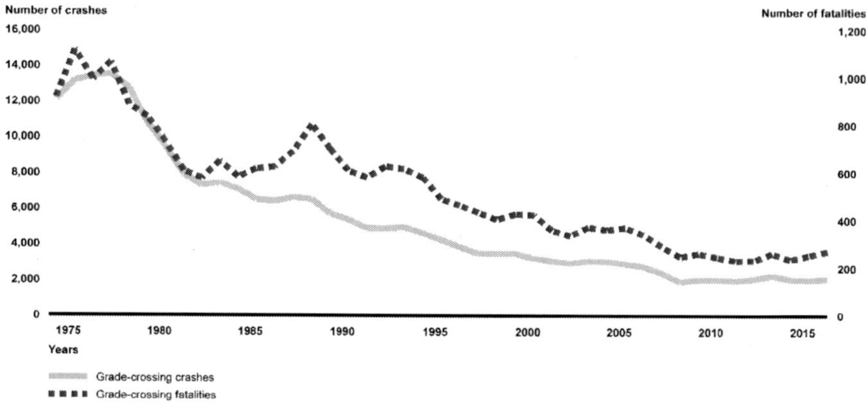

Source: GAO analysis of Federal Railroad Administration data GAO-19-80.

Figure 1. Crashes as Highway-Rail Grade Crossings and Fatalities from 1975-2017.

The Section 130 Program

As a set-aside portion of FHWA's much larger Highway Safety Improvement Program (HSIP), the Section 130 Program provides funds to state DOTs for the elimination of hazards at highway-rail grade crossings.[8] States determine what improvements need to be made at grade crossings. FHWA has oversight responsibilities regarding the use of federal funds as part of its administration of federal-aid highway programs and funding,

---

[7] FRA faces an emerging challenge in dealing with expected increases in freight rail traffic. FRA has estimated that the amount of freight shipped in the United States would increase by 1.1 billion tons (about 9 percent) across all modes from 2010 to 2020, with about 176- million tons of the increased amount shipped by rail. According to the Association of American Railroads, this includes the rapid increase in freight rail traffic related to energy production, both in the transport of materials such as sand for use in hydraulic fracturing and the shipment of crude oil from fields.

[8] Under amounts authorized by the Fixing America's Surface Transportation (FAST) Act, between fiscal years 2016 and 2020, individual state Highway Safety Improvement Program apportionments ranged from approximately $2.2 billion to an estimated $2.4 billion. Pub. L. No. 114-94 (2015).

including HSIP funds.[9] FHWA uses a statutory formula to distribute to states Section 130 Program funds, which averaged $235 million per year during the last 10 years (fiscal years 2009 through 2018). Section 130 Program projects are funded at a 90 percent federal share, with the state or the roadway authority funding the remaining 10 percent.[10] States have 4 years to obligate their program funds before they expire, meaning that in any given fiscal year, states can obligate funds appropriated in that year as well as any unobligated funds from the previous 3 fiscal years.[11] In addition, states may choose to combine funds from multiple years to fund relatively expensive projects.

The Section 130 Program's requirements direct states to establish an implementation schedule for grade-crossing-safety improvement projects that, at a minimum, include warning signs for all public grade crossings. Grade crossings are generally categorized as "active" or "passive" depending on the type of traffic control devices that are present. As of July 2018, according to FRA's National Highway-Rail Crossing Inventory, there were approximately 68,000 public grade crossings with electronic, or active, traffic control devices in the United States. Another approximately 58,000 public grade crossings have passive traffic-control devices, which include signs and supplementary pavement markings.[12] The requirements also specify that at least 50 percent of Section 130 Program funding must be dedicated to the installation of protective devices at grade crossings, including traffic control devices.[13]

---

[9] Federal assistance for highway and bridge infrastructure—about $40 billion each year— is distributed through multiple formulas and discretionary grant programs collectively known as the federal-aid highway program. States have flexibility to use federal-aid highway program funding outside the Section 130 Program to address rail-highway crossing safety improvements.

[10] Certain grade crossing projects funded with other Highway Safety Improvement Program funds may be eligible for a 100 percent federal share. 23 U.S.C. § 120(c). Currently, the Section 130 funding is a 90 percent federal share. See Pub. L. No. 100-17, § 121 (1987); Pub. L. No. 109-59, § 1401(d) (2005).

[11] 23 U.S.C. § 118(b).

[12] As discussed below, we identified data reliability issues related to the inventory, which may cause these statistics to be out of date.

[13] In guidance to states, FHWA has specified that protective devices are grade-crossing improvement projects such as installing signs and pavement markings, upgrading warning devices and traffic signals, illuminating grade crossings, and improving the surface at a grade crossing.

States can use remaining program funds for any hazard elimination project.[14] States may also use program funds to improve warning signs and pavement markings or to improve the way the roadway aligns with the tracks (e.g., to ensure low-clearance vehicles do not get stuck on the tracks). In addition, states can use up to 2 percent of the funds to improve their grade-crossing inventories and to collect and analyze data. See Figure 2 for examples of the types of projects eligible for Section 130 Program funds and graphical depictions of grade crossings before and after safety improvements have been made.

The Federal Role in Grade-Crossing Safety

FHWA and FRA are the primary agencies responsible for safety at grade crossings, and they both play key—yet distinct—roles. FHWA oversees the Section 130 Program and monitors states' uses of program funds through 52 division offices located in each state, the District of Columbia, and Puerto Rico and through headquarters staff in Washington, D.C. In addition, FHWA's division staff reviews states' processes for prioritizing and selecting grade-crossing-safety improvement projects. FHWA does not evaluate the appropriateness of individual grade-crossing projects, but instead helps states determine that projects meet program eligibility requirements. Division staff assists in the implementation of Section 130 Program state-administered projects, and they may participate in state DOT-led, on-site reviews of grade crossings under consideration for Section 130 Program projects. FHWA headquarters staff is responsible for FHWA-wide initiatives, such as working with stakeholders to establish standards for traffic control devices and systems at grade crossings and for engineering oversight of state-administered safety improvement projects.

---

[14] Pursuant to statute, the types of eligible projects have changed over time. For example, the FAST Act amended Section 130 project funding eligibility to include projects to eliminate hazards posed by idling trains that block grade crossings. Pub. L. No. 114-94, § 1412.

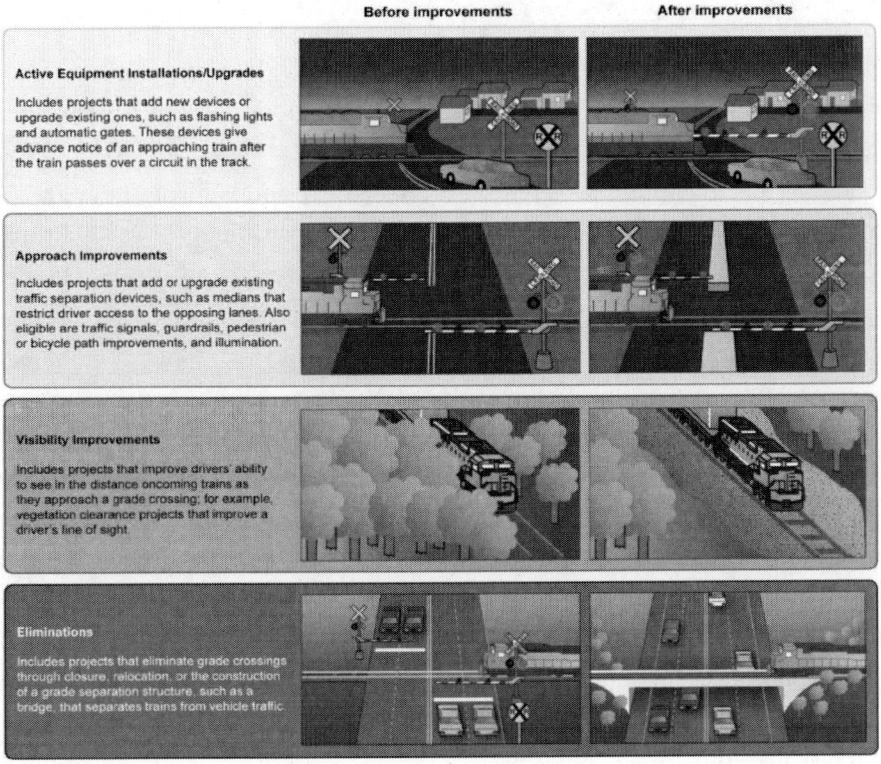

Source: GAO analysis of DOT information | GAO-19-80.

Figure 2. Examples of Eligible Projects for the Railway-Highway Crossings Program with Before and After Views of Safety Improvements

FRA provides safety oversight of both freight and passenger railroads by:

- collecting and analyzing data;
- issuing and enforcing numerous safety regulations, including on grade-crossings' warning systems;
- conducting focused inspections, audits, and accident investigations; and
- providing technical assistance to railroads and other stakeholders.

Specifically, FRA oversees rail safety through eight regional offices and through headquarters staff in Washington, D.C. Regional staff monitor railroads' compliance with federal safety regulations through inspections and provide technical assistance and guidance to states. In 2017, FRA created a new discipline for grade-crossing safety and is hiring new grade-crossing inspectors.[15] These inspectors conduct field investigations, identify regulatory defects and violations, recommend civil penalty assessments when appropriate, and may participate in state-DOT-led teams that conduct on-site reviews of grade crossings to evaluate potential safety improvements. According to FRA documentation, FRA's new inspectors will also work with a variety of stakeholders to institute new types of training, explore new safety concepts and technologies, and assist in the development of new or modified highway-rail grade-crossing-safety regulations, initiatives, and programs. The inspectors will also work with FHWA and other DOT operating administrations in a cooperative effort to improve grade-crossing safety. FRA regional staff also investigates select railroad crashes, including those at grade crossings, to determine root causation and any contributing factors, so that railroads can implement corrective actions.[16]

FRA headquarters staff develops analytical tools for states to use to prioritize grade-crossing projects. In addition, headquarters staff manages research and development to support improved railroad safety, including at grade crossings.

FRA's Office of Railroad Safety maintains the National Highway-Rail Crossing Inventory database and the Railroad Accident/Incident Reporting System on grade-crossing crashes. Both states and railroads submit

---

[15] FRA's 342 regional safety inspectors formerly covered five safety disciplines—track; signals and train control; motive power and equipment; operating practices; and hazardous materials.

[16] FRA criteria for grade-crossing accident investigations generally involve: serious injury or fatality to persons being transported in a commercial motor vehicle or school bus; three or more motor vehicle occupant fatalities; or without a fatality, but involving credible evidence of a malfunction or failure of an active-warning device. The National Transportation Safety Board (NTSB) also conducts selected accident investigations, including at grade crossings. NTSB's Office of Highway Safety investigates significant crashes that are likely to impact the public's confidence in highway transportation safety, generate high public interest, or highlight national safety issues.

information to FRA's crossing inventory, which is designed to contain information on every grade crossing in the nation. Railroads submit information such as train speed and volume; states submit information such as highway speed limits and average annual daily traffic. The Rail Safety Improvement Act of 2008 added requirements for both railroads and states to periodically update the inventory; however, the Moving Ahead for Progress in the 21st Century Act (MAP-21) repealed a provision providing DOT authority to issue implementing regulations that would govern states' reporting to the inventory. According to FRA officials, while FRA's regulations do not require states to report the information, FRA encourages them to do so. FRA regulations require railroads to report and update their information in the inventory every 3 years or sooner in some instances, such as if new warning devices are installed or the grade crossing is closed. FRA's accident system contains details about each grade-crossing accident that has occurred. In addition to submitting immediate reports of fatal grade-crossing crashes, railroads are required to submit accident reports within 30 days after the end of the month in which the accident occurred and describe conditions at the time of the accident (e.g., visibility and weather); information on the grade crossing (e.g., type of warning device); and information on the driver (e.g., gender and age).

FRA Has Focused Research on Understanding and Addressing Risky Behavior by Drivers at Grade Crossings

Research Sought to Identify Risk Factors at Grade Crossings and Understand Driver Behavior

In its role overseeing grade-crossing safety, FRA has sponsored a number of research efforts to better understand the causes of grade-crossing crashes and identify potential ways to improve engineering, education, and enforcement efforts. For example, FRA sponsored an in-depth data analysis of grade-crossing crashes to better identify which crossing characteristics increase the risk of an accident.[17] The report, issued in 2017, found that the volumes of train and vehicle traffic at a crossing are the biggest predictors of grade-crossing crashes.[18] Changes in vehicle and train traffic therefore affect the annual number of grade-crossing crashes. For example, as highway traffic decreased in 2008, possibly due to the economic recession and higher gas prices, so too did the number of grade-crossing crashes. As previously noted, FRA expects that the number of grade-crossing crashes will likely grow with anticipated increases in future train and highway traffic. As discussed below, vehicle and train volume are included in the U.S. DOT Accident Prediction Model, which some states use to select grade-crossing improvement projects.[19] According to FRA officials, FRA is using the results of this recent in-depth data analysis to, in part, evaluate whether additional risk factors, such as the number of male drivers or trains carrying toxic materials, should be added to the model.

Source: GAO. | GAO-19-80.

Figure 3. Examples of Driver Behavior Contributing to Highway-Rail Grade-Crossing Crashes.

[17] Federal Railroad Administration, *In-Depth Data Analysis of Grade-crossing Accidents Resulting in Injuries and Fatalities* (May 2017). We did not review the analytical sufficiency of FRA's report, as it was beyond the scope of this engagement.

[18] Train speed had a significant effect on the injury and fatality rate. The report also found that grade crossings with multiple traffic lanes and railroad tracks increase accident risk, as does proximity to a highway intersection.

[19] The US DOT Accident Prediction Model is a multi-step model that uses grade-crossing characteristics and accident history to predict the number of crashes per year at a grade crossing and the severity of predicted crashes.

FRA has targeted other research into understanding driver behavior at grade crossings, which is the leading cause of crashes. According to FRA's accident data, in 2017, 71 percent of fatal crashes at public grade crossings occurred at those with gates. In 2004, the DOT Inspector General (IG) reported that 94 percent of grade-crossing crashes from 1994 to 2003 could be attributed to risky driver behavior or poor judgement. State officials we spoke with explained that drivers may become impatient waiting at a grade crossing and decide to go around the gates. Drivers may also line up over the grade crossing in heavy vehicular traffic, and be unable to exit before the gates come down. See Figure 3 for examples of risky driver behavior at grade crossings.

To better understand driver behavior, FRA sponsored a John A. Volpe National Transportation Systems Center (Volpe Center)[20] study that recorded and analyzed drivers' actions as they approached grade crossings.[21] The researchers found that almost half of drivers were doing another task, such as eating, and over a third did not look in either direction while approaching passive grade crossings. We have previously reported, and many stakeholders we interviewed agreed, that in light of inappropriate driver behavior, technological solutions alone may not fully resolve safety issues at grade crossings.[22] In addition, public-education and law-enforcement efforts can augment the effectiveness of technological solutions. According to FRA officials, they shared information on driver education with DOT's National Highway Traffic Safety Administration (NHTSA) as NHTSA works more closely with states on driver education manuals. According to DOT officials, NHTSA updates its driver education materials every 2–3 years and plans to consider including grade-crossing-safety materials in the next versions.

---

[20] The John A. Volpe National Transportation Systems Center conducts transportation research for DOT administrations and other entities.

[21] FRA, *Driver Behavior Analysis at Highway-Rail Grade Crossings using Field Operational Test Data— Light Vehicles* (May 2013). We did not review the analytical sufficiency of FRA's report, as it was beyond the scope of this engagement.

[22] GAO/RCED-95-191.

FRA Works with States to Research New Safety Measures to Address Risky Behavior at Grade Crossings

FRA is also working with states and localities to research and develop new protective devices and other safety measures targeted at improving driver behavior at grade crossings. As most fatal crashes happen at grade crossings already equipped with gates, FRA and state and local agencies are exploring whether additional safety measures can improve safety at those locations. For example, in 2016 and 2017, FRA's Grade Crossing Task Force[23] worked with the Volpe Center and the City of Orlando to test whether photo enforcement at grade crossings could reduce risky driver behavior. The City of Orlando installed automated photo-enforcement devices at a grade crossing, and instead of issuing fines to drivers who had violated its warning devices, sent drivers a warning notice and educational safety materials. Eight months after the photo-enforcement system was installed, grade crossing violations decreased by 15 percent. While FRA judged these enforcement efforts successful at changing driver behavior, a 2015 FRA whitepaper noted that photo enforcement equipment is costly—on average costing over $300,000 per crossing to install and operate for 2 years—and may not be cost-effective for most grade crossings.[24] FRA found that due to costs and state laws prohibiting photo-enforcement, only two photo-enforcement cameras were currently in operation at grade crossings across the country.

States, localities, and FHWA are also exploring whether new types of pavement markings at grade crossings can improve driver behavior. According to DOT officials, FHWA is working with two states to develop new cross-hatch pavement markings for grade crossings that would comply with the Manual on Uniform Traffic Control Devices, similar to the "don't

---

[23] FRA created the Grade Crossing Task Force after 6 people died in a grade-crossing accident involving a commuter railroad in 2015. According to FRA, the taskforce brainstorms new ideas and oversees grade crossing projects in the areas of enforcement, education, engineering, data analysis, and research.

[24]. FRA, *The Use of Automated Enforcement of Traffic Laws at Highway-Rail Grade Crossings* (October 2015). According to this whitepaper, as of October 2015, 27 states have laws allowing the use of technology to enforce compliance with traffic laws, with 8 states specifically mentioning grade crossings.

block the box" type pavement markings used in intersections. FHWA also worked with a city to test the use of in-roadway lights to delineate the crossing. (See Figure 4).

Source: Federal Highway Administration. | GAO-19-80.

Figure 4. Photos of In-Roadway Lights That Delineate a Grade Crossing.

FRA and state DOTs are also trying to improve pedestrian safety at grade crossings by developing new safety measures. Grade-crossing accidents involving pedestrians are less frequent than those involving automobiles at grade crossings but have a higher fatality rate. While pedestrians were involved in only 9 percent of accidents at public crossings in 2017, almost 40 percent of fatal grade-crossing accidents involved pedestrians.[25] To try to improve pedestrian safety, in 2012 the Volpe

[25] Though not discussed in this report, trespasser fatalities, another source of pedestrian rail fatalities, remain an on-going challenge for railroads. The rates of trespasser fatalities have seen little improvement in recent years. According to DOT officials, in 2017, 575 people died and another 505 were injured in railroad trespassing incidents. The sheer amount of railroad track throughout the United States makes preventing trespassers difficult to address, and trespassing cannot be easily predicted or controlled. (GAO-14-85).

Center worked with New Jersey Transit to study whether adding additional pedestrian gate skirts— hanging gates that further block a crossing (see Figure 5)—would prevent people from ducking under the gates.[26] The Volpe Center reported that these new gates had mixed success. While incidents of people going under and around the gates decreased, more people chose to cross the tracks in the street rather than at the sidewalk.

Source: Federal Railroad Administration. | GAO-19-80.

Figure 5. Photos of Gate Skirts for Pedestrians in Matawan, New Jersey.

Finally, FRA is exploring new automated and connected vehicle technologies that could reduce risky driver behavior at grade crossings. FRA, FHWA, and officials from one state we interviewed said they anticipate that such technology will be critical to further improving safety. Specifically, FRA and FHWA are coordinating with DOT's Intelligent Transportation Systems Joint Program Office to develop pilot technology that would enable crossing infrastructure or trains to communicate wirelessly with vehicles. Vehicles can use this information to warn the driver that a crash or violation is imminent, or integrate with onboard active safety systems. According to FRA officials, they completed a proof of concept in 2013 and completed and tested a prototype of the technology in 2017. DOT officials said that DOT does not have a time frame for when automakers might begin incorporating such connected vehicle technologies

[26] FRA, Effect of Gate Skirts on Pedestrian Behavior at Highway-Rail Grade Crossings (December 2013).

and noted that retrofitting older cars with new equipment will likely make this a long-term effort.

FRA shares information on its research in various ways with state DOTs, because states are responsible for deciding which safety measures to install at grade crossings. Specifically, FRA and FHWA jointly hold quarterly webinars with stakeholders, including state DOT officials, and conduct presentations at highway-rail safety workshops. Information on safety measures such as grade-crossing devices, signs, and markings are also included in the *Railroad-Highway Grade Crossing Handbook*.[27] According to DOT officials, the handbook was developed jointly by FHWA and FRA. The last version of the handbook was updated in 2007 and includes some out of date information. FRA and FHWA officials said they began working on an update in 2017, but missed the July 2018 target completion date. According to FHWA officials, updating the handbook is a complex undertaking that has taken more time than they anticipated due to the extensive collaboration required among stakeholders. FHWA officials said they anticipate completing the update during the spring of 2019.

STATES USE A RISK-BASED APPROACH FOR PROJECT SELECTION AND MAY USE FRA DATA

States Consider Risk when Identifying Grade-Crossing Improvement Projects

The risk of crashes at public grade crossings within a state factors into states' selection of over 1,000 new Section 130 Program projects nationally each fiscal year. FHWA requires states to develop a grade crossing program that considers relative risk.[28] FHWA officials said they review the methods that states use to select projects to ensure that risk is

[27] FHWA, Railroad-Highway Grade Crossing Handbook: Revised Second Edition (August 2007).

[28] 23 C.F.R. § 924.9(a)(4)(ii).

considered. According to a 2016 academic study of 50 states, most states use mathematical formulas, or “accident prediction models,” to help assess risk and identify grade crossings for potential projects.[29] More specifically, these accident prediction models use factors such as grade crossing characteristics and accident history to rank grade crossings by risk. DOT provides one such model—the Accident Prediction Model—and some states have developed their own models.[30] The study reported that 19 states used DOT’s model and 20 states used a different model.[31] It also found that the DOT and commonly used state models include some similar grade-crossing characteristics to predict accident risk. For example, the selected models reviewed all considered vehicle- and train-traffic volume, which FRA has found to be the strongest predictors of grade-crossing crashes.

FRA makes its Accident Prediction Model available to states online through its Web Accident Prediction System. This system is an online tool that uses FRA’s crossing inventory, crossing collision history, and the DOT Accident Prediction Model to predict accident risk for grade crossings in each state. Only one of the eight states in our review used the system as its primary source for ranking grade-crossing risk. Most of the other states perform their own calculations to rank grade crossings. Officials from two states said that they believe their state-maintained data are more reliable than FRA’s crossing inventory and explained that they go directly to their contacts at railroads to get updated information on factors such as train volume.

Accident prediction models are only one source of information states use when selecting Section 130 Program projects. According to the state officials we spoke with, a variety of other considerations can also influence their decisions, including the following:

---

[29] Benjamin R. Sperry, Bhaven Naik, Jeffery E. Warner, *Evaluation of Grade Crossing Hazard Ranking Models*, a report prepared at the request of the Ohio Department of Transportation, May 2016.

[30] We did not assess the quality or accuracy of DOT’s model, as it was beyond the scope of this engagement.

[31] Eleven states did not use models. For example, officials from one state DOT told us they maintained lists of grade crossings that needed certain types of upgrades.

- Proximity of projects together along a railroad "corridor" in order to gain efficiencies and reduce construction costs.
- Requests from local jurisdictions or railroads. These stakeholders may have information on upcoming changes at a grade crossing, such as higher train volume or new housing developments nearby, which would increase risk but would not be reflected yet in the accident prediction model.
- Availability of local funding to provide the required 10 percent match for Section 130 Program projects, while trying to spread the funds fairly across the state.

States may also consider grade crossings that have had close calls in the past, such as where a car narrowly avoided being hit by a train. FRA does not require railroads to report on these close calls, or "near misses;" however, according to state officials, railroads sometimes provide this information to states on an ad-hoc basis. State officials from four of the eight states we spoke with said they considered near misses when selecting Section 130 Program projects. A 2004 Volpe Center report noted that studying close calls was a proactive way to improve safety.[32] According to the report, FRA sponsored a workshop to learn about the benefits of collecting and analyzing close calls. However, stakeholders we interviewed noted challenges formalizing near-miss reporting. For example, Volpe Center officials said these reports are subjective in nature—what one engineer considers a close call, others may not.

FRA developed another online tool—GradeDec—to allow states to compare the costs and benefits for various grade-crossing improvement projects. GradeDec uses models to analyze a project's risk and calculate cost-benefit ratios and net present value for potential projects. FRA provides state DOTs with on-site GradeDec workshops upon request. While FRA officials noted that many state and local governments have registered to use the program, none of the state officials we spoke with identified GradeDec as a tool that they use to conduct cost-benefit analysis.

---

[32] Volpe Center, Proceedings of the Human Factors Workshop: Improving Railroad Safety through Understanding Close Calls (May 2004).

Officials from two state DOTs we spoke with said that cost-benefit analyses could help them better identify and select the most cost-effective crossing safety projects in the future.[33] According to the academic study of 50 states noted above, because of limited funding for grade-crossing improvements, states should consider the life-cycle costs of the projects as well as net present value to help select projects.[34] As discussed later in this chapter, the small number of crashes at grade crossings can make it challenging to distinguish between different projects in terms of their effectiveness in reducing accidents.

Finally, after they have considered risk factors and created a list of potential grade crossings for improvement, state officials, along with relevant stakeholders from railroads and local governments, conduct field reviews of the potential projects. According to state officials, these reviews help identify grade-crossing characteristics that may not be included in the accident prediction models, such as vegetation that would obstruct drivers' views.

FRA Has Taken Steps to Improve Inventory Data and Is Formalizing How Inspectors Will Validate the Data's Accuracy

In 2008, legislation was enacted mandating reporting by states and railroads to the National Highway-Rail Crossing Inventory.[35] However, the fact that reporting to the inventory remained voluntary until 2015 has had lingering effects on the completeness of the data in the inventory. In 2015, as mandated by statute, FRA issued regulations requiring railroads to update certain data elements for all grade crossings every 3 years.[36] However, our analysis of FRA's crossing inventory found that 4 percent of

---

[33] Officials from one state reported using GradeDec to perform "what-if" analyses, to predict, for example, the effect of increased traffic on a grade crossing's accident risk.

[34] B. Sperry, B. Naik, J. Warner, *Current Issues in Highway-Rail Grade Crossing Hazard-Ranking and Project Development*, Journal of the Transportation Research Board,vol.2, No. 2608 (2017).

[35] Pub. L. No. 110-432, § 204 (2008).

[36] 49 C.F.R. § 234.409. FRA regulations do not require railroads to periodically update inventory records for grade-separated grade crossings or closed grade crossings.

grade crossings were last updated in 2009 or earlier. In addition, because MAP-21 repealed DOT's authority to issue regulations that would govern state reporting to the inventory, state reporting of grade-crossing data remains voluntary, according to FRA officials, and all state-reported information is not complete. Our analysis of state-reported data in FRA's crossing inventory found varying levels of completeness. For example, while some state-reported data fields were almost entirely complete, 33 percent of public grade crossings were missing data on posted highway speed. We also found that of the crossings for which states reported the year when the highway-traffic count was conducted, 64 percent of the highway-traffic counts for public grade crossings, another important risk factor, had not been updated since 2009, or earlier. According to the 2015 final rule, FRA will continue to evaluate whether additional regulations to address state reporting are needed to maintain the crossing inventory's accuracy.[37]

FRA officials told us that improving inventory data will help them better deploy their limited resources, particularly their grade-crossing inspectors, and said that they have taken steps to help improve the data. In 2017, FRA regional officials conducted field reviews to verify the latitude and longitude data for grade crossings in the inventory, data that states are responsible for updating. In addition, FRA expects its grade-crossing inspectors as part of their inspections to review and identify issues with the railroad- and state-reported inventory data. According to FRA officials, FRA has begun to both transition its 19 grade-crossing managers into grade-crossing inspectors and also hire new inspectors, for an eventual total of 24 inspectors and eight regional specialists to supervise their activities.[38]

To help ensure railroads' compliance with crossing inventory regulations, officials said that the inspectors will use spot checks to validate the inventory data by comparing grade-crossing characteristics in the field with the information railroads submitted to the inventory. In

---

[37] 80 Fed. Reg. 746, 748 (Jan. 6, 2015).

[38] According to FRA officials, current grade-crossing managers may choose to transition to being grade-crossing inspectors or regional specialists, or maintain their current position.

addition, FRA has incorporated information on inventory-reporting requirements into the grade-crossing inspectors' training. Finally, FRA is currently developing guidelines for the grade-crossing inspections similar to those for other FRA safety disciplines. FRA headquarters officials acknowledged that they are still clarifying the details for the inspections that will be included in the compliance manuals that inspectors will use.[39] Specifically, they said they are still determining appropriate inspector workloads and drafting specific guidelines that will need to be integrated into FRA's regional inspection plans.

FRA officials said they are working to develop and make available inventory inspection guidance to the grade-crossing managers and inspectors by December 31, 2018. In the meantime, FRA held training that included information on inventory-reporting requirements. In August 2018, FRA developed guidance for grade-crossing inspections specific to quiet zones in response to a recommendation we made in 2017.[40] It is important that FRA meets its goal to issue similar guidance specific to reviewing the accuracy of the inventory data, as FRA cannot have reasonable assurance that inspections that are already under way are being conducted in such a manner that would allow them to consistently identify data reliability issues at each crossing.

States Reported Challenges Implementing Certain Project Types and Measuring Projects' Effectiveness, and FHWA's Efforts to Assess the Program's Effectiveness Have Limitations

About 75 percent of all Section 130 Program projects states implemented in fiscal year 2016 involved installing or updating active grade-crossing equipment, including warning lights and protective gates

---

[39] FRA has developed a manual for each of its other five disciplines. For example, FRA's manual for the operating practices discipline includes: pertinent laws and regulations, inspector best practices, field-reporting procedures and forms, and illustrative examples of non-compliance issues.

[40] GAO, Railroad Safety: Quiet Zone Analyses and Inspections Could Be Improved, GAO-18-97 (Washington, D.C.: October 2017).

(see Figure 6).[41] The prevalence of this type of project is in part due to the Section 130 Program requirement that states spend at least 50 percent of funds on protective devices. Other than eliminating a grade crossing, adding protective devices has long been considered the most effective way of reducing the risk of a crash.

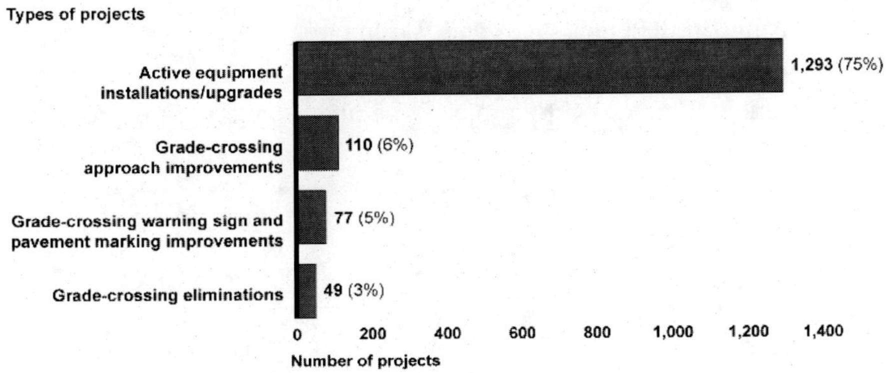

Source: GAO analysis of Federal Highway Administration information. | GAO-19-80.
Note: The Federal Highway Administration's data from fiscal year 2016 were the most recent data available.

Figure 6. Railway-Highway Crossings Program's Most Common Project Types Identified by States in Fiscal Year 2016.

Officials from six of eight state DOTs we interviewed told us that the numbers and types of grade-crossing projects they implement are dependent on the amount of Section 130 Program funding they receive and the cost of the projects. As previously described, funds are set aside from the Highway Safety Improvement Program and distributed to states by a statutory formula that includes factors such as the number of grade crossings in each state. Officials from six of the eight state DOTs we spoke to agreed that the set-aside nature of the program was crucial in allowing them to implement projects, many of which they said would not have been possible without Section 130 Program funds. For example, many said the formula funding ensures that grade-crossing projects are completed along with highway safety projects, particularly given the fact that fatalities

[41] FHWA's project data from fiscal year 2016 were the most recent data available.

resulting from grade-crossing crashes account for so few when compared to highway deaths. Overall, fatalities resulting from grade-crossing crashes account for less than 1 percent of all highway-related fatalities.

In fiscal year 2018, the funds distributed ranged from a low of approximately $1.2 million for eight states and Washington, D.C., to over $16 million for California and over $19 million for Texas.[42] The number of grade crossings in the eight states and Washington, D.C. ranged from 5 to 380, while California had almost 6,000 and Texas had over 9,000. Project implementation costs varied by project type and ranged widely depending on project scope. Based on 2016 DOT data, some typical project costs ranged as follows:

- adding signs to passive grade crossings—$500 to $1,500;
- adding flashing lights and two gates to passive grade crossings—$150,000 to $300,000;
- adding four gates to grade crossings with flashing lights—$250,000 - $500,000;
- closing a grade crossing—$25,000 to $100,000; and
- separating a grade crossing from traffic (Grade Separation)—$5 million to $40 million.[43]

State officials we spoke with cited several challenges in pursuing certain types of controversial, innovative, and expensive projects that could help them address the evolving nature of risk at grade crossings and difficulty in measuring the effectiveness of their projects. First, most state DOT officials said that the cost of grade-separation projects and, at times, the controversy of eliminating grade crossings through closure reduces the

[42] States can use Section 130 Program funds for other highway safety projects if they demonstrate they have met their safety needs for installing or upgrading protective devices. 23 U.S.C. § 130(e)(2). FHWA reported in 2016 that the District of Columbia and Hawaii, with less than 10 active public grade crossings each, were the only states to have obligated program funds for purposes other than grade-crossing projects. According to FHWA officials these two states used program funds for other Highway Safety Improvement Program projects such as traffic signals and intersection improvements.

[43] Costs for grade separation can range widely due to differences in the number of highway lanes and railroad tracks, as well as the lengths of bridges built to traverse the tracks.

number of these projects, while acknowledging that they are the most effective ways to improve safety. These types of projects made up only 3 percent of Section 130 Program projects in fiscal year 2016 (see fig. 6). Grade-separation projects are often more expensive than the annual Section 130 Program funding available to states. In 2018, only eight states received annual Section 130 Program funding sufficient to fund a $7-million grade-separation project. As discussed previously, to fund relatively expensive projects, states may choose to combine funds from multiple years. Also, states and railroads may make incentive payments to localities for the permanent closure of a grade crossing.[44] In addition to the cost, most state DOT officials reported challenges obtaining local support for closing grade crossings. They said closures may inconvenience residents who use the road and force emergency responders to take longer routes, potentially slowing response times. Grade-separation projects address these safety concerns and may be more agreeable to residents, but they are substantially more expensive. While up to $7,500 in Section 130 Program funding can be used to help incentivize communities to close grade crossings, officials from some of our selected state DOTs said this amount is generally not enough to persuade local officials to support the closing.

Second, officials from many state DOTs we interviewed also reported that the requirements of the Section 130 Program create challenges for them in implementing what they considered to be innovative projects. For example, the program requirement that 50 percent of funds be used on protective devices, combined with what one researcher described to us as the tendency by states to implement "known" projects—i.e., protective devices—may impede states' selection of new, more innovative safety projects. Officials we interviewed from many state DOTs described challenges related to the program's requirements. They noted that they are prevented from using Section 130 Program funds for new types of safety technologies not yet incorporated into FHWA's Manual on Uniform Traffic Control Devices. As noted previously in this chapter, outside the

---

[44] 23 U.S.C. § 130(i).

Section 130 Program FHWA is working with states and localities to explore whether new types of pavement markings at grade crossings, not in the manual, can improve driver behavior. One state DOT official we interviewed suggested changes to allow states to fund one grade-crossing pilot project per year or to use a set percentage of program funds to finance a pilot project that could help them explore promising but as yet unproven technologies.

Third, state DOT officials from four of the eight selected states also said it can be difficult to find funding for the required 10 percent state match. As previously mentioned, while certain rail-safety projects are eligible for up to 100 percent federal funding, Section 130 Program projects are funded at a 90 percent federal share. According to DOT documentation we reviewed, only some states have a dedicated source for such a match, and state DOT officials from one of our selected states said their state cannot use state funds for the 10 percent match. Some state DOT officials said this situation can drive project selection. For example, they sometimes chose projects based on which localities or railroads were willing to provide matching funds or offer cost savings.

Finally, many state officials cited challenges in measuring the effectiveness of grade crossing projects in reducing crashes or the risk of crashes. In particular, state officials we spoke to said it can be difficult to use before-and-after crash statistics as a measure of effectiveness because of the low number and random nature of crashes. Also, as FRA research has shown and as FHWA and FRA have noted, reporting on before-and-after grade-crossing accident statistics can be misleading, given the infrequency of crashes and crashes that are not the result of grade crossing conditions.[45] States' required Section 130 Program annual progress reports to the Secretary of DOT call for states to report on the effectiveness of the improvements they made.[46] FHWA reporting guidance suggests they

[45] See, for example, Federal Railroad Administration, *Proceedings of the Human Factors Workshop: Improving Railroad Safety Through Understanding Close Calls* (April 2003) and Federal Highway Administration, Federal Railroad Administration, *Noteworthy Practices Guide: Highway-Railway Grade Crossing Action Plan and Project Prioritization* (November 2016).

[46] 23 U.S.C. § 130(g).

define effectiveness as the reduction in the number of fatalities and serious injuries after grade-crossing projects were implemented, consistent with statutory requirements. In addition, FHWA guidance states that consideration should be given to quantifying effectiveness in the context of fatalities and serious injuries.[47] However, states often report no differences in crashes after specific projects were implemented, and there have been instances where states reported a slight increase in crashes. Such an increase does not necessarily mean that the project was not effective in reducing the overall risk of a crash. Also, not all projects are implemented at grade crossings where there has been a crash.

Among other information, states also typically report information on funding and data on the numbers and types of projects implemented. In addition, the extent to which states report projects' effectiveness varies greatly. Given states' responsibility for implementing the Section 130 Program and the differences in the amounts of funding they receive, FHWA officials said states should determine and report on the appropriate effectiveness metrics for their programs. According to FHWA officials, during the 2017 reporting year, a few states requested examples of what to include when reporting effectiveness, and FHWA responded with examples of various methods they could use, such as a benefit-cost ratio or the percentage decrease in fatalities, serious injuries, and crashes. Regardless of the difficulty in measuring the effectiveness of specific projects, most state DOT officials we interviewed stressed the importance of the Section 130 Program in funding grade-crossing projects.

FHWA Reports Provide Limited Insight into the Program's Effectiveness, and FHWA Has Not Evaluated Program Requirements in Light of Changing Risk Conditions

FHWA's biennial report to Congress is intended to provide information to Congress on the progress being made by the states in

---

[47] FHWA, Office of Safety, *Railway-Highway Crossings Program Reporting Guidance* (Feb. 22, 2013).

implementing projects to improve safety and, in addition, make recommendations for future implementation of the program. FHWA reviews states' annual Section 130 Program reports and uses them to formulate the report to Congress every 2 years. FHWA's 2018 report highlights that the Section 130 Program has seen great success since 1975, with a decrease of approximately 74 percent in fatalities at the same time that there was an increase in vehicle and train traffic. The report described the latest available 10-year trend, from 2007 to 2016, as showing a 31 percent decrease in fatalities. Fatalities have also decreased when adjusted for train traffic. However, FHWA officials acknowledged in interviews with us that crashes and fatalities have remained constant since about 2009, with more recent data showing a slight increase in fatalities over the last 2 to 3 years, data that are consistent with the increases in overall roadway fatalities. The officials said increased train- and vehicle-traffic volumes could be contributing to that increase, in addition to other factors, such as more bicycle riders and pedestrians using grade crossings. As described earlier, states have generally already used Section 130 Program funding to address safety at the riskiest grade crossings by adding protective measures, typically lights and gates. Yet crashes continue to occur at these improved grade crossings. Given these trends and the challenges discussed earlier related to the requirements of the Section 130 Program, it is not clear whether the program remains effective in continuing to reduce the risk of crashes and fatalities at grade crossings.

As required, FHWA's biennial report includes a section on "recommendations for future implementation" of the Section 130 Program. As part of this, FHWA reports on challenges and actions being taken to address them. FHWA's 2018 report identified one of the same challenges we heard about from state DOT officials related to the inability or unwillingness of local agencies to provide matching funds and the relatively low amount of funding designed to incentivize localities to close crossings. FHWA reported on its efforts to address these challenges, including by providing guidance, resources, and supportive training to states and local agencies and serving as a clearinghouse for innovative methods of supporting projects. However, with the exception of the funding challenge, FHWA's most recent report does not include the other challenges state officials identified to us related to the requirements of the Section 130 Program discussed above. These include program funding requirements that may impede innovative approaches and the difficulties of using before-and-after crash statistics to measure effectiveness.

Many state DOT officials we spoke with said there may be an opportunity to more broadly assess the Section 130 Program at the national level. It could be more informative to comprehensively assess more detailed crash trends, such as those that look forward over multiple years across the more than 1,700 crashes nationwide, rather than on the approximately 35 that occur on average within a state, and identify strategies to address those trends. Doing so could help FHWA learn more about why crashes are continuing and what types of projects may be effective. There could be ways to evaluate the program in a more comprehensive way; many state DOT officials we interviewed told us such a comprehensive evaluation could help improve program effectiveness in a number of ways, including by enabling the program to better keep up with the rapid pace of technological change and reexamining eligibility requirements that limit the flexibility of states to consider other types of projects beyond engineering. Also, most state DOT officials we interviewed agreed that education and enforcement efforts are crucial to further improving safety, as did 8 out of 10 other stakeholders we spoke to, as well as officials from Volpe Center and NTSB. However, according to FHWA officials, those project types are not allowed under the Section 130 Program's requirements. The officials said FHWA has partnered with FRA and NHTSA on research efforts, such as driver-behavior studies, to inform grade-crossing safety issues. However, the officials said that FHWA has not conducted a program evaluation of the Section 130 Program to consider whether the program's funding and other requirements allow states to adequately address ongoing safety issues such as driver behavior. FHWA officials said that there is no federal requirement for them to conduct such a program evaluation.

We have previously reported that an important component of effective program management is through program performance assessment, which helps establish a program's effectiveness—the extent to which a program is operating as it was intended and the extent to which a program achieves what the agency proposes to accomplish.[48] This type of evaluative information helps the executive branch and congressional committees make decisions about the programs they oversee. Assessing program performance includes conducting program evaluations, which are individual systematic studies that answer specific questions about how well a program is meeting its objectives.[49] In addition, federal internal-control standards state that management should identify, analyze, and respond to significant changes in a program's environment that could pose new risks.[50]

FHWA officials said the fact that crashes and fatalities have held steady while the volume of train and vehicle traffic has increased is an indication that grade-crossing safety has continued to improve. However, specific to fatalities per million train-miles, FHWA's 2018 biennial report shows this rate to be fairly constant since 2009. As noted previously, FRA expects train and traffic volumes to continue to increase and has expressed concern that grade-crossing crashes and fatalities may also increase. Without conducting a program evaluation, FHWA cannot ensure that the Section 130 Program is achieving one of the national goals of the federal-aid highway program, to reduce fatalities and injuries.[51] In addition, It is difficult to see how FHWA, in its biennial reports to Congress, could make informed recommendations for future program implementation without conducting a program evaluation to assess, among other things, whether program requirements first established some four decades ago continue to

---

[48] GAO, Program Evaluation: Strategies to Facilitate Agencies' Use of Evaluation in Program Management and Policy Making, GAO-13-570 (Washington, D.C.: June 26, 2013); Performance Measurement and Evaluation: Definitions and Relationships, GAO-11-646SP (Washington, D.C.: May 2011); and Managing for Results: Enhancing Agency Use of Performance Information for Management Decision Making, GAO-05-927 (Washington, D.C.: Sept. 9, 2005).

[49] GAO, Veterans Justice Outreach Program: VA Could Improve Management by Establishing Performance Measures and Fully Assessing Risks, GAO-16-393 (Washington, D.C.: Apr. 28, 2016).

[50] GAO, Standards for Internal Control in the Federal Government, GAO-14-704G (Washington, D.C.: September 2014).

[51] 23 U.S.C. § 150(b).

reduce fatalities and injuries. We note that as part of a program evaluation, some changes that FHWA, working with FRA, identifies as potentially having merit to improve the program's effectiveness could require a statutory change.

Conclusion

The continued number of crashes and fatalities at grade crossings with devices intended to warn of a train's presence calls into question whether the Section 130 Program is structured to help states continue making progress toward the national goal to reduce fatalities and injuries. An evaluation of the program's requirements could help determine whether Congress should consider better ways to focus federal funds to address the key factor in crashes—risky driver behavior. An FHWA program evaluation could also help determine whether, for example, states could more strategically target emerging safety problems if changes were made to the types of projects eligible for funding under the Section 130 Program. FRA's new grade-crossing inspectors are meant to increase the effectiveness of FRA's rail-safety oversight activities, and accordingly, these FRA inspectors, along with FRA researchers, may be well positioned to help FHWA evaluate potential changes to improve the effectiveness of the Section 130 Program.

Recommendation for Executive Action

The Administrator of FHWA, working with FRA, should evaluate the Section 130 Program's requirements to determine whether they allow states sufficient flexibility to adequately address current and emerging grade-crossing safety issues. As part of this evaluation, FHWA should determine whether statutory changes to the program are necessary to improve its effectiveness (Recommendation 1).

Agency Comments

We provided a draft of this chapter to DOT for review and comment. In written comments, reproduced in appendix II, DOT concurred with our recommendation. DOT also provided technical comments, which we incorporated as appropriate.

Susan A. Fleming
Director, Physical Infrastructure Issues

Appendix I: Objectives, Scope, and Methodology

This chapter examines (1) what has been the focus of Federal Railroad Administration's (FRA) grade-crossing-safety research, (2) how states select and implement grade-crossing projects and what railroad- and state-reported data are available from FRA to inform states' decisions, and (3) the challenges states reported in implementing and assessing projects and the extent to which the Federal Highway Administration (FHWA) assesses the program's effectiveness. The scope of this work focused on the nation's more than 128,000 public grade crossings. We did not include private grade crossings, as states can only use Railway-Highway Crossings Program (commonly referred to as the Section 130 Program) funds to improve safety at public grade crossings. While FRA provides safety grants to address rail issues, including for grade-crossing projects, we focused our work on the Section 130 Program because it is the primary source of federal funding directed at grade-crossing-safety improvement.

For each objective we reviewed: pertinent statutes and FHWA and FRA regulations and documents; interviewed FHWA and FRA program officials in headquarters; and conducted in-depth interviews with a non-generalizable sample of organizations that included officials from 4 freight and passenger railroads, 12 state agencies from 8 states, 6 FRA regional offices, and 8 FHWA state division offices. We also spoke with representatives from relevant associations and officials from NTSB and Volpe Center. We selected these organizations based on our initial background research, prior work, and input from other stakeholders, among other things. See the paragraph below for additional selection details and Table 5 for a complete list of organizations we spoke with.

We selected eight states as part of our non-generalizable sample for interviews. These states included Arizona, California, Florida, Illinois, Missouri, New Jersey, North Carolina, and Pennsylvania. The states were selected to include a mix of state experiences based on a variety of factors, including the number of grade crossings and crashes at those crossings, and the amount of Section 130 Program funding they received. Specifically, we selected four states from those in the top 25 percent of all states in terms of their number of grade crossings and the amount of Section 130 Program funds they received. We selected the other four states to include a mix of these factors. We also considered geographical diversity and recommendations from FRA and FHWA officials. Within these eight states, we conducted in-depth interviews with FHWA division staff, FRA regional staff, and state officials. A variety of state agencies administer the Section 130 Program within their state; the state officials we spoke with from our eight selected states worked for agencies such as state departments of transportation, corporation commissions, and public utility commissions. We also spoke with a non-generalizable sample of four railroads: Amtrak, CSX, Norfolk Southern, and Sierra Northern. We selected railroads based on a variety of factors including geographic location and stakeholder recommendations.

We also conducted additional work related to each of the objectives. To describe the focus of FRA's grade-crossing-safety research, we examined FRA research aimed at understanding the causes of grade-crossing crashes and identifying potential improvements and described FRA efforts to test new approaches that could improve safety. We did not assess the quality of FRA's research, as that was beyond the scope of this engagement. Instead, we described the nature of the research. We also spoke with FRA research and development staff, Volpe researchers, and state partners about this work.

To describe how states select and implement grade-crossing projects, and what FRA data are available to inform their decisions, we reviewed an academic study that included a literature review and interviews with state officials to describe how states select Section 130 Program projects.[52]

Table 1. Electronic Testing of National Highway-Rail Grade Crossing Inventory– Missing Data

Data element	Number of missing values (out of 130,449 total values)
Weekly train movement	379
Highway speed limit	42,575
Type train service	31,271
Annual average daily traffic	1,429
Number of traffic lanes	1,046
Smallest crossing angle	871
Latitude	706
Longitude	706
Highway traffic signal controlling crossing	676
Regularly used by school bus	472
Roadway gate arms	307
Max timetable speed	536
Day through-train traffic	40
Night through-train traffic	92

Source: GAO analysis of U.S. Department of Transportation information. | GAO-19-80.

We spoke with the researcher and determined the study to be reliable for the purposes of our reporting objectives. We also spoke with officials from our eight selected states, FHWA division staff, and FRA regional staff, and reviewed the states' 2017 Section 130 Program reports. As part of this objective, we also assessed the reliability of data reported for all railroads in FRA's National Highway-Rail Crossing Inventory data as of August 31, 2018. For public grade crossings that were not closed, we examined a selection of fields within the database to identify the frequency of missing data (see Table 1), data anomalies (see Table 2), relational

[52] Benjamin R. Sperry, Bhaven Naik, Jeffrey E. Warner, *Evaluation of Grade Crossing Hazard Ranking Models,* a report prepared at the request of the Ohio Department of Transportation, May 2016.

errors, where two related data fields had values that were incompatible (see Table 3), and when the data was last updated (see Table 4). Specifically, we conducted the following electronic tests on the crossing inventory data to determine if they were within reasonable ranges, were internally consistent, and appeared complete:

Table 2. Electronic Testing of National Highway-Rail Grade Crossing Inventory– Data Anomalies

Data element	Values we considered outside the normal range	Number of values outside the normal range
Max timetable speed	<1 or >150	1,968
Longitude	For states except Alaska: <-124 or >-66 For Alaska: <-165 or >-132	162
Annual Average Daily Traffic	<1 or >999,999	13
Latitude	For states except AK: <24 or >49 For AK: <50 or >71	10
Weekly train movement	<0 or >999	0
Highway Speed Limit	<0 or >120	0
Roadway gate arms	<0 or >99	0
Number of traffic lanes	<0 or >9	0

Source: GAO analysis of U.S. Department of Transportation information. | GAO-19-80.

Table 3. Electronic Testing of National Highway-Rail Grade Crossing Inventory–Relational Errors

Data relationship error	Criteria	Number of errors
Crossings with gates are missing information on gate configuration	Gates>0 and Gate Configuration is blank	19,506
Crossing with school busses do not have the number of school busses listed	School buses=1 and School bus count is blank	438
Freight-only lines have passenger counts listed	Type of train service is "11" and Passenger count>0	105

Source: GAO analysis of U.S. Department of Transportation information. | GAO-19-80.

Before conducting our analysis, we filtered the inventory data to only include open, public, at-grade crossings. To understand FRA's efforts to improve its crossing inventory data, we interviewed FRA regional and headquarters staff and reviewed job descriptions for FRA's new grade-crossing inspectors.

Table 4. Electronic Testing of National Highway-Rail Grade Crossing Inventory–Date Updated

Data element	Before 1/1/1980	From 1/1/1980 to 12/31/1989	From 1/1/1990 to 12/31/1999	From 1/1/2000 to 12/31/2009	From 1/1/2010 to 8/31/2018	Missing
Revision date	99	942	1,044	3,611	125,554	0
Year of train count data	41	500	6	129	97,033	33,541
Year of annual average daily traffic	2,405	29,924	11,660	37,877	47,497	1,887

Source: GAO analysis of U.S. Department of Transportation information. | GAO-19-80.

Finally, to determine the challenges states reported in implementing and assessing grade-crossing safety projects and the extent to which FHWA assesses the program's effectiveness, we reviewed program requirements and state project data and other components from FHWA's 2016 and 2018 Section 130 Program biennial reports to Congress. We also reviewed FHWA's summary of fiscal year 2018 program funds provided to states and federal laws and guidance related to implementing projects and measuring performance. We interviewed state DOT officials from the eight selected states and other stakeholders on the challenges states reported in implementing and assessing projects, and FHWA and FRA officials for their perspectives on managing the program, including how FHWA measures performance and assesses program effectiveness. We compared information collected from FHWA and FRA to federal internal-control standards and criteria on program evaluation identified in our previous work.

Table 5. List of Organizations Interviewed by GAO

Name of Organization	Type of Organization
Federal Government	
FRA Headquarters	Federal Government
FRA Region 1	Federal Government
FRA Region 2	Federal Government
FRA Region 3	Federal Government
FRA Region 4	Federal Government
FRA Region 6	Federal Government
FRA Region 7	Federal Government
FHWA Headquarters	Federal Government
FHWA Arizona division office	Federal Government
FHWA California division office	Federal Government
FHWA Florida division office	Federal Government
FHWA Illinois division office	Federal Government
FHWA Missouri division office	Federal Government
FHWA New Jersey division office	Federal Government
FHWA North Carolina division office	Federal Government
FHWA Pennsylvania division office	Federal Government
The Volpe National Transportation Systems Center	Federal Government
National Transportation Safety Board	Federal Government
State Agencies	
Arizona Department of Transportation	State Agency
Arizona Corporation Commission	State Agency
California Department of Transportation	State Agency
California Public Utility Commission	State Agency
Florida Department of Transportation	State Agency
Illinois Department of Transportation	State Agency
Illinois Commerce Commission	State Agency
Missouri Department of Transportation	State Agency
New Jersey Department of Transportation	State Agency
North Carolina Department of Transportation	State Agency
Pennsylvania Department of Transportation	State Agency
Pennsylvania Public Utility Commission	State Agency
Railroads	
Amtrak	Railroad
CSX	Railroad
Norfolk Southern	Railroad
Sierra Northern	Railroad

Table 5. (Continued)

Name of Organization	Type of Organization
Others	
American Association of Railroads	Trade Association
American Association of State Highway and Transportation Officials	Transportation Association
American Shortline and Regional Railroad Association	Trade Association
Operation Lifesaver	Safety Organization
Joyce Rose (WSP USA)	Transit and Rail Safety Consultant
Benjamin Sperry (University of Ohio)	Academic

In addition, we reviewed FHWA and FRA documents designed to guide states, such as the Grade Crossing Handbook, the Manual on Uniform Traffic Control Devices, the Action Plan and Project Prioritization Noteworthy Practices Guide, and other related documents. We conducted this performance audit from November 2017 to November 2018 in accordance with generally accepted government auditing standards. Those standards require that we plan and perform the audit to obtain sufficient, appropriate evidence to provide a reasonable basis for our findings and conclusions based on our audit objectives. We believe that the evidence obtained provides a reasonable basis for our findings and conclusions based on our audit objectives.

APPENDIX II: COMMENTS FROM THE DEPARTMENT OF TRANSPORTATION

U.S. Department of Transportation
Office of the Secretary of Transportation

Assistant Secretary for Administration

1200 New Jersey Avenue SE
Washington, DC 20590

OCT 26 2018

Susan A. Fleming
Director, Physical Infrastructure Issues
U.S. Government Accountability Office (GAO)
441 G Street NW
Washington, DC 20548

Dear Ms. Fleming:

The Federal Highway Administration (FHWA) and the Federal Railroad Administration (FRA) are committed to enhancing safety at or near public rail-highway crossings. Over the last 10 years, the number of fatalities at rail-highway crossings decreased by 31 percent while train and vehicle traffic increased. Fatalities at rail-highway crossings now comprise less than 1 percent of total highway fatalities. The FHWA's Railway-Highway Crossing Program (Section 130 Program) provides states funding to address safety at grade crossings. This annual set-aside program, which set-aside $235 million in Fiscal Year 2018, is a small portion of the $40 billion Federal-aid Highway Program. The purpose of the program is to eliminate hazards at rail-highway crossings. The FHWA's continued emphasis on safety targets have focused States' efforts on streamlining processes, implementing systemic safety improvements, developing innovative methods, and applying noteworthy practices from other States.

In addition, FHWA continues to take the following actions to effectively implement the Section 130 Program:

- Establish State flexibility to use State-specific, data-driven processes for managing their rail-highway crossing program to ensure that States can target Federal-aid investments to reduce rail-highway crossing deaths and serious injuries;
- Offer technical assistance to States as they administer and manage their programs;
- Assist states to determine the most effective processes for selecting, prioritizing and evaluating grade-crossing safety improvement projects that meet their needs;
- Partner with various stakeholders from public and private organizations to improve safety on the Nation's rail-highway crossing sites in a coordinated manner;
- Collect annual outcome program evaluations and partner with States on their program reviews; and
- Submit biennial reports to Congress—seven to date—that include State program implementation efforts, program effectiveness findings, and evaluation of State programs and recommendations for future program implementation.

Further, FRA has taken actions to improve rail-highway safety. For example, FRA has created a Grade Crossing Discipline, consisting in part, of twenty-four regional inspectors and eight regional specialists who perform inspections of railroad Emergency Notification Systems to ensure compliance with FRA regulations. FRA's inspectors also inspect quiet zones—grade crossings where train horns are not routinely sounded—to ensure crossing safety enhancements are properly maintained and remain in place. Finally, FRA inspectors plan to work with railroads to ensure the grade crossing inventory data is accurate and updated in accordance with the regulations.

Upon review of the GAO's draft report, we concur with the recommendation that FHWA, working with FRA, determine whether the Section 130 Program requirements allow states sufficient flexibility to adequately address current and emerging grade-crossing safety issues. We will provide a detailed response to the recommendation within 60 days of the final report's issuance.

Sincerely,

Keith Washington
Deputy Assistant Secretary for Administration

INDEX

A

B

C

D

E

F

G

H

I

L

M

N

S

T

U

V

W